HOUSE AND PSYCHOLOGY

HOUSE AND PSYCHOLOGY

Humanity Is Overrated

EDITED BY TED CASCIO AND
LEONARD L. MARTIN

WILEY

John Wiley & Sons, Inc.

Published by John Wiley & Sons, Inc., Hoboken, New Jersey
Published simultaneously in Canada

For general information about our other products and services, please contact our Cus-tomer Care Department within the United States at (800) 762-2974, outside the United States at (317) 572-3993 or fax (317) 572-4002.

Wiley also publishes its books in a variety of electronic formats and by print-on-demand. Some content that appears in standard print versions of this book may not be available in other formats. For more information about Wiley products, visit us at www.wiley.com.

Library of Congress Cataloging-in-Publication Data:

  House and psychology: humanity is overrated / edited by Ted V. Cascio and Leonard M. Martin.
    p. cm.
    Includes bibliographical references and index.
    ISBN 978-0-470-94555-1 (pbk); ISBN 978-1-118-11458-2 (ebk);
ISBN 978-1-118-11459-9 (ebk); ISBN 978-1-118-11460-5 (ebk)
  1. Helping behavior.   2. Personality.   I. Cascio, Edward V., date.
  II. Martin, Leonard M., date.
  BF637.H4H68 2011
  791.45'72—dc23
                                                2011024781

Printed in the United States of America

10 9 8 7 6 5 4 3 2 1

Contents

Acknowledgments:
Literary Health Assurance

This project was truly a team effort. Please join us in expressing gratitude to those who chipped in.

First and foremost, we would like to thank our amazing contributors, without whom this book would have been impossible. Their extraordinary scholarship, literacy, and diligence rendered our work as editors about as easy as "making Scarlett Johansson look pretty" (House in "Fetal Position"). *Muchas gracias a todos y todas!*

For providing creative and editorial feedback, we are grateful to Laura Buffardi, Edward J. Jackson, and Patricia and Joseph Cascio, as well as to students from our adjustment and social psychology courses at the University of Georgia (and, in particular, for his extremely valuable assistance locating quotes, thanks to Timothy Pierce-Tomlin!).

Introduction
An Ailment-Free Primer

Take caution: you're about to enter the extraordinary mental universe of the brilliant, bombastic, bile-belching doctor of medicine referred to simply as House. How's that for a hook? No good? Okay, scratch that. Let's get a little closer to the subject. If a real hook were to become elongated and flame-tipped, it would embody something relevant to House, namely, his cane. This book is about objects such as flame-tipped canes, giant tennis balls, monster trucks, Game Boys, and adult magazines; well . . . not really. If you believe that, then you may need to be admitted under the care of a certain eminent diagnostician (who'd frankly be happy to take your case to get out of clinic duty). Relax, you probably have time to swing by the bookstore register before you start hemorrhaging rectal blood.

Let's try this again. You're reading this book to gain a fresh, sophisticated perspective on House and the other members of the Princeton-Plainsboro staff, right? You're a "smart" person. You're an enthusiastic fan of *House*, you're looking for something fun to read, and you have the urge to learn what other "smart" people think about one of your favorite TV shows. (Okay, I think we're on the right track now.)

If so, you're not alone. Adoring audiences around the world seek a deeper understanding of *House*, an amazingly complex show just spoiling for careful and incisive analysis. Reading this book will enable you to become not only an even smarter person in general, but a smart fan of *House* in particular (that is, you may experience increased intracranial pressure). What you do with your new, enlightened perspective is completely up to you: impress your friends, write a term paper, post on Internet *House* forums . . . whatever. Or, you could simply bask in the glory of the newfound heights of your *House* fanaticism. This book is meant to bolster your *House* expertise by imparting psychological principles. It is ultimately intended to be fun but not completely frivolous, which, come to think of it, echoes the overall tone of *House* perfectly. House himself just might consider this book "cool."

Of course, another possibility is that House would dismiss everything here as pretentious psychobabble. We (the editors) have taken every precaution to avoid including anything flimsy or resonant with "pop" psychology in this book. In other words, don't expect the sort of soothing platitudes and affirmations found on *Dr. Phil*. Since some of you are here primarily to take a peek at the holy grail of knowledge that research psychologists have unearthed (i.e., you're here to learn more about psychology for itself and for its own sake), this book is chock-full of scientifically valid, research-based psychological knowledge; so much so, that it would serve quite well as a supplemental text for psychology instructors at high schools and universities. As instructors ourselves, we can't think of a better way to make learning psychology fun.

We solicited essays from well-respected research psychologists, and we ended up with an awesome group of world-renowned experts who also happen to love *House*. This book comprises an anthology of the essays submitted to us by these experts. Each essay examines instances and characters from *House* through the lens of psychological theory and research. While some essays deal with a topic or topics that you will naturally find more interesting than others, we think that all of them focus on subject matter that is generally appealing and fundamental to *House*. Our objectives as editors were to celebrate *House*, as well as disabuse you, the reader, of certain illusions you may have about human nature. We are pretty sure that House, the man who once said that "humanity is overrated," would endorse those aims and recommend this book to his many, many friends.

So join us as we decrypt the diagnosticians and solve the psychological puzzles of Princeton-Plainsboro!

PART ONE
The Good: Unlimited Vicodin

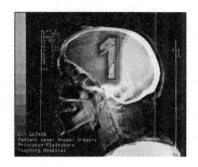

In the Patient's Best Interests?

Perspectives on Why We Help Others

TED CASCIO

Feeling sick? I recommend Princeton-Plainsboro Teaching Hospital. The doctors and the nurses there are exceptionally skilled. They don't save everyone, but they do have a very high success rate—even for extremely rare and difficult cases. The staff can be summarized in two words: they help. As Cameron puts it in the pilot episode, "Isn't treating patients why we became doctors?" I have to admit that there is at least one doctor on the staff who may seem a little rude and obnoxious—even cruel—but does that matter if you get better?

Actually, it does seem to matter. Although the sort of beneficence practiced by doctors is surely valuable, maybe even virtuous, helping's ultimate moral status is seldom clear-cut. We wonder. And even when we feel pretty sure, we tend to be critical. Cameron, in particular, has frequently been forced to bear criticism for her seemingly reflexive self-sacrificial tendencies. She's even been accused by House and others of having a sort of helping pathology. On their so-called date that kicked off season 3, House accurately (and in typical point-blank fashion) identifies this supposed condition as the primary basis for her romantic involvement with him:

> House: You have no interest in going out with me. Maybe you did, when I couldn't walk, when I was a sick puppy that you could nurture back to health. Now that I'm healthy there's nothing in it for you.
> Cameron: You are not healthy.
>
> —"Meaning"

And yet Cameronesque fervor is clearly not a necessary precondition for helping. Most people (including House) help one another. We are psychologically predisposed to both care about and do something about the suffering of others. That is interesting, because things could have been so different. Why aren't we selfish instead? Shouldn't we all simply pursue our own self-interests? Does it really make sense to sacrifice our time, energy, money, and sometimes lives for the sake of another person's well-being? If so, why?

Psychology offers some interesting insights into these cosmic questions that you might not have thought to consider, and it challenges some prevailing assumptions. One of these assumptions is that people help out of genuine concern for other people's well-being. That assumption has been challenged. Another is that people help because they are strongly compelled by their unique dispositions to do so—or not—depending on some, usually hazy, notion of "character." Helping doesn't happen by accident; rather, it is character-driven. That assumption has also been challenged. Another doozy is that only human beings help one another or, at minimum, that human and animal helping are fundamentally and qualitatively different. This assumption has been challenged since the days of Darwin.

You will walk away from this chapter with a better understanding of the truly complex underpinnings of helping behavior. You will see why helping is not quite the pure, wholesome act it's usually depicted as. At least, that's not the whole story. This may alter your perspective on *House*, on your friends and family, and even on what it means to be human (as well as humane). Finally, I hope this chapter convinces you to become less self-centered and to make helping people in need a fundamental concern in your own life. We'll start with the various motives that inspire helping. When people help one another, are they actually just trying to indirectly help themselves?

Isn't All Helping Actually Egoistic?

Consider that doctors may help patients for many different reasons. They may help because they

1. Want to relieve the patient's suffering
2. Are simply doing their jobs
3. Enjoy the challenge of the diagnosis and the treatment
4. Are seeking fame and power
5. Hope that doing so will bring attention to their research project or their pet disease
6. Want to feel like Superman (or Superwoman)

Notice anything about this list? Only the first item reflects helping in the pure selfless or altruistic sense. In each of the other examples, the doctor helps primarily to benefit himself or herself. The patient may get better, but this is merely a side effect of a selfish or egoistic motive.

Egoistic helping is motivated by a desire to advance the interests of the person doing the helping, rather than those of the person in need. We saw House engage in egoistic helping when he becomes convinced (correctly, of course) that one of the actors on *Prescription: Passion*—his favorite soap opera—has a life-threatening medical condition. House decides to intervene by abducting him from the set of the show and chauffeuring him to Princeton-Plainsboro in order to be treated. When the unfortunate fellow finally realizes what is going on, House willingly admits that "I don't care if you die, but if Brock Sterling dies, Anna never finds out he's the father of Marie's baby" ("Living the Dream"). This is a classic (and pretty hilarious) instance of egoistic helping. House does this type of thing frequently. In this case, he is concerned for the other man's life only insofar as the man's continued existence is necessary to keep the story line alive on his favorite TV show. Egoistic helping at its best.

House's general assumption seems to be that people are apt to deceive themselves and others about their true motives for helping. According to House, when we say that our motive for helping another person strictly involves concern for his or her welfare, the true motive is often one that is more egoistic and likely to benefit us directly. It's no surprise, then, that House harbors suspicions about motives and generally distrusts people's claims about what inspires their helping behavior.

For example, many doctors may claim that they chose their profession because they "want to help people." As usual, however, House is not shy about proposing alternatives:

> House: People act in their own self-interests. You're all here because you're happy to be here or at least because it's your best option.
> Kutner: I'm here because I want to help people.
> House: No, you're here because it makes you feel good to help people. Taub and Foreman are here because they've got no other viable choices, and Thirteen is desperate to make her life matter before it's over.
> —"The Greater Good"

House is what we'll call an egoistic reductionist. His cynical interpretation of people's helping behavior is part of his larger philosophy about why anyone does anything. According to him, every act is ultimately in the service of self-interest. As House puts it in a conversation with Wilson:

> Wilson: Apologies aren't supposed to make you feel better, they're supposed to make the other person feel better.
> House: In order to make you feel better.
> —"Under My Skin"

One psychological hypothesis that jibes neatly with House's interpretation of helping is called the *negative state relief hypothesis*. It suggests that individuals help in order to reduce the sense of guilt that they would experience if they didn't help. This is a form of egoistic helping, even if the other person ends up being benefited.

Sometimes House—and the negative state relief hypothesis—is right on target. At some point toward the end of season 5, Kutner ominously fails to show up for the morning differential (we learn later that, sadly, this is because he committed suicide). When House begins to "politely inquire" into the situation, Taub, of all people, attempts to defend Kutner by devising an excuse for him, something House naturally finds suspicious. He doesn't believe Taub would help without a direct personal incentive. House's doubts are later vindicated when it is revealed to him that earlier, Taub dishonestly claimed credit for one of Kutner's diagnostic ideas, a transgression that elicited the guilt that impelled him to come to his friend's assistance. Despite Taub's best efforts, House is never fooled. Later, sizing up the situation in characteristically cynical terms, House affirms with relish, "I thought maybe you were lying to cover for Kutner, which sounds noble, except you're doing it out of guilt instead of love" ("Simple Explanation"). This example perfectly illustrates the negative state relief hypothesis. When guilt reduction is the driving force behind our actions, any helping that might follow is egoistic in nature.

Are egoistic hypotheses such as these enough to explain all helping behavior? Probably not. A series of studies by Dan Batson and his colleagues demonstrated that altruistic helping is a real phenomenon. Imagine that you are a participant in one of these studies. You show up for an experiment on "task performance and impression projection under stressful conditions." You learn that you are participating with another person named Elaine. Your responsibility is to observe Elaine as she performs a number of tasks under stressful conditions. Stressful conditions? Yes, Elaine will be receiving mild electric shocks.

As the experiment continues, though, Elaine begins to react. The shocks do not seem so mild to her. In fact, Elaine's facial expressions and body movements clearly indicate that she is in distress. The experimenter notices this, too, and interrupts the trial in order to ask Elaine if she is doing all right. Elaine explains that "as a child she had been thrown from a horse onto an electric fence." She goes on to inform the experimenter that she suffered a bad trauma and in the future might react strongly to even mild shocks. Still, Elaine claims that she wants to continue with the study.

So, here's the problem: the experiment requires that one person receive some mild shocks while another person observes. Elaine, however, is clearly suffering. As the observer, you can see this. The experimenter asks you if you would be willing to take her place. If you had the chance to take her place, would you? In other words, would you take the shocks so that Elaine doesn't have to?

Suppose these were your only options: take the other participant's place or stay and observe her suffer. In situations like this in which escape is not an option, people usually help Elaine. After all, if you can't leave, then the only way you can reduce your distress (i.e., guilt) is to keep the other person from suffering.

Yet what if you were presented with the option to leave immediately? You won't have to watch Elaine agonize. The really interesting finding of Batson's studies is that when people have this option to leave, they still volunteer to take her place. Even though leaving would be the easiest way to relieve their distress, people pursue the less pleasant, more altruistic alternative of helping Elaine.

Still, critics (such as House) might claim that the prospect of physical escape did not seem sufficient to participants in this study because it could not have relieved their guilty conscience. Follow-up studies have ruled out this alternative. These experiments found that even when participants had options that would allow them to escape without having guilty afterthoughts (such as claiming impediments to helping or noting the inaction of others who could help), they still helped, regardless. Studies such as this specifically contradict the negative state relief hypothesis because participants do not pursue easier alternatives to helping that could just as effectively reduce their guilt. They instead pursue the more difficult and less egoistic option of genuine helping.

We can thus conclude that helping is motivated at least at times by altruistic, in addition to egoistic, motivations. Altruism seems to be real. It's important to note that we can't conclude that people *never* help for purely egoistic reasons, only that this is not *always* the *only* impetus for helping.

Characterless Helping: The Influence of Situations

In addition to altruistic and egoistic motives, research has demonstrated that helping is caused in part by factors that seem random, arbitrary, or both, such as our moods, whether we're in a hurry, the gender and attractiveness of the person in distress, whether other people happen to be around and are looking, and levels of ambient noise. The absurdity of some of these "situational" factors that determine helping is truly amazing. Studies show that nice weather, visualizing a vacation in Hawaii, and eating cookies all serve to increase helping.

The list goes on, but we will limit our discussion to one situational factor that seems especially relevant to *House*: the degree to which we feel similar to the person in need of help. Generally speaking, we are more likely to help those who are similar to us than those who are dissimilar. This is referred to as the *similarity bias*. It's a subtle and disquieting form of reflexive favoritism. Frequently, we aren't even aware that it is factoring into our decisions, and the criteria we use to gauge this similarity can be ludicrously superficial, such as the type of clothes someone happens to be wearing.

As rational as House is, he is not immune to this sort of influence. Take, for example, an instance involving a patient whose medical condition resulted in frontal lobe disinhibition. This ailment causes the patient to experience great difficulties in refraining from uttering all kinds of offensive opinions and attitudes; he has lost the ability to censor his true thoughts, which is greatly undermining his relationships with his family and friends. Sounds familiar, right? Sounds a lot like House. Just as we would predict in light of the similarity bias, House is more compassionate toward this patient than usual. He shows some genuine empathy. In an uncharacteristic move, House petitions Chase to perform a risky surgery in order to cure this patient's symptoms, which at this point are non-life-threatening:

> Chase: You want me to help you? Tell me why.
> House: Why what?
> Chase: Why you care. The puzzle's solved. The guy's alive. And the odds of coming out of this surgery with that same status aren't that great.
> House: My patient has a quality-of-life issue.
> Chase: He says awful things. Hardly a medical condition.
> House: When he leaves here, he's going to lose his family. He's going to alienate the people he works with, and if he ever finds a friend who's willing to put up with his crap, he'll be lucky. Until he drives them away, too.
> Chase: I'll see what I can do.
>
> —"The Social Contract"

House's desire to prevent this patient's long-term suffering goes above and beyond his usual level of concern. This increased compassion is presumably the result of their apparent similarities and potential for shared destinies. The situation is one main cause of House's helping, and we are all likewise subject to situational influences such as these.

So what? Who cares? Well, the fact that these random situational cues determine helping suggests that *character* is much less important than once thought in deciding who engages in helping behavior. It is not so much our stable personalities that lead to acts of helping, but rather the ephemeral and often arbitrary environments in which we find ourselves. Character still matters, but it has to share a large portion of the responsibility for helpful acts with factors for which we can't so readily take credit. House would have no problem admitting that he helped a patient simply because "She was hot!" Would you be comfortable admitting the same?

Our Selfish Pedigree

Finally, I will address the perspective that evolutionary biology has on helping. This train of thought begins with the idea that many, if not all, of the moral sentiments we find in human beings can also be found in animals. For example, many animals have been observed helping one another. Even feelings such as empathy and reciprocity (the compulsion to return a favor or redress an offense) are experienced by animals. It is these same very basic emotions that stimulate human helping. Thus, human helping is not qualitatively different from animal helping. When considered in this light, helping may be no more than a biologically useful behavior, despite the way it feels to us when we do it or the value we place on it in our society. We do it because it works. It helps the species. It transmits our genes.

In terms of evolutionary biology, if life can be said to have a purpose, it is to pass on our genes. The thoughts, feelings, and behavior of the organism are simply the means by which this happens. People may help because it feels good or because they are motivated to relieve the suffering of another person, but ultimately they do it because they possess genes passed down from helpful ancestors who were themselves benefited by being helpful. These selected-for genes generate instinctual helping behavior in us that we attempt to consciously make sense of with labels such as "altruism" and "morality."

From this perspective, all helping is selfish. It serves to transmit our genes to the next generation—the ultimate egoistic act. Thus, we should be likely to help others only to the extent that doing so helps accomplish this task. In other words, we should be more likely to help close relatives (who possess our genes) and others who are likely to help us in return (because that should increase our chances of surviving and reproducing). Both of these strategies serve to increase the biological "fitness" of the organism.

On the whole, House seems to agree with the biological theory, as we can see in one of his remarks:

> House: There's an evolutionary imperative why we give a crap about our family and friends. And there's an evolutionary

imperative why we don't give a crap about anybody else. If we loved all people indiscriminately, we couldn't function.

—"TB or Not TB"

Yet House discounts two very large categories of people (i.e., non-relatives and nonfriends) that we should have good cause to help. In addition to genetic similarity, there is also the issue of reciprocity. If we can expect to get something in return, we should be motivated to help. Accordingly, House seems to have some difficulty accounting for why people help as liberally and frequently as they do. He often explains away helping, or "niceness," as a genetic anomaly or deficiency:

Kutner: Niceness is a defect?
House: Three cavemen see a stranger running toward them with a spear, one fights, one flees, one smiles and invites him over for fondue. That last guy didn't last long enough to procreate.

—"No More Mr. Nice Guy"

Actually, that last guy may have survived the longest if his dinner invitation resulted in generous reciprocal rewards from his guest (how-ever far-fetched that possibility might be in this particular example).

Hence, there is a compelling case to be made against House's pessimistic outlook on kindness. Kindness or niceness is probably not maladaptive, as he asserts. That's a pretty common misperception on *House*, because Foreman also seems disinclined to sympathize with those who engage in difficult or potentially risky acts of self-sacrifice, a sentiment that frequently strains his relationship with Cameron. Once, while reflecting on her conscious and informed decision to marry a terminally ill man, he remarks, "She married a dying guy. She has issues" ("Under My Skin"). Ouch.

Tying the Perspectives Together

So, why do we help? Is it because of (a) egoistic motives, (b) altruistic motives, (c) situations, or (d) biological factors? The answer is (e) all of the above, and that is the main point of this chapter. Discounting the influence of any of these causes is too simplistic to provide an accurate explanation for helping behavior. As painful as it may be, we should come to terms with the fact that helpful people are not always simply trying to do the "right thing." When people choose to help, they may be doing so for many reasons. They do so partly for the sake of the individual in need but also to advance their own interests. Some factors that promote helping are disconcertingly arbitrary, and others are never processed consciously.

This has implications for how we understand what's going on at Princeton-Plainsboro. "Antihero" is a label frequently applied to House, and he has certainly done much to earn this reputation. He intentionally helps many and yet readily acknowledges his pervasive egoism and wide-ranging "wickedness." He is always refreshingly candid. More traditional heroes are less candid and, not coincidentally, less capable of such keen introspection. This is a big part of what makes House so unbelievably appealing.

Yet House errs in fancying himself, as well as others, wholly egoistic. He mistakenly thinks that all heroes are, like him, 100 percent self-serving. This is the particular House-ism that psychological research disputes. House's views on helping depart radically from the mainstream, and it appears that in the process of becoming polarized, these views have also become oversimplified. It's never as simple as the either/or proposition between altruism and egoism that House seems to presuppose. Altruism and egoism operate in tandem at different levels (both biological and psychological) to produce helping, and, in addition, other causes—such as environmental factors—have little, if anything, to do with this distinction. Given all of the evidence, House's egoistic reductionism seems ill-advised.

On the other hand, House is doing the right thing by disparaging the "good guy" archetype. We want to believe that helping should be heart-warming, that the "good guy" helped out of a single-minded preoccupation with the welfare of the person in distress, that his motives were "pure." As an entertaining refutation of this myth, we have House, who does many good deeds without always (or

even frequently) being altruistically motivated. He calls attention to
the limits of language every time he demonstrates the compatibility
between misanthropy and philanthropy. He pushes the boundaries of
morality and thereby helps us define it.

One of the funnier and more ironic things about *House* is that
the *most* misanthropic doctor is also usually the one *most* capable of
helping his patients. Inveterate do-gooders seem to recognize this
incongruity, but Wilson, at least, won't let it diminish the tremendous esteem he maintains for his old friend: "He saves lives. People
that no one else can save. And, no matter how much of an ass he is,
statistically, House is a positive force in the universe" ("Merry Little
Christmas").

SUGGESTED READINGS

Batson, C. D., B. D. Duncan, P. Ackerman, T. Buckley, and K. Birch (1981). Is
    empathic emotion a source of altruistic motivation? *Journal of Personality
    and Social Psychology, 40,* 290–302.
Cialdini, R. B., M. Schaller, D. Houlihan, K. Arps, J. Fultz, and A. L. Beaman
    (1987). Empathy-based helping: Is it selflessly or selfishly motivated?
    Journal of Personality and Social Psychology, 52, 749–758.
Cunningham, M. R. (1979). Weather, mood and helping behavior: Quasi-
    experiments with the sunshine Samaritan. *Journal of Personality and Social
    Psychology, 37,* 1947–1956.
Darley, J., and C. Batson (1973). From Jerusalem to Jericho: A study of situa-
    tional and dispositional variables in helping behavior. *Journal of Personality
    and Social Psychology, 27,* 100–108.
Dawkins, R. (1976). *The Selfish Gene.* New York: Oxford University Press.
Eagly, A. H., and M. Crowley (1986). Gender and helping behavior: A meta-
    analytic analysis of the social psychological literature. *Psychological Bulletin,
    100,* 283–308.
Emswiller, T., K. Deaux, and J. E. Willits (1971). Similarity, sex, and requests for
    small favors. *Journal of Applied Social Psychology, 13,* 284–291.
Isen, A. M., and P. F. Levin (1972). The effect of feeling good on helping:
    Cookies and kindness. *Journal of Personality and Social Psychology, 21,*
    384–388.
Matthews, K. E., and L. Canon (1975). Environmental noise level as a deter-
    minant of helping behavior. *Journal of Personality and Social Psychology,
    32,* 571–577.

Rosenhan, D. L., J. Karylowski, P. Salovey, and K. Hargis (1981). Emotion and altruism. In J. P. Rushton and R. M. Sorrentino (eds.), *Altruism and Helping Behavior.* Hillsdale, NJ: Lawrence Erlbaum Associates.

Satow, K. L. (1975). Social approval and helping. *Journal of Experimental Social Psychology, 11*(6), 501–509.

West, S. G., and T. J. Brown (1975). Physical attractiveness, the severity of the emergency and helping: A field experiment and interpersonal simulation. *Journal of Experimental Social Psychology, 11*, 531–538.

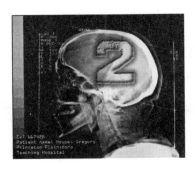

Authenticity in the House

Will the Real House Please Stand Up?

BRIAN M. GOLDMAN AND SAMUEL J. MADDOX

House has many characteristics that captivate and amuse his fans. There's his caustic humor, his razor-sharp wit, and his profound narcissism. For many of us, though, there is also a lingering question: When we see House engage in his repulsive, yet fascinating and provocative, behavior, are we seeing the real House or are we seeing antics House uses to mask his true self? To phrase the question in psychology terms, we may wonder whether House is being authentic.

The formal psychological definition of authenticity is not far off from our common understanding of the term. Individuals are authentic to the extent that they act in ways that are congruent with their genuine thoughts, feelings, and values. In everyday language, we might describe authenticity with a phrase such as "keeping it real." In one study, adolescents defined "true-self behaviors" as "saying what you really think or feel" and "expressing your honest opinion." When they were asked to define "false self-behaviors," they used phrases such as "being phony," "hiding your true thoughts and feelings," or "saying what you think others want."

On the surface at least, House seems to pass the authenticity test. He prizes rationality and seldom holds back in disclosing uncomfortable truths. Yet he is also manipulative, sarcastic, and an admitted liar. So, which is it? Should we credit House with a brusque, irascible sort of authenticity?

In this chapter, we hope to go beyond a broad, intuitive understanding of authenticity and really flesh out what it means to be authentic and why it is good to be authentic. This will help us decide whether House's apparent authenticity qualifies as real psychological authenticity. In doing so, we will explore different ways in which authenticity is defined. We will also discuss research findings that highlight what it means to be authentic, and we will evaluate House's authenticity in terms of these definitions and findings.

It Feels Good to Be Me: Perspectives on Authenticity and Well-Being

Generally speaking, authenticity is good. People who are authentic are more likely than those who are not authentic to experience a range of healthy, positive psychological states, and they are less likely to experience a range of negative, maladaptive psychological states. Such benefits occur regardless of the domain in which individuals experience authenticity.

For example, people differ in the extent to which they express their true selves in the various social roles they play, such as employee, friend, or son/daughter. This is referred to as role authenticity. Consider House. He is more himself around his friend Wilson than around Officer Tritter, who has the power to punish him for his inappropriate behavior. People who claim to have high role authenticity generally say they experience less stress, less depression, fewer physical symptoms, and more satisfaction than people who report low role authenticity. People also differ in the extent to which they act in accord with their true selves in the context of their romantic relationships. How many times have we seen House pretend to be a new, improved person? Yet we know he is only scheming to get Cuddy to like him. Obviously, this is an example of low relationship authenticity—and, as you might expect, this is not good. People who are high in relationship authenticity report greater relationship commitment and satisfaction than do people who are low in relationship authenticity.

We can also talk in terms of dispositional authenticity. This reflects the extent to which people act in accordance with their feelings and values in a wide range of situations, roles, and relationships. People who are high in dispositional authenticity report greater life satisfaction, more frequent positive emotions (e.g., happy, joyful, inspired, and pleased), fewer maladaptive coping styles (e.g., using alcohol or drugs to manage stress), and fewer negative emotions (e.g., feeling irritable, frustrated, and upset).

So, generally speaking, authenticity is good, but it can't be that simple, can it? Is it really good to say whatever you think and feel in all situations, regardless of the costs? Let's find out by "playing House."

Break Out the Whiteboard: Is This Guy Authentic or Not?

Imagine that you are in the differential room with your diagnostic team at Princeton-Plainsboro. You are reviewing the case of a patient named "Gregory." The patient has come to you with a mysterious condition. So, you start by getting the patient's history. You learn that the patient's friends and colleagues uniformly describe the patient as someone who "acts as he pleases." Interestingly, the patient describes himself using the same terms. Clearly, this is a person with a strong sense of self. Is this good or bad, though? Is the patient simply being selfish or narcissistic? Or is he behaving authentically? How can we tell?

Further on in the patient's charts you learn that your patient does what he wants to do even when it involves cheating and lying and even when it is clear he will suffer negative consequences as a result. You learn, for example, that your patient's behaviors resulted in his being fired and incarcerated and on the brink of death on multiple occasions. Yet he continues "doing whatever he pleases."

Is this really what it means to be authentic? There is one way to find out. If the patient is being authentic, then he should display other symptoms associated with authenticity. For example, he should feel happy, joyful, pleased, and satisfied in his life, as well as with his social roles and his close relationships. At the same time, he should rarely feel irritable or have to resort to drug use to cope with his stress.

If this patient were House, as the thinly veiled allusions to him may have led you to suspect, then you may also have realized that House displays few of the positive characteristics associated with authenticity and many of the negative characteristics associated with a lack of authenticity. What is going on here? How is it that House appears in many ways to be highly authentic, yet he seems to reap none of its benefits?

I Do What I Want vs. I Own What I Am

Authenticity is more than simply "doing what you please." It involves "owning" one's personal experiences, including one's thoughts, emotions, and needs. According to humanistic psychologists such as Abraham Maslow and Carl Rogers, authenticity reflects being *self-actualized* and a *fully functioning* person. These qualities emerge as people discover their true inner nature, and they realize (e.g., put into action) their deepest potentials and capabilities. To be self-actualized, a person must first satisfy a broad set of physiological and psychological needs, including love, belongingness, and esteem. Considering House's penchant for prostitutes, his physiological need for sex may be satisfied but a slew of unrealized potential love interests (Stacy, Cameron, Lydia, Cuddy) likely keeps his psychological need for love unmet. Authenticity also involves becoming a more complete or fully functioning person. To be fully functioning, people must develop *congruence* between their self-concept (i.e., beliefs about themselves) and their experiences. This involves freely behaving in accord with beliefs that reflect who people really are, rather than trying to live up to an image that reflects who they imagine themselves to be or feel they have to be.

Let's apply this to House. In "Ugly," House's treatment of a patient with a severe malformation was documented by a film crew. House responds sarcastically to the filmmakers' inquiries and frequently attempts to ditch them. Despite such attempts, the final edited cut of the documentary portrays House as a hero, and when he sees it, he gets upset. This example illustrates House's desire to typify an image or a persona that presents him in a particular light (well, maybe "darkness"). Yet his persistent attempts to highlight his "bad" qualities and conceal his good ones are at odds with the fact that House has chosen a profession where he does good deeds and saves and improves countless patients' lives. By attempting to play the role of "antihero" while being a doctor, House places himself in situations where he is not fully meeting his psychological needs (e.g., pissing others off is not a very effective strategy for satisfying needs such as love or belonging), nor is he achieving congruence with his true self. As a result, House keeps himself from becoming a more fully functioning person, which includes becoming the heroic doctor that he clearly has the potential to be.

Kernis and Goldman have taken the initial theoretical ideas about authenticity a step forward—or maybe it was four steps forward. In their view, authenticity reflects how much people typically *know* and *accept* who they really are and *act* in ways that express their true selves. Specifically, dispositional authenticity involves four components: (1) *awareness*, (2) *unbiased processing*, (3) *behavior*, and (4) *relational orientation*. When people exhibit high amounts of authenticity in each of these components (assessed by the Authenticity Inventory, a questionnaire that examines how authentic people are in these components), they generally express their true selves fully and obtain substantial psychological benefits. Let's consider each component in turn.

The Doctor Will See You Now: Awareness

If you are honest with yourself, you may have noticed that you are not perfect. Maybe you've done a couple of foolish things or perhaps you've packed on a few (okay, more than a few) extra pounds. It can hurt to recognize these things in ourselves, but we have to if we want to be honest. Yet we don't have to be honest, do we? We can remain "blissfully ignorant," and that's the difference. Authentic people are aware of their strong points, as well as their weak points. Inauthentic people are unaware of aspects of themselves, and this often comes at a cost.

For example, think about House's prolonged addiction to painkillers. By living in denial and being unaware of the toll that his substance abuse is taking, House winds up going to jail courtesy of Officer Tritter in season 3's "Que Sera Sera," almost overdoses on methadone in the "The Softer Side" in season 5, and gets fired after screaming to the whole hospital that he had slept with Cuddy when in fact it was a substance-induced hallucination in the season 5 finale, "Both Sides Now."

In short, the awareness component of authenticity refers to the degree to which people fully know and understand their true self-aspects, such as their motives, desires, values, personality traits, and strengths and weaknesses. It also reflects the extent to which people are motivated to learn about these self-aspects and their role in behavior. In the season 6 premiere, "Broken," House's life is in shambles, and he has to be hospitalized for detoxification and psychotherapy treatment. Although he clearly needed to be "fixed," House initially refuses psychotherapy, and he consents to it only when his psychiatrist, Dr. Nolan, will not recommend to the medical board that House return to practicing medicine unless he undergoes therapy. House's lack of motivation to explore his deepest thoughts and feelings and learn about what brought him to his breaking point illustrates an example of low awareness. People high in awareness tend to agree with statements such as the following: "I am in touch with my deepest thoughts and feelings," "I have a very good understanding of why I do the things I do," and "For better or for worse, I am aware of who I truly am."

As individuals function with greater awareness, they become more knowledgeable and understanding of themselves. They realize that even though they may display one particular self-aspect more strongly than others, they also have other aspects of themselves. An extravert, for example, may sometimes desire to be alone. A very masculine person may have some feminine qualities. People who are high in awareness know this and are aware of their inconsistencies, contradictions, mixed motives, feelings, and inclinations.

In "Honeymoon," House reveals to Wilson that Mark, a dying patient who is the husband of his past love Stacy, is not responding to the treatment, and that he has mixed feelings about it: "Some part of me wants him to die. I'm just not sure if it's because I want to be with her or because I want her to suffer."

This scene illustrates the complexity of the awareness component. Rather than being clueless about what he's feeling and why he's feeling it (which would reflect low levels of awareness), House is fully aware of what he is feeling (that part of him wants Mark to die). He has also narrowed the range of causes to two possibilities, which both pertain to his feelings for Stacy. Presumably, House was still angry with Stacy for making the medical decision that resulted in him being a cripple (and letting Mark die could be sweet revenge), and he was still in love with her (and letting Mark die would allow them to be together). Overall, House's recognition of his conflicting feelings about Mark's mortality and his authentic exploration of the causes for these feelings reveal an instance in which House is functioning with high amounts of awareness.

Give It to Me Straight. I Can Take It: Unbiased Processing

Being authentic requires more than merely not being ignorant about our good, bad, and neutral qualities. It requires that like impartial judges, we continually and in "real time" consider self-relevant social feedback based on its veracity, rather than on its favorability. The unbiased processing component of authenticity involves the way in which people process and evaluate information about their personal qualities and abilities. When engaging in unbiased processing, people are motivated and able to assess both their positive and their negative qualities in an objective, nondefensive, and openly accepting manner. They aim to evaluate themselves without having to deny, distort, or ignore information that is relevant to accurately discerning their strengths and weaknesses. People who are low in unbiased processing tend to agree with statements such as "I am very uncomfortable objectively considering my limitations and shortcomings," "I find it very difficult to critically assess myself," "I often deny the validity of any compliments I receive," and "I find it difficult to embrace and feel good about the things I have accomplished."

Consider House's authenticity in the episode "Poison." House assumes that his teen patient was poisoned by a chemical identified on a canister label from the patient's home, and he recommends a treatment that would be fatal if his assumption is wrong. The patient's mother is aware of potential inaccuracies on the canister label, so she refuses House's treatment and confronts him, questioning his judgment and unwillingness to listen to her. Unfazed by the mother's concerns and fully convinced of his foolproof judgment, House approaches Cuddy for assistance in removing the mother's authority to decide her son's treatment. He reasons that they could argue that the mother is mentally ill, but Cuddy offers a more unbiased and realistic appraisal of the situation: "Her only sign of mental illness is that she disagrees with you!"

We all make mistakes, even distinguished doctors. In this case, House is wrong about what poisoned the teen. Yet not all people are willing to objectively acknowledge their limitations, are they? House's discomfort with accepting his shortcomings results in an unrealistic and inflated sense of confidence, even in situations when it is unwarranted (his patient could have been killed). In circumstances such as the episode "Poison," his overconfidence is not based on merit; it is based on his biased refusal to accept that he has anything but infallible judgment. Even after repeated failed attempts at treating the patient, House is still compelled to rigidly accept the same convictions and confidence in his judgment without any alteration, without any inkling of doubt, and without any reservations about acting on these beliefs. Such conclusions are echoed in House's subsequent attempt to persuade the mother to accept his latest proposed treatment. House approaches the mother to discuss the case while he waits for Chase to carry out his instructions to pretend to be someone from the Centers for Disease Control (from whom the mother was awaiting a second opinion) and call the mother to inform her that they are unable to assist her.

Mom: "What makes you think you're right this time?"
House: "The same reason as last time."

House's limited unbiased processing compromises his effectiveness as a doctor and prevents him from learning how to become a better one. His reluctance to objectively see his judgment as anything less than perfect requires that he selectively ignore information (in this case, intimated by the mother and by Cuddy). This information was both relevant for him to consider in the immediate situation for his patient's care and in its aftermath for more generally informing his understanding of how his overconfidence affects his medical practices. House's limited unbiased processing squanders his chance to learn valuable lessons about himself and expand the reach of his self-knowledge and understanding. It also keeps him from behaving congruently with the full scope of his true self-aspects.

Let's Take a Closer Look: Awareness and Unbiased Processing—the Ingredients of an Authentic Self-View

Nobody really wants to "fake it" in life or do what they dislike. What we really want is to do what feels right, and when we act on our likes, desires, values, preferences, and so on (think burgers, fries, and milk shakes), it feels good. But what if we don't really know what we like? Or, what if we were wrong, and we've convinced ourselves otherwise (think of all of the brussels sprouts you might've missed)? To address this, we need to take a closer look at the awareness and unbiased processing components so we can better understand what a person is "being authentic" to.

Awareness and unbiased processing work in tandem in the development of authenticity. When functioning authentically, people typically feel as if they know and understand themselves (high awareness). They are also accepting of themselves, and they seek to objectively assess their qualities, both good and bad, as they really are (high unbiased processing). In short, they develop an authentic self-view that reflects completeness, accuracy, and balance. Consequently, they behave in ways that reflect who they really are.

Let's apply this logic to House. If House's behavior is in accord with an authentic self-view, then that behavior is attuned to a deep sense of self-awareness, understanding, and accuracy in his knowledge about his true qualities. Alternatively, if he possesses an inauthentic self-view, then rather than reflecting on the knowledge and understanding of his full self-aspects, House's self-view would be incomplete and inaccurate. It would reflect only the self-aspects that he willingly perceives in himself, which are tainted by widespread biases and distorted appraisals. In this case, even when he is "keeping it real," he is being true only to the uninformed and/or misinformed self-view that he perceives in himself.

At times, House may appear to be highly aware and unbiased in his processing of his true self because he openly embraces having characteristics that others deem undesirable (e.g., embarrassing or socially offensive self-aspects). For example, consider the following exchange between Wilson and House in "Honeymoon" concerning House's struggle in treating Stacy's husband, Mark, as his patient.

> Wilson: You have to treat this like a regular case. Be yourself: cold, uncaring, distant.
> House: Please don't put me on a pedestal.

While such comments may be dismissed as mere sarcasm, they also provide insight into House's capacity to at times acknowledge and even embrace self-aspects that others would likely resist and struggle to recognize they possess. Yet is he willing to acknowledge and accept those qualities that he does not deem pedestal worthy?

Open Up and Say Ahhh: Authentic Behavior and Not Being a Jerk

Before answering the prior question, let's consider a study by Lakey, Kernis, Heppner, and Lance. The study examined the relation between dispositional authenticity and defensiveness. Participants completed the Authenticity Inventory and then a standardized interview that asked them to verbally describe their actions and feelings surrounding past events that were unpleasant, perhaps even threatening, to think about. For example, times when they had "broken the rules" or had "sexual feelings for someone other than their partners." Thinking about such events is likely to be unpleasant for anyone, but the study's findings indicated that highly authentic people (with high AI scores) were particularly open and honest about it, and that highly defensive and guarded reactions were more likely when people were low in authenticity.

The findings suggest that when put to the test of facing unpleasant truths about themselves, highly defensive people balk. Rather than objectively acknowledge their unpleasant truths, they simply deny, ignore, or alter their recollections and interpretations of events in exchange for a more pleasant fiction. In doing so, they respond in ways that show blockages or deficits in the functioning of an authentic view.

Consider the actual responses from a participant who was rated to be highly defensive. When asked about breaking the rules, instead of openly reflecting on an event, the participant laughed and replied, "What do you mean by the rules?" Having eventually recalled an instance, the participant tried to avoid seeing the past misbehaviors objectively and instead downplayed their negative implications. The participant proclaimed, "I guess in high school I cheated on a couple of tests. I guess that's breaking the rules." By having rationalized and reinterpreted the events in selective ways, the participant denied having felt any negative feelings at all. When asked how it made him or her feel, the participant replied, "I felt good because I got a higher grade. I didn't feel bad."

The defensiveness study may help shed light on whether House's behaviors are in accord with an authentic or an inauthentic self-view. Does House typically perceive (high awareness) and openly appraise (high unbiased processing) his undesirable self-aspects, and how does he behave when faced with having to consider these self-aspects? Consider again the "Poison" episode, which is representative of House's typical problems with achieving and maintaining an authentic self-view. Blockages in his awareness and unbiased processing exist, and this makes House defensive. We see this in his overconfidence and lack of awareness about his imperfect judgment and his selective dismissal of contrary opinions. Prior to merely trying to trick the mother into accepting his treatment, by eliminating the CDC as an alternative opinion, House more forcibly attempted to persuade her. Keep in mind, in the exchange that follows, that House has actually misdiagnosed her son, and therefore his treatment would be fatal. House confronts the mother and mocks her decision to refuse treatment, while sarcastically reading a phony waiver form aloud.

> House: I understand many doctors consider my decision to be completely idiotic. . . .
> Mom: Why are you doing this?
> House: . . . but I am convinced that I know more than they do. . . . Besides I enjoy controlling every aspect of my son's life even if it means his death.
> Mom: Who are you?
> House: I am the doctor who is trying save your son; you are the mom who's letting him die!

By functioning without an authentic self-view and acting in accord with an inauthentic self-view, House shows just how maladaptive his extremely defensive reactions can be. House's behaviors reveal the positive biases and distortions in how he appraises himself and the negative biases and distortions in how he appraises others. Clearly, this is a dangerous mix. House's misguided attempt to persuade the mother is fueled by his biased conviction about his foolproof judgment, and thus he thinks he's saving the patient. Also, House's malicious attack on the mother is fueled by his biased convictions about the other's foolish judgment and broader shortcomings; therefore, he thinks she would risk her son's life. A later exchange between the mother and Foreman illustrates House's thought process and the damage that results from his behaving in accord with his biased beliefs.

Mom: My God, the things he [House] said.

Foreman: Dr. House wanted your son to get the medicine he needed. He was willing to do whatever it took to make that happen.

Mom: The wrong kind of medicine.

Foreman: He didn't know that. At the time it was our only choice.

Mom: He would have known if he had listened to me.

Foreman: He listened. He just assumed you were wrong. To be honest, that's true of most of our patients.

Mom: [*Laughs*] You are just as pompous and superior as he is!

Foreman's comments reveal the negative beliefs that House imposes on others ("he just assumes" they are wrong) and the manipulative tactics he defaults to when dealing with others (he "is willing to do whatever it takes"). These inclinations are telling of House's Machiavellian qualities. Research shows that people who report high Machiavellianism hold negative and cynical beliefs about others, and they feel, when dealing with others, that others can and should be manipulated. For example, they agree with statements such as "all people have a vicious streak that comes out when they're given a chance," and "anyone who completely trusts anyone else is asking for trouble." With such beliefs in mind, high Machiavellians exhibit a "cool detachment" that makes them less emotionally involved with other people, with sensitive issues, or with saving face in embarrassing situations.

Such characteristics help account for House's caustic approach with the mother in the "Poison" episode, and they apply more broadly to his interpersonal dealings (recall the earlier example of Wilson's advice to House: "Be yourself: cold, uncaring, distant"). With a cavalier attitude about how his accusations and dismissing of others may cause them to feel hurt and offended and little concern over being construed as "pompous and superior," House is compelled to simply "say what he really thinks." Unfortunately what he really thinks about others may be unfounded and distorted, based on the negative biases of his Machiavellian leanings.

Recent research shows that higher dispositional authenticity is associated with less reported Machiavellianism. This suggests that perhaps by "keeping it real" with themselves, people may also be empowered to "keep it real" with others, interacting nondefensively without negative prejudices and preemptive agendas to manipulate others. By behaving in step with the deficits in his authentic self-view, House restricts his range of possible behaviors with others to a limited set of options. This steers him more toward defensiveness and Machiavellianism (distrust, cynicism, and so on) and less toward openness and honesty, especially when dealing with those he is closest to.

Through the Stethoscope—Heartbeats and Heartaches: An Authentic Relational Orientation

The final component of authenticity, called relational orientation, reflects the extent to which people generally value and achieve being their true selves in close relationships. An authentic relational orientation involves being genuine, rather than fake, in one's interpersonal relationships. This means being open and truthful in disclosing and expressing one's true self-aspects (both positive *and* negative), rather than deliberately falsifying the impressions one makes on close others or neglecting to express key aspects of who one really is. People who score high on the relational orientation component of authenticity agree with statements such as: "I want people with whom I am close to understand my strengths and weaknesses," "I make it a point to express to close others how much I truly care for them," "My openness and honesty in close relationships are extremely important to me," and "I want close others to understand the real me, rather than just my public persona or image."

House's deficits in his authentic self-view keep him from fully being his true self in his close relationships. Consider the prior relational orientation statements as they apply to House. For example, by being unaware of or unwilling to recognize his caring for close others, he fails to express it to them. When he is open and honest, it is usually only to divulge aspects of himself that he wants close others to see, which allow him to play up the image of the "coolly detached, all-knowing doctor."

By being open and honest in self-disclosing their inner feelings, people help cultivate close relationships that are built on mutual trust and intimacy. These characteristics are difficult for House to achieve because he is reluctant to express or even acknowledge having positive feelings such as concern, empathy, pride, or love. How often do we, for example, hear House express feeling grateful for Wilson's devoted friendship or give even a half-hearted "good job" to affirm his medical team? In short, House hides his more vulnerable emotions—the very emotions that are vital in establishing warm, accepting, and supportive relationships. Alternatively, House does willingly express negative emotions, such as contempt, anger, and annoyance. The barrage of criticisms, accusations, insults, and provocations that House freely hurls at others ultimately prevents him from developing close relationships. Consider the episode "Love Hurts" and the buzz-kill response that House provides on his date with Cameron, after she attempts to establish intimacy.

> Cameron: I want to know how you feel about me.
> House: You live under the delusion that you can fix everything that isn't perfect. That's why you married a man who was dying of cancer. You don't love. You need. And now that your husband is dead, you're looking for your new charity case. That's why you're going out with me. I'm twice your age, I'm not great looking, I'm not charming, I'm not even nice. What I am is what you need. I'm damaged.

Okay, so House admitted he's "not great looking," but are his shared revelations truly an act of relational authenticity? Is House simply "keeping it real" by being brutally honest? Notice that House never expresses his *feelings* for Cameron. He merely evokes his familiar persona of "all-knowing doctor" and expresses with "cool detachment" a harrowing clinical interpretation of Cameron.

House's behavior with Cameron fits with a general pattern that he exhibits in his close relationships, in which he uses verbal attacks to avoid self-disclosing positive and affectionate feelings. This dynamic is almost formulaic—when people attempt to connect with House, he rebuffs their attempts in a hostile way and belittles them for trying, which makes them leery of doing so again. Consequently, House's defensive inclinations to avert authentically exploring, acknowledging, accepting, and expressing his positive relational feelings with close others only pushes them away.

Psychological theory and research suggest that a sense of connectedness and positive intimate relationships is at the core of people's psychological well-being and their psychological needs. By eroding the quality of his close relationships House not only hurts others, he also hurts himself. So, why might he be compelled to undermine his own and others' well-being? House's eulogy at his father's funeral in "Birthmarks" provides insight into answering such questions and reveals a case in which the apple doesn't fall far from the tree.

> House: There's a lot of people here today, including some from the corps and I noticed that every one of them is my father's rank or higher, and this doesn't surprise me. Because, if the test of a man is how he treats those he has power over, it is a test my father failed. This man who we pay homage to—he was incapable of admitting any point of view other than his own. He punished failure. He did not accept anything less than [*pauses—presumably "perfection"*]. . . . He loved what he did. He saw his work as some kind of a secret calling more important than any kind of personal relationship. Maybe if he'd been a better father, I'd have been a better son. But for better or for worse, I am what I am because of him.

A Diagnosis Awaits: How Authentic Is House Overall?

House's poignant insights during his eulogy for his father actually provide an accurate summary for his own authenticity. Overall, House may "act as he pleases," but he doesn't authentically "own" who he is. House exhibits moderate amounts of dispositional authenticity.

Dispositional authenticity reflects a dynamic interplay between four components. It involves establishing an authentic self-view in which one is in touch with one's true self (awareness component) and is bias-free in how one evaluates the full range of his or her qualities (unbiased processing component). It also involves acting in accord with one's true self (behavior component) and being genuine in one's close relationships (relational orientation component). House exhibits deficits in establishing an authentic view. So, by acting in accord with his limited authentic self-view, House often resorts to maladaptive and destructive behaviors in general and in close relationships. House easily gets defensive and fails to admit to points of view other than his own. He is not accepting of others' foibles and fails the test of power by severely condemning them. He places a premium on his work, rather than on personal relationships. Take it or leave it, for better or for worse, House is who he is.

SUGGESTED READINGS

Gillath, O., A. K. Sesko, P. R. Shaver, and D. S. Chun (2010). Attachment, authenticity, and honesty: Dispositional and experimentally induced security can reduce self- and other-deception. *Journal of Personality and Social Psychology*, 98(5), 841–855.

Harter, S. (2002). Authenticity. In C. R. Snyder and S. J. Lopez (eds.), *Handbook of Positive Psychology* (pp. 382–394). Oxford, England: Oxford University Press.

Kernis, M. H., and B. M. Goldman (2006). A multicomponent conceptualization of authenticity: Theory and research. In M. P. Zanna and M. P. Zanna (eds.), *Advances in Experimental Social Psychology*, Vol. 38 (pp. 283–357). San Diego: Elsevier Academic Press.

Lakey, C. E., M. H. Kernis, W. L. Heppner, and C. E. Lance (2008). Individual differences in authenticity and mindfulness as predictors of verbal defensiveness. *Journal of Research in Personality*, 42(1), 230–238.

Maslow, A. H. (1968). *Toward a Psychology of Being*, 2nd ed. Oxford, England: D. Van Nostrand.

Rogers, C. R. (1961). *On Becoming a Person: A Therapist's View of Psychotherapy*. Boston: Houghton Mifflin.

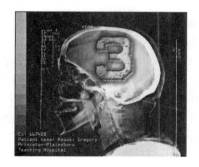

The Creative Side of House
It's the Last Muse on the Right

LILE JIA AND EDWARD R. HIRT

One of the more fascinating aspects of *House* for many of us is to watch the differential diagnosis process unfold as House guides his medical team down one blind alley after another until finally happening on the ultimate solution that solves the case. (Well, most of the time.) House likens the diagnostic task to a puzzle and revels in exploring the myriad possibilities that may underlie the set of symptoms experienced and/or reported by the patient. We marvel at his uncanny ability to take incongruous or seemingly meaningless clues and ultimately experience that moment of revelation when it all makes sense, and the brilliant solution to an ostensibly intractable problem is obtained. In many ways, House channels the creative process right before our eyes.

When we think of individuals throughout history and literature who exemplify the kind of insight, genius, and creativity that House exhibits, what names come to mind? Sherlock Holmes?

Albert Einstein? Wolfgang Amadeus Mozart? Vincent van Gogh? Can we put our beloved House in the same elite category as these fellows? Well, he certainly fits the personality profile of the tortured artist. He is a master diagnostician who commands the awe and respect of his colleagues. Yet he is also in constant pain, popping Vicodin every five minutes. He has difficulty communicating and relating to people (with the notable exception of the autistic boy from "Lines in the Sand" or the priest from "Unfaithful"). He seems lonely and miserable, unless he has a challenging case to distract and consume him. Finally, he shows disdain and a blatant disregard for social norms and rules, encouraging his team members to (among other things) illegally break into a patient's home to gather information relevant to the diagnosis.

> Chase: He thinks outside the box, is that so evil?
> Foreman: He doesn't know where the box is!!
> —"Occam's Razor"

Indeed, the idea that creativity and madness are intricately related dates back to Aristotle. Moreover, some contemporary researchers believe that people who are gifted with such astute powers of observation and creativity are more prone to suffer from mental disorders such as depression, schizophrenia, and bipolar disorder than their noncreative counterparts. Drug addiction, alcoholism, and suicide are all common symptoms in these individuals. While there is some intuitive appeal to this perspective that creative people are somewhat different from the rest of us, brilliant but one step away from going "over the edge," research in social psychology has tended to focus on the orientations of creative individuals that facilitate their insight. This perspective argues that we can all have creative moments, times where things just click. But these moments for many of us seem elusive, and it begs the question of how someone like House can be so insightful when those around him, equally motivated to nail the diagnosis and treat the patient successfully, struggle to fit the pieces together. In this chapter, we will explore what factors contribute to House's insight, as well as how much control he has over his creativity.

Do (Creative) Clothes Make the Man?

One of the most notable traits of House is his willingness to take risks. It seems that everyone else around him is afraid of making the wrong move, a move that might hurt or potentially kill the patient, but House is open to what he calls "exploratory treatment" in order to ascertain what is wrong with a patient. While others around him chastise him as insensitive or uncaring, our man House is simply willing to try something radical if he feels it will provide valuable information in correctly diagnosing the malady affecting a given patient. Consider the following exchange between House and Cuddy from "Pilot":

> Cuddy: I'm stopping the treatment.
> House: She's my patient.
> Cuddy: It's my hospital.
> House: I did not get her sick, she is not an experiment, I have a legitimate theory about what's wrong with her.
> Cuddy: With no proof.
> House: There's never any proof. Five different doctors come up with five different diagnoses based on the same evidence.
> Cuddy: You don't have any evidence. And nobody knows anything, huh? Then how is it that you always assume you're right?
> House: I don't, I just find it hard to operate on the opposite assumption. And why are you so afraid of making a mistake?
> Cuddy: Because I'm a doctor. Because when we make mistakes, people die.

Certainly, we can see both sides here. Most of us would probably side with Cuddy on this issue, because the risk of making a mistake with someone's life is enough of a deterrent to take a safer, more conservative approach. Yet House adheres to a different perspective, one that research has shown to facilitate greater creativity and out-of-the-box thinking. Unconventional approaches to treatment that may foster valuable information in diagnosis often entail greater risks. House is not afraid to accept these risks in exchange for the potential payoff of the correct diagnosis and the successful treatment of the patient. Recall his unconventional approach to the treatment of Rebecca later on in "Pilot":

> House: How long do we have?
> Foreman: If it's a tumor, we're talking a month, maybe two; if it's infectious, a few weeks; if it's vascular, that'll probably be fastest of all, maybe a week.
> House: We're gonna stop all treatment.
> Foreman: So we're just gonna do nothing? We're just gonna watch her die?
> House: Yeah, we're gonna watch her die. Specifically, we're gonna watch how fast she's dying. You just told us each diagnosis has its own time frame. When we see how fast it's killing her, we'll know what it is.

This approach seems heartless to Foreman but ends up providing crucial information in saving Rebecca's life. Only someone like House is willing to consider a riskier, more radical approach, one that might incur potential criticism, derision, and ridicule from others, but one that has the creative potential for breaking new ground. Indeed, many of the most creative theories and discoveries in history involved stepping outside of conventional thinking and proposing ideas that seemed ludicrous and/or heretical at the time.

One could say that creative geniuses must then be mavericks, people who enjoy bucking social conventions, traditional ways of thinking, and the status quo. A mode of thinking that promotes this kind of orientation is known as *promotion focus*. Promotion-focused individuals view opportunities in terms of their potential for success, growth, and accomplishment. Promotion focus leads people to approach situations because of their potential gain. In contrast, *prevention-focused* individuals view situations in terms of their potential for failure or punishment and thus are motivated to avoid situations that pose a threat to their sense of safety and security. Research has shown that promotion-focused individuals are more likely to take calculated risks if they believe these can lead to significant payoffs down the road, whereas prevention-focused individuals are highly risk averse, fearful of doing anything that may result in negative consequences or losses. House most certainly exemplifies promotion focus and expresses disdain for those who can't see the value in taking the necessary risk to get the diagnosis right. "Why are you so afraid of making a mistake?" says House in "Pilot." Indeed. Spoken like a card-carrying promotion-focus poster boy!

Haven't We Been Over This Already?

We are all familiar with the quote "If at first you don't succeed, try, try again." For the members of House's team, this phrase adequately characterizes the process illustrated in episode after episode, as the physicians struggle through diagnosis after diagnosis, most of which turn out not to be supported by test results and treatment outcomes. Given the host of potential diagnoses available for the set of symptoms experienced by these patients, it is not surprising that House and his team must often return to the drawing board and gather additional evidence to support or rule out various possibilities. One of our favorite parts of every episode is watching the interactions of the team members when they gather and brainstorm possible diagnoses for the patient. Someone will throw out his or her best guess, only to have it ruled out by House as unlikely, and this process continues until the team reaches some consensus that a given diagnosis is plausible enough to merit additional scrutiny and testing.

The dynamics of these group interactions illustrate an important aspect of creativity in groups. Individuals who are low in *the psychological need for closure* are people who are likely to explore all of the possibilities and angles of a given problem before rendering a decision or a judgment. They solicit input from a variety of sources, gather as much information as they can, and are open to the consideration of any and all alternatives. In contrast, individuals high in the psychological need for closure have little tolerance for ambiguity and often "jump the gun" in making quick decisions. Although the decisiveness of people who are high in the need for closure may be considered an asset under some conditions (e.g., time pressure), research has shown that individuals and groups that are low in the need for closure tend to be more creative and ultimately perform better. Certainly, the careful and thorough consideration that House and his team give to all of the potential diagnoses during these brainstorming sessions is a hallmark of low need for closure individuals.

How is it that low need for closure translates into more creative thinking and performance? Well, the most obvious characteristic is the willingness to gather as much data as possible. Tests are ordered, exploratory treatments are attempted, and results are monitored. Based on these results, possibilities remain viable or are discarded. This aspect doesn't seem particularly unique to House, though, as opposed to any good physician or diagnostician. Yet another key element of low need for closure that really sets House apart from the rest of the field is his willingness to revisit previously rejected alternatives in light of new evidence. It is House's uncanny ability to consider multiple possibilities, even previously discarded or rejected ones, that makes him the creative genius that he is. As an example, consider the episode "Lines in the Sand," in which the team is trying to diagnose the source of an autistic boy's heart and lung problems. House initially orders an analysis of a stool sample, testing for possible parasites, but the test comes back negative. They explore other possibilities, including cancer, cirrhosis, or a tumor, with little success.

> Foreman: What are you looking for?
> House: He's telling us what he's seeing, telling us exactly what was wrong with him, drawing them for us over and over again. Nobody knew how to speak autistic.
> Dominic: What are you talking about? What was he seeing?
> House: Hello, my pretties. It's not a tumor, Foreman, it's worms swimming in his eye. Animal makes potty in the sandbox, boy plays in the sandbox, boy eats the sand, you can probably tell where this is going by now.
> Foreman: Stool samples were negative for parasites.

House: Raccoon roundworms are not excreted by their human host.

Foreman: Cameron tested the sand.

House: All of it? Worms spread from his gut to the rest of his body. Attacked his lungs, that's what made him scream and caused the effusion. Invade [*sic*] his liver, sending dead liver cells coursing through his system; it attacked his eye and the muscles surrounding it, making his eyeball do a back flip.

While everyone else takes the stool sample results as definitive evidence to rule out parasites and fails to consider this possibility, House is able to reconsider this possible diagnosis and ultimately resolve the puzzle.

Psychological research on creative problem solving has consistently demonstrated that people often have difficulty breaking out of "mental sets" or "functional fixedness." A favorite example of this is the Duncker candle problem. In this classic experiment, participants are given a candle, a box of thumbtacks, and a book of matches and are asked to attach the candle to the wall so that it does not drip onto the table below. Participants routinely try to attach the candle directly to the wall with the tacks or to stick it to the wall by melting it, but neither of these strategies is successful in completing the task. Almost no one thinks of using the inside of the box as a candle-holder and tacking this to the wall. Why do people miss this potential solution to the problem? Psychologists find that participants remain "fixated" on the box's normal function of holding thumbtacks and cannot reconceptualize a box of tacks as a "box" and "tacks," which would allow them to correctly solve the problem.

Yet House is not like the vast majority of the participants who perform the Duncker candle problem. House's extremely low need for closure allows him to see the various potential ways to view the symptoms presented to him. He also displays the ability to revisit previously rejected diagnoses (such as a parasite, in "Lines in the Sand") when new evidence implicates such a possibility, leaving the rest of his team scratching their heads. Obviously, we know that he revels in his ability to make these clever and creative diagnoses. Not only does it massage his ego, but it also seems to relieve some of his physical pain (as seen at the end of "Broken").

Uncovering the Method behind the (Creative) Madness

From the previous analysis, we have keenly witnessed the various traits and dispositions that our Vicodin-addicted doctor possesses that might have nurtured his creative thinking style. Those who aspire to imitate House's method of creativity should soon realize the immense costs (social relationships, for one) that this kind of lifestyle would incur. It's clearly not for the fainthearted!

Perhaps we can now vividly picture the annoying signature smirk on House's face, "I'm simply unique!" Is there any way to get at this guy? To make a dent in his massive ego? To mock him in a way that he has so often mocked everyone else? "But, as the philosopher Jagger once said," we hear House sneering from the corner, "you can't always get what you want." Indeed, we can't, but, as it turns out, if we delve deeper into the processes of creativity, we are able to respond to him exactly as Cuddy does by citing Jagger again in "Pilot," "If you try sometimes, you get what you need."

"Lymphoma, Tada!": House's Prowess in Logical Reasoning

What we need is simply to show that House's creativity is not based on the prized asset he is most proud of—rationality. House is so attached to his rationality that he rejects religion simply because it is not a product of logical reasoning.

> Sister Augustine: Why is it so difficult for you to believe in God?

House: What I have difficulty with is the whole concept of belief; faith isn't based on logic and experience.

—"Damned If You Do"

Certainly, a large part of House's "sick" brilliance comes from his Sherlock Holmes–esque deductive ability. For example, in "Pilot," House is able to deduce that a patient's wife is having an affair from the simple fact that the patient's skin has turned orange (due to over-consumption of both carrots and vitamins).

During medical diagnoses, House is also usually a few steps ahead of his team in reaching a preliminary conclusion based on the patient's symptoms. Indeed, he is not shy about flaunting his gift. In "The Tyrant," when House just returns from his rehabilitation and joins the team that Foreman now leads, he pretends to respect Foreman's authority by not speaking during the preliminary diagnosis. It then comes as no surprise that House creates all sorts of other disruptions to dominate the discussion. After the team finally reaches the diagnosis of lymphoma for the African dictator, House suggests to Foreman that he should close the blinds. As Foreman does that, the blinds reveal "LYMPHOMA, TADA!" obviously correctly predicted and written down by House in advance.

House's prowess in rational reasoning, however, is not the driving force behind his creative thinking. In the following discussion, we will talk about two forms of House's creative genius. One is his incredibly accurate first instinct at the very beginning of the diagnosis, and the other is his uncanny tendency to experience an *Aha!* moment after a long period of impasse. As the following exploration will demonstrate, neither form of creativity relies on logical reasoning, as House so mistakenly claims.

"All You Had Was a Hunch!": House's Scarily Accurate First Instincts

Cuddy has probably accused House many times of basing treatments on his intuition, or *hunches*, rather than on concrete evidence. In many cases, House develops a gut feeling about the cause of a patient's symptoms almost immediately. One thing about these first instincts is that they are generally controversial and based on shaky assumptions, hence Cuddy's objections. To Cuddy's chagrin, however, House's hunches are usually scarily accurate.

In "All In," for instance, a doctor reports to Cuddy about the conditions of a child experiencing bloody diarrhea when Wilson, Cuddy, and House are in the heat of a poker game.

> Doctor: Dr. Cuddy? Got one of your patients in the ER. Ian Alston. Six years old.
> Cuddy: Ah . . . Oh, I know him. What's the problem? I'm all-in.
> Doctor: Bloody diarrhea, hemodynamically stable, but he's been developing some coordination problems.
> Cuddy: It sounds like gastroenteritis and dehydration. Order fluids, and I'll take it on my service. Bet's to you, House.
> House: They scan his head?
> Doctor: No, why would they scan . . .
> Cuddy: Don't play games. You gonna call?
> House: How's the heart rate?
> Doctor: Stable.
> Cuddy: I'm sorry. House? It's gastroenteritis. I'm not going anywhere.

Our little Ian here does seem to suffer from a gastric flu, and Cuddy's diagnosis is as good as that of any other qualified doctor. Yet because of the suspicious coordination problems Ian has, House has a hunch that the child is suffering from the same unknown disease that killed a seventy-two-year-old patient twelve years ago (so he quits the poker game with a pair of aces). This is a highly far-fetched instinct for two reasons. First, the loss of coordination can simply be a complication from gastroenteritis. Second, on face value, there seems to be very little in common between a six-year-old boy and a female septuagenarian. Strangely enough, House insists on acting on his instinct, despite equally persistent opposition from Cuddy and his team. In the end, as in many other cases, House turns out to be right. His hunch saves the child's life!

What Cuddy has failed to understand is that instantaneous hunches from experts such as House provide valuable insight into the roots of the problem at hand. Research has shown that the first instincts of experts such as chess masters and experienced firefighters can be very accurate. Two key conditions make experts' gut feelings especially accurate: (1) when the environment is a *high-validity environment*, which provides information that is highly informative of the underlying cause, and (2) when experts have been allowed enough opportunities to learn the environment.

Medicine, as opposed to politics and the financial industry (do we need to say anything more about political pundits' *predictions* for election results and financial analysts' *forecasts* for the stock market?), is such a high-validity environment. Each symptom is very informative of the cause of the problem. After all, the pains and discomforts in our bodies have been designed by evolution to signal us that something is wrong. House, being a leading diagnostician in the country, should also be *quite* familiar with the medical world. In other words, the conditions are ripe for House's hunches to result in effective treatment.

What House fails to understand, conversely, is the source of his instincts. House defends his hunch to Cuddy, "I just find it hard to operate on the opposite assumption," making it sound as if the hunch comes from logical reasoning. If one takes a closer look at the case in "All In," it's plainly obvious that there's nothing wrong with assuming that the boy suffers from dehydration and gastroenteritis, based on his initial symptoms. So, where does House's creative intuition truly come from?

Researchers in general agree that our gut feelings come from unconscious (the use of *unconscious* is identical to what many refer to as *subconscious*) processes. Because our intuition is not based on conscious reasoning, we find it hard to describe how we arrive at these insights. It's easy to explain why we respond with "two" to "1 + 1 = ?" but it's difficult to explain why we feel someone is familiar even on our first encounter. Experts' gut feelings operate in a similar fashion.

They, too, sense a familiarity, endowed by their unconscious, in their hunch about a problem at hand. Especially creative flashes of intuition may occur to exceptional individuals such as House, but these are no more conscious than our daily mundane intuition is. Because of the unconscious nature of creative intuition, people attribute an almost magical aura to it.

"Rat, Blue, Cottage. Go!": The Associative Nature of the Unconscious

If the unconscious doesn't operate on logical reasoning, what does it ride on? After much effort to demystify intuition, psychologists largely agree that the unconscious relies on the activation of associative links among concepts stored in our memory to produce intuition.

Concepts are associated in our memory with varying strength. Things that tend to co-occur or share similar features are strongly associated with each other. For example, *pillow* is *strongly associated* with *sleep* because these concepts tend to co-occur on a daily basis, as opposed to with *fight*, which leads to a *weak* or *remote* association.

Flashes of creative intuition occur when people make remote or unusual associations between concepts. For instance, what is a creative answer to "name a mode of transportation"? We can easily agree that *dream*, as opposed to *car*, is a creative answer. Here, one has to make the unusual association between dream and mode of transportation, which both *take someone somewhere.*

To test whether one's propensity to make unusual associations is related to other forms of creativity, psychologists commonly use the remote association test (RAT). In this test, individuals are presented with groups of three words. Their task is to come out with a word that's commonly associated with all three of the words presented. Try an easy example: rat/blue/cottage. It doesn't take long for individuals to realize that the answer is the favorite food of cheese lovers. Yet it is more challenging and takes a long time for most people to figure out dive/light/rocket. It should come as no surprise that some people are better at RAT than others. More important, evidence suggests that individuals who excel in RAT tend to be more creative on other creativity tasks. (Hint for the hard RAT question: Have you ever wondered why it is blue in good weather?)

In fact, House would definitely excel on the RAT. Notably, the brainstorming session among members of his team at the beginning of any episode is strikingly similar to the RAT. House would name the symptoms and say, "Go!" The team's goal then is to find one or several promising causes that fit all of the symptoms. That's exactly how people solve the RAT. And House is usually the fastest. This gift for finding unusual and useful associations underlies his hunches, which are frequently so creative and so accurate.

Creative intuition thus occurs when the situation at hand triggers unusual associations with the underlying causes. Indeed, in "All In," House's intuition makes an exceptional association between the six-year-old and a seventy-two-year-old, which is why we immediately see it as creative intuition. As I have mentioned, this process happens automatically and is quite devoid of conscious processing. Logical reasoning comes in only when evaluating the validity of the diagnosis. The initial hunches House has, the initial bridging between remotely associated cases, contrary to what House believes, come from what he doesn't understand: his unconscious.

"I Had a Muse": House's *Aha!* Moments

Perhaps House is more famous for another type of creativity. We are all too familiar with the flow of a typical House episode. The team fails to correctly identify the reason a patient is dying and reaches an impasse. When all hope is lost, House suddenly experiences a creative insight while doing something completely unrelated to the diagnosis.

Take an example from the episode "Informed Consent." When the team is baffled by the symptoms of a dying old scientist named Ezra Powell, House suddenly receives an insight after staring at the red thong worn by the daughter of a clinic patient. Apparently, the red thong reminds him of Congo Red, a dye used to test for amyloidosis. When the team finds out that House's diagnosis is right, Foreman asks

House how he reached that conclusion. House is pretty honest this time and refers to the thong-sporting teenage girl as his *muse.*

Foreman: How the hell did you pull that out of . . .
House: Not out of mine. I had a muse.

Muses, Greek goddesses of inspiration, have been associated with creativity since time immemorial. Men often describe their creative insights, *Aha!* moments, as visits from muses. This analogy reveals important features of creative insights: that they are uncontrollable and seem to appear with no warning. Unlike logical reasoning, which is based on steps of induction and deduction that can be controlled by the mental path we take, creative enlightenment can only be hoped for.

House is no exception, and he has absolutely no control over his creative insight. This is evident when he can't solve a case in "Saviors," for he is visibly frustrated and worries that he may have "lost his mojo." House's mojo is actually his extreme tendency to be hit by creative insight. Yet if creative insight is not based on logical reasoning, where does House's mojo come from?

Graham Wallas first theorized the steps necessary for creative insight as preparation, incubation, insight, and verification. *Preparation* is the information collection phase, where one explores the various dimensions of the problem. *Incubation* is the stage where one abandons the focal problem while the creative solution is brewed in the unconscious. *Insight*, or illumination, is when creative insight rises into conscious awareness. *Verification* is the stage where creative insight is systematically scrutinized against reality and, if possible, improved on.

Preparation and verification are without doubt dictated by conscious reasoning, but what has been considered the passage to true insight, incubation, has long been recognized to involve the unconscious. Countless anecdotal accounts from famous scientists and artists suggest that the problem at hand has to be consciously ignored for a while so that the unconscious can offer a solution. For instance, G. Spencer-Brown has noted of Sir Isaac Newton that to arrive at the simplest truth, as Newton knew and practiced, requires years of contemplation. Not activity. Not reasoning. Not calculating. Not busy behavior of any kind. Not reading. Not talking. Not making an effort. Not thinking. Simply bearing in mind what it is that one needs to know.

—G. Spencer-Brown, *Laws of Form*

Nonetheless, due to the fact that the unconscious is notoriously difficult to study scientifically, the exact way in which the unconscious generates creative insight has been the subject of speculation.

For a long time, psychologists have assigned the unconscious an unceremonious role in incubation. Specifically, theorists believe that the unconscious simply allows incorrect initial strategies to fade away and be forgotten. The end result is that individuals would be able to look at the problem with a fresh perspective.

Such a passive role for the unconscious in the process of incubation has been challenged by recent research. Most notably, growing evidence suggests that the unconscious *actively* thinks. Indeed, it has been empirically demonstrated that the unconscious actively integrates and processes information in the absence of conscious processing.

Two characteristics of unconscious thought have been identified. One is that in situations where there is an overload of conflicting information, the unconscious is actually more capable in thinking than is the conscious. This is because conscious thought is limited by the number of thoughts we can hold in mind, whereas the unconscious does not have this restriction.

A typical case on *House* generally meets this condition. The patient usually has conflicting symptoms, each of which is related to a dozen different causes. In "Meaning," for example, to discover the cause of Richard McNeil's full-body paralysis, the team has to analyze eight years of the patient's medical history, which consists of a total of 214 symptoms. While this amount of information is guaranteed to result in information overload for the conscious mind, our unconscious can cope with it with no sweat.

Another feature of unconscious thought resonates with our discussion about first instincts. The unconscious is better than the conscious at discovering "weak" and unusual associations—a condition that is conducive to having creative ideas. Research has shown that although conscious thought processing has an advantage in solving easy RAT questions (concepts that are strongly associated), unconscious thinking makes the answers to really difficult RAT questions (e.g., down/question/check) very accessible in the mind. (Correct answer: mark.)

This research suggests that during incubation, when the conscious mind is distracted by other tasks, the unconscious does two things: (1) integrates a large body of information, and (2) finds the unusual connections among the concepts. Both of these processes are likely to lead to creative insight and are hindered when a person is consciously deliberating about the problem at hand. Thus, ironically, when House is playing a video game or watching *Prescription: Passion*, he's putting his unconscious to work!

The showdown between conscious and unconscious thinking can't be more telling than in "Meaning." In this episode, House diagnoses McNeil with Addison's disease, a disease that led to a corticosteroid imbalance that kept McNeil in a wheelchair. Cuddy, after disagreeing with House, eventually injects cortisol in McNeil and finds him standing up and hugging his wife and son. It is nothing less than a miracle to enable a patient to stand up again with a single injection, after he has suffered from full-body paralysis for eight years.

Does House's logical reasoning help him achieve this amazing feat? No. In fact, after House deliberates in front of the whiteboard filled with McNeil's symptoms of the previous eight years, he makes a *wrong* diagnosis that almost kills the patient (Chase and Foreman have to cut the patient's throat to save his life!). Yet when House puts aside the problem to go for a jog, an *Aha!* moment suddenly strikes him after he tries to cool himself down with a drink from a water fountain. He realizes that McNeil didn't dive into the swimming pool to commit suicide but to lower his body temperature, which finally leads House to the right diagnosis.

In other words, House's creative brilliance comes from his powerful unconscious, not from the logical reasoning that he is so proud of. His conscious brain simply can't deal with all of the information at once. Who is the fainthearted one now?

"You Owe Your Insight to the 'Mute Loser'": "Both Sides Now"

If we have only been taking hints, albeit strong ones, from House to infer how much he detests things unexplained by rationality, his comparison of the two halves of the globe in everyone's head is more revealing. In "Both Sides Now," the team admits a patient, Scott, who has undergone surgery that disconnects his left and right hemispheres, leaving his body functioning with two individual halves. In their first meeting, the team has the following wonderful exchange:

> Taub: Split brain. Right hemisphere controls the left and . . .
> House: Is making life miserable. Nonlogical thinkers often do.
> Thirteen: Current issue isn't the split brain. Surgery corrected . . .
> Foreman: You're dissing the right?
> House: Most people who have this operation don't notice they're missing anything. Left brain has language, arithmetic, rationality. Right brain is a mute loser.

House's opinion is clear. A person has to be a logical thinker to avoid a miserable life. The left brain is what makes life beautiful. A person is better off without the right brain.

Certainly, logical thinking may not involve major areas of the right brain, but when it comes to creative thinking, the right brain is exactly what makes House a terrific diagnostician. For a long time, the right brain has been associated with divergent thinking, a potent thinking style for creativity. More recent neuroscience research has started to employ functional magnetic resonance imaging (fMRI), a technique that lights up the busiest parts of the brain, to study the *Aha!* experience. It's not surprising that increased activity in the right hemisphere, especially the region known as the anterior superior temporal gyrus, has been found to be responsible for generating creative insight.

The right hemisphere is not a mute loser. It may be quiet, but it's a hard worker. While the logical thinker, the left brain, is distracted by a sexy girl's thong or the endorphin rush after a jog, the nonlogical thinker within us is busy bridging remotely connected concepts, patterns, and events to solve the puzzle. It then selflessly supplies the answer to the conscious mind. The left brain, which is in charge of language and conscious output, thereupon takes the credit and fools even arguably the smartest doctor on television.

We feel deviously joyous to realize that our badass doctor is as helpless as we are in achieving creative insight. He is also clueless about and in denial of a fact that even his subordinate Foreman knows: "Right brain's advantage is that it isn't logical, doesn't choose which details to look at, makes connections you could never see. You owe your insight to the 'mute loser.'"

Although this ought to twist the knife into House's ego, the more sympathetic among us could find solace when House eventually acknowledges that "my [right] brain was trying to tell me" after realizing that he has had a slip of tongue (pancreatic cancer) about the cause of the incessant squawking of an eighty-year-old patient later in the episode.

Perhaps we are simply deluding ourselves to believe that this realization would inflict any damage on the ego of our beloved House. Regardless, we hope that the present analysis will give us a greater appreciation of things we can do to be more creative and of the role the unconscious and the right brain play in creativity. From now on, like House, let's take more risks, focus more on the potential gains in life, and feel freer to revisit abandoned opinions. Unlike House, however, let's not ignore the whispers of our unconscious and the mute "loser"—that's our muse singing.

SUGGESTED READINGS

Dijksterhuis, A., and T. Meurs (2006). Where creativity resides: The generative power of unconscious thought. *Consciousness and Cognition, 15,* 135–146.

Friedman, R. S., and J. Forster (2001). The effects of promotion and prevention cues on creativity. *Journal of Personality and Social Psychology, 81,* 1001–1003.

Schooler, J. W., and J. Melcher (1995). The ineffability of insight. In S. M. Smith, T. B. Ward, and R. A. Finke (eds.), *The Creative Cognition Approach* (pp. 97–133). Cambridge, MA: MIT Press.

Spencer-Brown, G. (1972). *Laws of Form.* New York: Julian Press.

Bowden, E. M., M. Jung-Beeman, J. Fleck, and J. Kounious (2005). New approaches to demystifying insight. *Trends in Cognitive Sciences, 9,* 322–328.

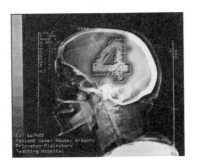

Love, Liking, and Lupus

House and Relationships

LINDSEY M. RODRIGUEZ AND C. RAYMOND KNEE

After watching the staff members of Princeton-Plainsboro Teaching Hospital interact with one another, it is easy to come to the conclusion that romantic relationships are more trouble than they are worth. After all, our romantic partners can make us jealous (Cameron and Chase), do things to us behind our back (House, anyone?), and distract us from our work (Foreman and Thirteen). Even when we finally find true love, we may lose it to death (Cameron's first husband). Why even try?

Just as the first diagnosis on any *House* episode is never correct, so it is with this conclusion. It is not correct. Relationships are worth having—even if they can be difficult. When people are in a romantic relationship, they are better adjusted than when they are not in a relationship—and this is true at both the physical level and the psychological level. In this chapter, we tour the life of a relationship. We start with people's initial beliefs about relationships. Do we believe that we are destined for one true love? Do we believe that we have to work at relationships to allow love to develop? Next, we discuss initial attraction. Why are we drawn to some people more than others? After that, we discuss love and relationship maintenance. How can we keep the love alive? Finally, we end (sadder but wiser) with break-ups and loneliness. After reading this chapter, you will have a better sense of romantic relationships—not only at Princeton-Plainsboro but also in your own life.

Relationship Beliefs: It's All in Your Head

Chase and Cameron are a very cute, attractive couple. Yet they initially did not seem particularly well suited to each other. They seemed incompatible, right down to the different beliefs they held about the ideal structure and development of relationships. We see this early on during the fledgling stages of their attraction in "Insensitive":

> Cameron: The point here is to make things simpler, not more complicated. Someday there'll be time to get serious about someone. Meanwhile, we already had sex once and didn't get weird about it.
> Chase: I get it. I get it. So, what if I'm offended by your judgment?
> Cameron: Then you're not the man I'm looking for.

We can see Cameron here almost talking herself out of something she knows she wants (i.e., Chase). She seems to be looking for that "special someone" when Chase, a perfectly suitable partner, is standing right in front of her! Her preexisting beliefs about the ideal form that romantic relationships should take determine her treatment of Chase at this and subsequent stages of their partnership. Evidently, she feels that they will not easily be able to work through their differences.

Individuals may differ in the degree to which they think relationships are destined, as well as the degree to which relationships involve growth and change. Those who endorse a *destiny belief*—epitomized by Cameron—think that potential relationship partners are either meant for each other or not. Those who endorse a *growth belief*—epitomized by Chase—think that successful relationships are developed and cultivated through mutual experiences (even conflict).

Those with strong destiny beliefs place heavy emphasis on making a good impression during the beginning stages of the relationship and are sensitive to early indications that the relationship cannot succeed. They tend to seek out the "one perfect person" and reject flawed potential partners rather quickly. In "Don't Ever Change," Taub talks to a Jewish patient named Yonatan whose wife (Roz) was overcome by a mysterious condition during their wedding ceremony, which took place earlier in the day. In the classic Hasidic tradition, the wedding was arranged, and the two had not dated in the time preceding their wedding. Nevertheless, Yonatan is grief-stricken at the prospect of losing Roz because he apparently feels that their union was the result of cosmic destiny. He exhibits a very strong destiny belief in the following conversation with Taub:

Taub: You'd find someone else.
Yonatan: There isn't someone else.
Taub: You've had three dates.

Those with strong growth beliefs, on the other hand, weigh first impressions of compatibility less heavily and instead emphasize the dynamic aspects of closeness, understanding, and development over time. They believe that successful relationships evolve from the resolution of risks, challenges, and difficulties, rather than from their absence. In "Ignorance Is Bliss," Wilson talks to House about Cuddy and Lucas, providing an excellent example of the perspective that people with growth beliefs have: "If they stay together, then my meddling won't matter. In fact, if they survive it, it might even make their bond stronger."

People can be high or low in both destiny and growth beliefs, and neither belief is necessarily better than the other. Both beliefs reveal a somewhat optimistic and romantic view of relationships, in that believing in destiny gives a relationship a special and unique meaning (*Our love is written in the stars!*). Similarly, believing in growth (or the idea that *practice makes perfect!*) could make one assume that all relationship obstacles can be overcome.

Not only do people differ in their initial beliefs about the nature of romantic relationships, they also differ in their beliefs about close relationships more generally. Can you depend on other people? Are you a person worth loving? Are you generally more committed to your relationship than your partner is? Interestingly, the answers to these general questions may come (in part) from early relationship experiences with family members and can be seen in adult romantic relationships as attachment styles.

Fungus or Parasite: How Am I Attached to Thee?

Our attachment style is a general perspective that we bring into our relationships. It comes from the fact that compared to other species, humans are dependent on parents for a relatively long time. As infants, we almost immediately prefer faces and voices that are familiar to us. When children feel that they lack a secure base (a parent on whom they can rely and trust), they may become silent, terrified, and withdrawn. As children, we come to learn whether we can trust our close others to support us in times of need (both emotionally and physically). This learning develops into a general attachment perspective that we then carry with us into later romantic relationships. Indeed, individuals do exhibit attachment styles that remain relatively stable throughout adulthood.

Studies have shown that almost seven in ten individuals were brought up in comfortable, safe environments. These individuals demonstrate *secure attachment*, a generally trusting attachment style that allows individuals to have faith in their relationships during difficult times. They find it easy to become close to others and do not worry about becoming too dependent. Securely attached relationships tend to be the most satisfying. For example, when Cuddy decides to adopt a child, she realizes that she needs a reassuring and stable partner. Knowing House's track record of being unreliable leads her away from him and toward someone more dependable, such as Lucas, in "Known Unknowns":

> Wilson: Oh . . . how did you like '80s night?
> Cuddy: House talked with you?
> Wilson: I was being subtle about it. You left suddenly. I know House can be a little much sometimes . . .
> Cuddy: No, he was sweet. I just know better than to rely on that.
> Wilson: He's trying.
> Cuddy: Yeah, I know. I'm a mother now. I need a guy I can count on every single day. That's never been House.

Being secure in a relationship is not the only possibility, however. Those with an *anxious-ambivalent* style may have been raised with inconsistent or "hot-and-cold" parenting. As a result, they come to believe that they are not worthy of love and spend a lot of time seeking approval from others. In adult relationships, they tend to be less trusting and more jealous and controlling and are more likely to agree with the statement "I find that others are reluctant to get as close as I would like." When Cameron and Chase begin dating, Cameron acts as if it is a matter of convenience. As the relationship progresses, however, her conversation in "Known Unknowns" with Foreman suggests that she has become (overly) suspicious that Chase may be having an affair.

> Cameron: Chase went to the gym five times this week.
> Foreman: Okay.
> Cameron: One of those times I followed him.
> Foreman: What?
> Cameron: I followed him. And yes, I know how humiliating that admission is.
> Foreman: Where'd he go?
> Cameron: The gym, that time. But I know that something's—
> Foreman: I'm stopping you right there. This is a conversation you should be having with Chase, not me.

Cameron: I've tried having this conversation with Chase.
Foreman: No sign of tears. It's not bulimia.
Cameron: Is he having an affair?
Foreman: No.
Cameron: Why should I believe you?
Foreman: You shouldn't, you should believe him.

Cameron and House could hardly be more different with regard to their perspectives on relationships. While Cameron is so concerned with her relationship that she discloses embarrassing information to other people (representing *anxious-ambivalent* attachment), House becomes uneasy talking about his own relationships beyond a superficial level and usually deflects by making a joke, as he does here with Cuddy in "Love Hurts":

Cuddy: What happened in your last relationship, it's no reason to wall yourself off from people forever.
House: Wow. Well, you've certainly given me a lot to think about. If only I was as open as you.
Cuddy: Well . . .
House: Actually, it was your blouse I was talking about.

Avoidant children may be a product of somewhat neglectful parenting and, as adults, tend to be less trusting and less invested in relationships (as seen by House in the previous bit of dialogue). They are more likely to engage in casual sex and to agree with the statement "I am uncomfortable getting close to others." House's behavior reflects avoidant attachment on the basis that he regularly employs the services of prostitutes and refuses to connect with others on an intimate level. He confirms this tendency in "Private Lives" when he says, "Connections are for airports. For people, we have three hundred cable channels."

House has a reputation for remaining emotionally distant, as seen in his many deflections with Cuddy. Cameron recognizes his lack of concern for love in "Safe" when she tells him, "Love is an emotion certain people experience, similar to happiness. No, maybe I should give a more relatable example." Even more clearly, Cameron sums up House's lack of trust in intimate relationships from their conversation in "Heavy":

> Cameron: I'm the only one who's always stood behind you when you've screwed up.
>
> House: Why? Why would you support someone who screws up?
>
> Cameron: Because I'm not insanely insecure. And because I can actually trust in another human being and I am not an angry, misanthropic son of a bitch.

Knowing our own (or our close others') attachment style may help us understand why we behave the way we do. While attachment styles do lay a foundation for future relationships, it is certainly possible for someone's style to change based on his or her adolescent and adult relationship experiences. Also, our own emotional beliefs are just one element of determining what kinds of relationships we will have. There are other factors that determine whether attraction will bloom, and we now turn to a few of these.

Interpersonal Attraction

As is apparent from watching seasons of *House*, close relationships can begin in the most awkward and unexpected circumstances, as well as in more traditional ways. Psychologically, a crucial first step always involves attraction, which can be thought of as a sort of force that draws two people together, making them want to be in each other's company and possibly form a lasting relationship. It makes sense that we are attracted to those whose presence is rewarding and gratifying to us. Some of the things that attract us to others are physical attractiveness, physical proximity, and similarity.

Physical Attractiveness: We Like People Who Are Beautiful

Although relationships cannot survive on physical appearances alone, they certainly matter in the beginning. In "Private Lives," Chase has a difficult time believing that appearances are so important in the early stages of a relationship, but House and Wilson understand the reality:

House [*To Chase*]: Life is a beauty pageant. Little girls kiss frogs and expect them to turn into you.
Chase: So you attribute every relationship I've ever had to the height of my cheekbones?
Wilson: Not the whole relationship, just the beginning.

In fact, House bets Chase that even if he pretends to be unemployed, lazy, and boring at a speed-dating session, he will still get a dozen numbers. House is right. This is because most people have a considerable preference for attractive, rather than unattractive, potential partners. Even babies spend more time looking at attractive faces. In fact, studies have found that after an initial date, attractiveness matters more than anything else (such as humor, intelligence, similar values, and personalities) in predicting whether people will desire a second date.

Psychologists have learned the importance of being attractive. The *what-is-beautiful-is-good effect* suggests that we assume that physically attractive people are better than others on unrelated traits. For example, attractive people are believed to be happier, warmer, more popular, more intelligent, and more successful. Interestingly, not only are attractive people considered superior in many other characteristics, they are also more likely to be offered jobs, *and* their annual salaries are actually higher than those of less attractive people! For example, Wilson alludes to the real reason House hired Dr. Terzi in "Ugly":

House: I think she might be an idiot.
Wilson: Who?
House: But she can't be an idiot. She was in the CIA, for God's sake.
Wilson: The Bay of Pigs was a daring triumph.
House: She had good ideas in Langley.
Wilson: All your ideas.

House: She was able to identify that they were good ideas.
Wilson: Stab in the dark here. Is she pretty?
House: She's new. She's nervous.
Wilson: She's a C cup?
House: She said one dumb thing in a differential. They all say
    dumb things in differentials.
Wilson: A D cup?

Knowing the importance of appearing attractive to others, people spend much of their time trying to convince others that they are appealing, charming, and desirable. *Self-presentation* refers to our desire to present a positive image to other people. We excuse, justify, and rationalize as necessary to increase our self-esteem, and these tendencies become even more noticeable in situations where we expect to be judged or want to be accepted—such as an initial romantic encounter with an attractive person. One common self-presentational strategy is *ingratiation*, where, in an effort to gain acceptance from others, we do things such as emphasize shared interests, give compliments, and describe ourselves in a desirable manner. In "Private Lives," Thirteen remembers her first love for his self-presentational tactics:

The first person I ever fell in love with turned out to be a total tool. He came across all funny and charming and thoughtful, but it was an act. He saw something he wanted, and he knew he had to act a certain way to get it.

Although a degree of putting on our best behavior is initially beneficial, pretending to be something we're not has never served a relationship well in the long haul.

Appearing desirable is one important factor for attraction to take place, but it is irrelevant if two individuals do not often cross paths. Physical proximity is also an important predictor of attraction.

Proximity: We Like Those Who Are Close By

Think for a moment about how you came to know your five closest friends. Did you work together? Did you meet several times through mutual friends or through a club or a sport? Now, consider how many close friendships (e.g., House, Wilson, and Cuddy) and relationships (e.g., Cameron and Chase, Thirteen and Foreman, Wilson and Amber) are a result of individuals working together at Princeton-Plainsboro Hospital. When choosing a school to attend, a job for work, or a neighborhood in which to live, we may not realize that we are also choosing the people with whom we will meet and form close relationships. Studies have shown that there is truth in this phenomenon (termed *propinquity*). Those who work in close proximity to one another are more likely to form close relationships. Also, the more we are around something, the more we grow to like it. Hypothetically, if House were to want a relationship with Cuddy, he should make sure to be around her all of the time (which he does!). In your own life, have you ever wondered why people who are initially attracted to one another "miraculously" wind up close by for one reason or another? This is propinquity at work.

Similarity: We Like Those Who Are Like Us

House reluctantly agrees to speed-date in "Private Lives" and rejects every potential date except for one. Interestingly, the only woman he is (temporarily) attracted to is one who displays her fondness for puzzles by carrying around a crossword puzzle. In addition to physical attractiveness and proximity, people like those who have much in common with them. Similarity is attractive with factors such as demographics, values, and personalities. People who are similar to each other like each other more, especially as time goes by. In fact, although the old saying "opposites attract" is still commonly heard in conversation, research overwhelmingly supports the notion that similarity (rather than complementarity) leads to attraction.

Have you ever wondered why attractive people are usually seen dating (and marrying) other attractive people? Decades of studies have shown that similarity is a common and significant cause of both attraction and progression into more loving and committed relationships. Indeed, the *matching hypothesis* suggests that partners who are equally attractive are more likely to stay together and be more satisfied. This is especially true among lovers but is also true among friends.

Relationship Maintenance: Keeping the Love Alive

Though it does not always happen, interpersonal attraction sets the stage for love to emerge. The following section details current studies on love and other relationship-maintenance strategies that we use to help our romantic relationships thrive.

Positive illusions: we are who our partners think we are.

Factors that distinguish happy and unhappy couples compose a large part of relationship research. Studies have looked at the thought processes of both types of couples and found that satisfied couples exaggerate the positive aspects of their partners and relationships. During the early, passionate stage of a relationship, people generally think of their partners more optimistically than their partners think of themselves. These *positive illusions* are generally beneficial in that they allow us to perceive our partners' potential flaws in a more generous way and foster greater satisfaction, love, and trust.

As relationships develop, we learn more and more about our partners. Still, rarely do we know our partners as well as we think we do—instead, we overestimate the similarity that actually exists between ourselves and our partners. Interestingly, how similar two people think they are (*perceived similarity*) is more important for marital satisfaction than how similar two people actually are (*real similarity*). House understands this in "TB or Not TB" when he says, "We are who people think we are. The reality is irrelevant."

Positive illusions are often seen on *House* when the source of the patient's ailment is something that he or she has been hiding from the partner. For example, Hank, a former baseball player in "Sports Medicine," adamantly denies using steroids, even though all of the evidence points directly to it. His girlfriend, Lola, stands by his side, (mistakenly) believing that he would never do such a thing.

House: You see, kidneys don't wear watches. Sure, gallbladders do, but it doesn't matter, 'cuz kidneys can't tell time. Steroid damage could take years.

Lola: No steroids. How many times does he have to tell you?

House: I don't know. How many times did he lie about cocaine before coming clean with the league?

Hank: That is completely different.

House: Oh, that's right, I remember. You never did come clean. The league was out to get you, they faked the blood tests, you had to get yourself a lawyer—

Lola: If Hank says he never used steroids, that's the truth.

House: That's too bad. Because our theory is that the kidney damage is caused by A, and everything else is caused by B. The beauty of this theory is that we can treat A and B. But if you add the kidney symptoms back into the mix, then we are looking at another letter altogether, one that is apparently not in the alphabet.

Lola: Get another explanation.

House: Okay. Yeah. Think I've got one in my other pants. [*Starts to leave*]

Hank: Hold on. [*House turns around*] Five years ago, Bangor, Maine. My pitching coach had me on something, I never knew what it was.

House: And you never tried too hard to find out, either.

Hank: I gained 12 pounds of muscle in, like, 4 weeks. [*To Lola, who looks troubled*] I'm sorry, baby.

Even though Lola is wrong, she idealizes Hank's behavior and stands by him. When we have highly favorable perceptions of our partners, the relationships benefit—we interpret their behavior in positive ways, and we are more willing to commit ourselves to maintaining the relationships. Studies have shown that people who initially see each other in the most positive fashion have the most satisfying and long-lasting relationships. If a relationship continues to grow this way, it may develop into love.

Love: Psychological Vicodin

"Cameron, I love you. [*She opens her mouth in shock, and he swabs the inside of her cheek.*] Get your test results tomorrow."

—House (after learning that Cameron postponed an HIV test), "Need to Know"

Love is a complex concept that psychologists, philosophers, and soap opera writers have tried to define and explain for centuries. Psychologist Robert Sternberg proposed a theory of love that explains both the emotions involved and the way they change over time. Love is said to have three different components: passion, intimacy, and commitment.

Once reunited in season 6, Wilson and his ex-wife, Sam, exemplify *passion*. Passion involves sexual interest and strong feelings of physical and romantic attraction to the other person. It is characterized by high physiological arousal and, like Wilson and Sam, makes people want to spend every waking moment together (even if that means kicking House out!).

The second ingredient in Sternberg's theory of love is *intimacy*. Intimacy is a feeling of closeness and mutual understanding and concern for each other's happiness. We often see Cuddy and Lucas discussing how much they care about each other—they are displaying intimacy. In "Private Lives," House's patient has difficulty expressing herself to her boyfriend while simultaneously writing personal thoughts and feelings in her online blog. When Chase brings up how unusual it is to share such intimate details with random strangers, she responds by asking him about his romantic relationships. He tells her that his recently ended, and she offers an astute insight about how a lack of intimacy can cause individuals to lead emotionally separate lives. She asks Chase, "You saw each other every day, right? How much did you tell her about what you were thinking? Or did you just end up talking about where you were going to dinner and who needed to do the laundry?" Likewise, in "Open and Shut," Wilson and Sam finally discuss how their marriage fell apart. Wilson learns that much of it was due to her believing there was a lack of intimacy.

> Wilson: You served me with divorce papers in the middle of a medical conference in New Orleans. I threw a bottle into an antique mirror.
>
> Sam: Oh, you exhibited an emotion? I didn't think you were capable!

Wilson: I loved you. I thought I would be following you to
   Baltimore.
Sam: How did you think that we still had a real marriage? We
   hadn't had a conversation in months!

These responses illustrate the importance of intimacy (or the cost
of a lack of intimacy) in relationships with those who are dear to us.
Are you looking for a way to increase intimacy in your relationship?
Don't act like House by avoiding personal topics. Try talking about
more than what happened in your day. Intimate conversations delve
deep into our most personal thoughts and feelings.

According to Sternberg, the third ingredient of love is decision
and *commitment*. Commitment can be thought of as an individual's intent to maintain a relationship and to remain psychologically
attached to it. Wilson perfectly expresses his commitment to House
without even realizing it in "Don't Ever Change":

Wilson: Why not? Why not date you? It's brilliant! We've known
   each other for years, put up with all kinds of crap from each
   other, and we keep coming back. We're a couple!
House: Are you still speaking metaphorically?

In this way, House and Wilson commit themselves to their friendship with each other—they decide to stay together through the good
times and the bad. Unlike the other two components, commitment
refers more to a conscious decision than to an emotion. It helps
solidify the trust and mutual feelings that keep a couple (and in this
example, a close friendship) together during periods of conflict or
dissatisfaction (which we know—at least with House—will happen!).

Commitment promotes *accommodation*, and Wilson epitomizes
this in his relationship with House. An accommodative partner tol-
erates destructive behavior such as insults, sarcasm, and selfishness
without retaliating, as a sacrifice for the relationship. Over the years,
we have seen that no matter how many times House insults Wilson,
forces Wilson to buy him things, or tries to ruin his life and his relationships with others, Wilson does not reciprocate and is instead

consistently emotionally supportive of House. In fact, Wilson risks his career to protect House, which includes having his job terminated in the first season as Edward Vogler tries to dismiss House, and having his practice damaged by Detective Michael Tritter in an investigation of House's narcotics consumption.

More generally, Sternberg says that passion, intimacy, and commitment are not three different kinds of love but, rather, elements of it. Thus, any given relationship can have different quantities of the components (while ideal relationships contain substantial amounts of all three). Also, the three elements typically vary over time. Passion can arise quickly but also tends to diminish as the relationship becomes more stable. Intimacy arises more slowly but can continue to increase for a long time. Commitments are usually made at particular points in time (e.g., engagement, marriage). A typical long-term relationship may at the beginning consist primarily of passion, but over time the commitment and intimacy increase as passion subsides.

Of course, passion, intimacy, and commitment are not the only things that change as a relationship grows. The self also changes, and it changes in direct connection to the relationship.

Self-Expansion: Stuck in a Rut

We want to become better and more interesting people as a product of our relationships. As time progresses and the relationship develops, it becomes increasingly important that the individuals learn new things and develop as well. What happens as time moves forward and couples fail to seek out stimulating activities together is evident in "Black Hole," as shown in this conversation between Taub and his wife, Rachel:

> Taub: We are arguing over couple yoga?
> Rachel: No, we're arguing over the fact that we don't ever do anything together anymore.
> Taub: We do things together all the time.
> Rachel: Really, like what? Besides sleeping, watching TV, and going out to dinner, what do we do together?
> Taub: We . . . you don't like going out to dinner?

In psychology, *self-expansion theory* states that an individual has the desire and ability to grow as a result of experiences gained from being in a relationship. We are happiest when enjoying novel and challenging activities that promote this personal growth. Studies have shown that participating together in stimulating activities is consistently associated with higher levels of relationship quality. Cameron understands the importance of passion and novelty in keeping love alive in "Clueless" when talking about an unconventional gift her patients gave each other: "His wife arranged it as an anniversary present. And if you ask me, if two people really trust each other, a threesome every seven years might actually help a marriage."

Although a threesome every seven years might cause more damage than it's worth, even small novel experiences can make a big difference in romantic relationships. We grow personally through incorporating our partners' unique qualities, resources, and perspectives as our own. Fresh, exciting activities can also boost our attraction for our partners because we tend to mistakenly attribute the reason to physiological arousal. For example, if we become aroused by a scary movie or an intense roller coaster in the presence of our partners, some of that arousal can lead us to believe that we must be really attracted to them!

Of course, not all emotion and change in a relationship are good. Sometimes a relationship can be threatened by issues of trust, deception, and jealousy.

Trust Me, I'm a Doctor

As noted by Cameron in the previous example, trust is a fundamental aspect of successful close relationships. If people believe their partners have good intentions and are committed to the relationship, they are more likely to feel comfortable becoming vulnerable (by doing things such as disclosing their desires, feelings, and concerns).

If they cannot trust that their partners will be present indefinitely, however, they may fear that being open will allow their partners access to information that can be used against them. A potential risk of trust is that it can make us vulnerable to those who wish to exploit it (such as House!). In "Family," House and Wilson discuss options with the patient's parents. House believes that worsening the infection will help determine what kind of infection it is, but Wilson doesn't agree. Later, House objects.

> House: All you had to do is say "Yes, I do." God knows, it's a phrase you've used often enough in your life.
> Wilson: It was a mistake every time. Give it a break. They said yes.
> House: That's not enough for you. You need them to feel good about saying yes.
> Wilson: I treat patients for months, maybe years, not weeks like you. If they don't trust me, I can't do my job.
> House: The only value of that trust is that you can manipulate them.
> Wilson: You should write greeting cards.

House often abuses the trust that others place in him for a single, overarching purpose: to be right and save lives. Although thankful for his behavior in the end, many times the patients first feel deceived.

Deception: Never Trust a Patient

> "It's a basic truth of the human condition that everybody lies. The only variable is about what."
>
> —House, "Three Stories"

The darker side of trust is deception. Deception is when you intentionally create an impression that you know is false. It is a common topic within the relationships of both the patients and the doctors on *House.* Similar to the famous quote from the first episode ("Pilot"), House says, "I don't ask why patients lie, I just assume they all do." Studies reveal that the most common type of lie is one that benefits or protects the liar, created to ward off embarrassment, guilt, or inconvenience or to seek approval or material gain. In "Joy to the World," a pregnant patient tries to protect herself by lying about her sexual activity. House, however, is concerned only with the truth.

Patient: I'm a virgin, so is my fiancé.
House: I believe him.
Patient: Are there other ways I could get pregnant? Like . . . sitting on a toilet seat?
House: Absolutely. There would need to be a guy sitting between you and a toilet seat, but, yes, absolutely.

People tell more self-serving lies (lies that benefit themselves) to strangers and acquaintances, but when people tell serious lies with the potential to destroy their reputations or close relationships, they are more likely to do so to their closest partners. For example, Cameron and Chase are happily married until Chase informs Cameron that he murdered the African dictator Dibala in "The Tyrant." Even though he did it because Cameron had a problem with the dictator's ethical position, his actions took place without her knowledge, and he does not tell her until much later. As a result, she feels that she can no longer trust him and leaves both her marriage with Chase and her position at Princeton-Plainsboro.

Jealousy: Me or Lupus?

Like deception, jealousy is also a negative emotional experience that can occur in close relationships. It results from the possible loss of a valued relationship to a real or imagined rival and involves feelings such as hurt, anger, and fear. While House outwardly dismisses any potential romantic emotions toward Cuddy, he displays a bit of jealousy in "Act Your Age":

House: You're trying to have sex with Cuddy.
Wilson: [*Offers House some of his food*] Fries?
House: You took her to a play, you only take women to plays because—
Wilson: No, *you* only take women to plays for that reason. That's your theory.

House: Okay, then why did you take her to a play?

Wilson: She's a friend.

House: A friend with a squish mitten.

Wilson: It is possible to have a friend of the opposite sex without—

House: Blasphemer! She's not a friend of the opposite sex, she's a different species. She's an administrator. She's going to eat your head after she's done.

Wilson: Yes, I slept with her.

House: Seriously?

Wilson: No.

House: Yes, you did.

Wilson: Yes, I did.

House: Seriously?

Wilson: No. You've got a problem, House.

Generally, people are more likely to become jealous when they are dependent on the relationship and when they feel inadequate to fulfill their partners' needs. An evolutionary psychological perspective suggests that jealousy may have evolved to motivate behavior that will protect our close relationships from the interference of others. In line with this perspective and in agreement with studies on attraction, men experience the most jealousy at the thought of their partners' sexual infidelity (*I could be raising a child who isn't mine!*), while women react most strongly to the threat of emotional infidelity from their partners (*He could be giving resources to a different family!*).

Deception, jealousy, and a lack of trust can be toxic for a healthy relationship. Relationships are like House's cases, in that no matter how hard we work to make them succeed, sometimes we lose them. Fortunately, we can take what we've learned from our failed relationships and improve our new ones.

Relationship Dissolution and Moving On

"Sometimes the best gift is the gift of never seeing you again."

—House, "Maternity"

Due to their highly emotional nature, jealousy and betrayal are more likely to occur in our intimate relationships than in relationships that are not as emotionally close. As we raise the stakes, intimacy allows for the potential of both precious rewards and painful costs. When asked to remember feeling deceived in the past, individuals report worse adjustment and higher anxiety when they tried to deny that it happened, dwelled on the negative effects of the experience, and resorted to drugs and alcohol. On the other hand, positive outcomes were associated with confronting the event, reinterpreting it in a positive way, and seeking support from family and friends.

Conflict is a natural part of relationships and should not be avoided for the sake of avoiding it. When problems arise, partners can choose to remain together and work on their issues or end the relationship. Relationships end for countless different reasons, some common ones being "growing apart" (a lack of intimacy, as in Sam and Wilson's prior marriage), an inability to manage work and home life (e.g., Thirteen and Foreman), or one partner not being able to regain trust after a betrayal (e.g., Chase and Cameron).

If the relationship partners desire to stay together after a betrayal, forgiveness may be necessary. Forgiveness, however, takes effort from both parties, and some individuals, such as House, prefer to say, "I don't care much for apologies" ("DNR"). Unfortunately for those who are like House, a possible effect of not forgiving is loneliness.

Close relationships fulfill our basic human need for belonging and caring for others. The need to belong is considered a need and not only a want, because when it does not happen, people suffer in more ways than simply being unhappy. In fact, the risk of death is higher among people without social connections than among those with them. Overall, recent studies have shown that the single best defense anyone can have against the risk of developing many mental and physical illnesses is being part of a large, supportive social network. Although less exciting than new love and less devastating than separation, keeping alive the successful relationships we have already formed can contribute substantially to achieving a fulfilling, rewarding life. Hopefully, reading this chapter has given you insight into both the relationships at Princeton-Plainsboro and those in your own life.

SUGGESTED READINGS

Aron, E. N., and A. Aron (2005). Love and expansion of the self: The state of the model. *Personal Relationships*, 3, 45–58.

Baumeister, R. F., and M. R. Leary (1995). The need to belong: Desire for interpersonal attachments as a fundamental human motivation. *Psychological Bulletin*, 117, 497–529.

Fraley, R. C., and P. R. Shaver (2000). Adult romantic attachment: Theoretical developments, emerging controversies, and unanswered questions. *Review of General Psychology*, 4, 132–154.

Knee, C. R. (1998). Implicit theories of relationships: Assessment and prediction of romantic relationship initiation, coping, and longevity. *Journal of Personality and Social Psychology*, 74, 360–370.

Rempel, J., J. G. Holmes, and M. D. Zanna (1985). Trust and close relationships. *Journal of Personality and Social Psychology*, 49, 95–112.

Sternberg, R. J. (1988). *The Triangle of Love: Intimacy, Passion, Commitment.* New York: Basic Books.

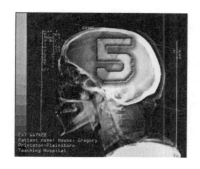

House and Happiness

A Differential Diagnosis

NANCY L. SIN, KATHERINE M. JACOBS, AND
SONJA LYUBOMIRSKY

People are drawn to activities and lifestyles that they believe will maximize their happiness. House, for example, enjoys solving medical puzzles, watching soap operas, attending monster truck rallies, and frequently pointing out the logical, physical, and moral deficiencies of others. These activities and preferences define a big part of House as a person, but he could choose to do very different things with his life. He could decide, for instance, to get married, spend less time at work, do community service, attend church, be nicer to Wilson, or practice meditation, but he doesn't. House probably expects that these choices would make him miserable.

The same general idea holds for Cuddy, Foreman, Chase, Thirteen, Taub, and, indeed, for all of us. We pursue what we believe will be the path to happiness, and we avoid or are indifferent to what we imagine will lead us to boredom or gloom. Some decisions, such as whether to pop a few Vicodins, might bring momentary pleasure; other decisions—for example, where to work or whether to form an intimate relationship—can provide lasting satisfaction. What choices have the characters of *House* made in their pursuit of happiness? And how likely are these choices to be effective in boosting their well-being? Psychology can provide some intriguing answers to these questions.

The characters on *House* display varying symptoms of happiness (and unhappiness). Together, we will embark on a differential diagnosis of what contributes to their—and everyone's—happiness. As with any proper differential diagnosis, we must first define happiness. Next we'll rule out the factors that do *not* enhance happiness. Finally, we will explore what actually makes us happy. (A note before we begin: This chapter addresses only the *controllable* characteristics of people's lives that promote or diminish well-being. Yet a large portion of happiness is determined by genetics—something that cannot be changed. Nevertheless, even a self-described "lonely, misanthropic drug addict" ["Wilson's Heart"] such as House has a considerable degree of control over his happiness.) Let us begin the differential diagnosis.

Happiness: What Are We Really Seeking?

Although the term *happiness* holds nuances in meaning for each person, researchers agree that a happy person frequently experiences positive moods (such as joy, affection, or pride), occasionally experiences negative moods (for example, guilt, sadness, or anxiety), and is generally satisfied with his or her life. This definition of happiness— also called *subjective well-being* or *hedonia*—is related to the pleasure principle. That is, the happiest people are those who often experience pleasure and seldom experience pain.

Another dimension of happiness is something psychologists and philosophers call *eudaimonia*. Based on Aristotle's definition, eudaimonia involves living a life of virtue and realizing one's fullest potential. As an illustration, imagine a person—say, Cameron—who is honest, sincere, and compassionate and adheres to her strong moral principles. Cameron even falls in love with and marries a dying man because she doesn't want him to be alone. She epitomizes eudaimonia, yet she appears to have higher subjective well-being (i.e., hedonia) than the other doctors. Like Cameron, people who strive toward their goals, practice good deeds, and have meaningful lives also tend to feel good, and vice versa. Thus, research and theory suggest that feeling good (hedonia) and doing good (eudaimonia) are intertwined and are both crucial components of happiness.

Everybody Lies about What Makes Them Happy

Everybody lies—from our parents and colleagues to the media and the larger culture. Claims are often made about happiness that are not necessarily true—at least, not true for all of us. Money, marriage, and parenthood are just a few of the ingredients in the recipe for happiness that our culture prescribes. These myths about happiness, which are perpetuated from one generation to the next, have an insidious influence. Most of us are convinced that attaining the goals valued by our society will provide us with enduring happiness. Yet evidence from research in the fields of psychology and economics suggests that we are often wrong.

Money

In "Here Kitty," Taub happens to run into his old friend Neil at the hospital. Neil claims to be the CEO of a large successful company (but we later find out that he is an impostor). After the two enjoy a few cigars and drinks together, Taub is tempted to quit his job at Princeton-Plainsboro to go into business with his long-lost friend. The appeal of this idea for Taub is simple: more money.

Many of us believe that if we only had more money, we would be happier. Yet—excluding those who live below the poverty line and cannot meet their basic needs for food, shelter, safety, or medical care—greater wealth generally does not lead to substantially greater well-being. For example, a number of countries have experienced dramatic economic growth in recent decades, but their citizens' happiness levels remain unchanged. In rich nations, including the United States, wealthy people are only slightly happier than those who have less money. Contrary to popular belief, rich folks do not spend more time in passive leisure activities, such as tanning by the pool or watching their flat-screen TVs. Instead, higher-income people are more likely than their lower-income counterparts to be engaged in stressful activities and to feel intense negative emotions, such as hostility and anxiety. Thus, we can be fairly certain that Neil is faking the relaxed vibe that supposedly comes with his wealth and power:

> Taub: You like your job?
> Neil: Same as you. Same as everyone. It has its ups and downs.
> Taub: You're lying to make me feel better.
> Neil: Yeah, it's the best. I'm in charge, you know? I'm a kid with toys.

Neil is merely emulating the stereotype that many of us have about very wealthy, powerful people. In reality, CEOs generally don't do "laid-back," and they may not do "happy," either.

What if you secure a substantial raise or win money because you, like House, try to "cure cancer by infecting a guy with malaria to win a $50 bet" ("5 to 9")? Research shows that the boost in your net worth will make you happier temporarily, but it will not create a long-term change in your well-being. One explanation for why more money does not bring lasting happiness is that people become accustomed to their higher standard of living and desire even more money to maintain their happiness, much as House needs increasingly larger doses of Vicodin to achieve the same pain-relieving effect. In addition, when people become wealthier, they tend to compare themselves to other wealthy people, rather than to their peers at their previous income levels. Thus, it makes sense that Foreman is upset when he thinks that his subordinate doctors earn more than he does, even though his current income level is probably sufficient.

Despite all of this evidence, money and happiness are indeed related in several ways. First, people who are relatively happier to begin with tend to earn more money at later points in time. That is, being happy may lead to financial prosperity, perhaps because happier people tend to feel competent, set high goals, expect success, and obtain more support. Second, you can buy happiness if you know where to spend your money. Spending on others will make you happier than if you spend the same amount on yourself. Taub could learn a thing or two about happiness from Cuddy, who donates to Amnesty International and is willing to pay for House to see a shrink. Taub is clearly motivated more by avarice than by generosity, and House knows it: "Knew it when I hired you. You'd eventually miss the money, being the big shot like your new CEO friend, if that night club stamp on your hand is any indication" ("Here Kitty"). In the end, Taub stays at Princeton-Plainsboro, but only because the opportunity to work at the higher-paying job vanishes when Neil is discovered and arrested. This ordeal does not alter Taub's opinion that money brings happiness, but Taub and all of us would probably be better off if we disabused ourselves of this false notion.

Marriage

When Foreman encourages a teenage patient, Stevie Lipa, to pursue a career in medicine, Stevie replies, "I see you with Drs. Chase and Cameron, and you all got empty ring fingers. You're alone" ("Needle in a Haystack"). Like most of us, Stevie believes marriage is a central goal in life, and that without marriage, we would be lonely and unhappy. Numerous studies conducted in diverse cultures do, in fact, demonstrate that married people are happier than those who are single, divorced, separated, or widowed. Yet the story about happiness and marriage does not end there.

Like other major positive life changes, getting married brings a boost in happiness, but that boost turns out to be only temporary. A fifteen-year study of more than a thousand Germans found that about two years after getting married, most people are back to their pre-marriage levels of life satisfaction. Those who wedded and got divorced quickly, however, did not experience substantial changes to their life satisfaction levels. After Cameron leaves in the sixth season, Chase goes back to working and refuses to talk about his failed marriage. Although it may appear that Chase is suppressing or denying his feelings, it could be that he is actively trying to move on. Chase will probably return to his old self quickly; Cameron, on the other hand, will need longer because she may still be recovering from the death of her first husband. Widowhood is associated with a long-lasting drop in life satisfaction, and some widows and widowers never fully recover.

Research evidence suggests not only that the happiness-boosting effects of marriage are short-lived but that it may actually be happiness that leads to marriage. In other words, the causal direction may be reversed. Longitudinal studies, which track people over a specific period of time, reveal that happier people are relatively more likely to get married and to stay married. And once happy people are married, they tend to feel more fulfilled and satisfied with their marriages than their less-happy married peers. After three unsuccessful marriages, Wilson would do well to enhance his own happiness before entering a fourth (hopefully, lifelong and satisfying) marriage.

Parenthood

Cuddy, like many people, really wanted a baby. She labored through fertility treatments and one unsuccessful adoption attempt before finally adopting her baby, Rachel. But does Rachel make her happier? In "5 to 9," we see Cuddy struggle with juggling the demands of being a single parent and a hospital administrator. Although most people believe that having children will make them happier, research suggests otherwise. Women with jobs outside the home rated caring for their children as only slightly more positive than doing more mundane tasks such as commuting to work and household chores. Furthermore, multiple studies have found that parenthood is associated with decreased happiness.

Why is parenthood linked to lower well-being? One possibility is that children interfere with basic needs, such as sleep or relationships with others. Another possible reason is that the short-term, day-to-day costs of raising children outweigh the long-term benefits. Cuddy experiences a great deal of stress from caring for her baby. For instance, in "Big Baby," Cuddy finds it hard to leave her crying baby with the nanny and feels that she should soothe Rachel herself. Cuddy also struggles with creating the mother-child bond: "I know I'm supposed to feel amazement. I'm supposed to love her. I just—I don't feel anything at all." It can be difficult to feel fulfilled as a parent when one has to cope with the everyday stresses of raising the child, as well as any larger issues, such as bonding. A third reason that parenthood may be associated with lower happiness is that the modern child-rearing environment is very different from that of our ancestors. For instance, there is less of a collective effort to raise children (for example, consider the saying "it takes a village"), which puts the burden solely on the parents' shoulders. That said, when Cuddy reflects on Rachel's childhood years from now, she will likely recall the happy moments and not remember the extent of her frustration and hardship.

The More Likely Culprits: What Actually Makes People Happy

Thus far in our differential diagnosis, we have ruled out three alleged sources of lasting happiness: money, marriage, and parenthood. The next step is to examine the life circumstances and the behaviors that do contribute to and sustain well-being for long periods of time. Here, House's maladaptive ways of interacting with the world are contrasted with the research evidence. Even for an individual who values logic, reason, and science, House easily could guess—without poring through journal articles—that he is obstructing his own path to happiness.

Friendship and Social Support

House seems to have few friends, which could be a major cause of his unhappiness. Data from nearly three hundred scientific studies, on average, revealed that you can predict a person's happiness based on his or her number of friends and the quality of those friendships. Fortunately, House has one friend he can rely on, Wilson, although the quality of their friendship is debatable. House and Wilson have radically different personalities. Wilson is an overly agreeable people-pleaser with a "need to be needed" ("Son of a Coma Guy"). In "The Social Contract," House says to Wilson, "You have no core. You're what whoever you're with needs you to be." House is correct, judging from Wilson's inability to furnish his condominium because he does not know what he likes or how to define himself. In stark contrast, House appears to be quite comfortable with who he is, contradictions and all. He has been described by his team as an "ass," an "emotionally stunted bigot," and an "angry, misanthropic son-of-a-bitch" ("No Reason," "Fools for Love," and "Heavy").

Why do these two polar opposite men have such a strong and enduring friendship? And how on earth could House possibly make Wilson happy? Perhaps the reason that their friendship works so well is that they have no social contract. They are not afraid to reveal to each other their true selves—whatever that may be for Wilson. In "The Social Contract," Wilson explains to House the value of their friendship:

> My whole life is one big compromise. I tiptoe around everyone like they're made of china. I spend all my time analyzing, "What will the effect be if I say this?" Then, there's you. You're a reality junkie. You'd smack me over the head with it. Let's not change that.

Friendship may promote happiness because friends offer both emotional and material assistance and protection from stress. According to the buffering hypothesis, social support is especially beneficial to a person's well-being when he or she is experiencing adverse life events. Wilson helps House through many stressful times, including the death of House's father and recurring problems due to House's Vicodin addiction. Although this friendship is often one-sided, House does reciprocate during Wilson's times of need. For instance, House allows Wilson to stay at his apartment when Wilson separates from his third wife. If only House would temper his rudeness and show more warmth toward others, he might form additional friendships and thus gain greater happiness.

Work

What motivates the diagnostic team to suffer through long hours at the hospital, perform illegal and unethical assignments (e.g., breaking into patients' homes), and tolerate House's insults and manipulation? Indeed, the extrinsic (or external) incentives are few—in Foreman's case, training under House is detrimental to his job prospects. These doctors are likely driven by rewards that arise from the nature of the work itself or intrinsic (internal) factors—the exhilarating rush of a fast-paced environment, intriguing diagnostic mysteries, and, perhaps most important, the satisfaction and pride that come from saving lives. In other words, the doctors are not motivated simply by an altruistic desire to help people; instead, as House puts it in "The Greater Good," "You're here because *it makes you feel good* to help people."

Meaning and Purpose

As the best diagnostic department in the country, House and his team have an unprecedented capacity to diagnose the rarest of medical conditions and to bring patients back from the brink of death. They are highly skilled and perhaps even uniquely gifted. Thirteen feels that exceptionally talented individuals have an obligation to society: "I don't care if Jonas Salk's life is a miserable shell. I just want him to cure polio" ("The Greater Good"). According to Thirteen, being a doctor is a selfless and noble profession that matters in the "big picture" but is mutually exclusive of hedonic happiness or pleasure ("The Greater Good"). She is echoing the common myth that having a purpose in life (a key component of eudaimonic well-being) limits a person from enjoying life. Yet research suggests that people who experience high eudaimonic well-being tend to be relatively happier and more satisfied with their lives.

The myth of eudaimonic well-being and hedonic well-being being mutually exclusive is further perpetuated by other characters on *House*. Specifically, in "The Greater Good," the patient Dr. Dana Miller asserts that her meaningful career did not make her happy. A former world-renowned cancer researcher, Dr. Miller describes her years of toil in the laboratory as what she was always *supposed* to do but never what she *wanted* to do. She gave up her medical and research career, despite her colleagues' fury and protests, and now dedicates her life to activities that provide pleasure. The following is a conversation between Taub and Dr. Miller:

> Taub: No offense, but you're not working. What does it matter if you spend a little time in bed?
>
> Dr. Miller: Not working doesn't mean I don't have places to go. I've got my book group, piano lessons, cooking classes. They make me happy.
>
> Taub: A warm apple fritter makes me happy. Doesn't fulfill me as a person.
>
> Dr. Miller: And working here does?
>
> Taub: If it didn't, I would have found a way to go back to tucking tummies.
>
> Dr. Miller: Good for you if your job fulfills you and makes you happy. That's rare.
>
> Taub: I didn't say I was happy. I loved being a plastic surgeon. The money, the lifestyle. And in a lot of ways, this job stinks. I'm making five bucks, I'm always annoyed, but—
>
> Dr. Miller: You can look yourself in the mirror and think, "I did something worthwhile today."
>
> Taub: Exactly.
>
> Dr. Miller: That's important. And I do miss that, but it just wasn't enough anymore.

Like Thirteen, Taub and Dr. Miller incorrectly believe that one cannot achieve both fulfillment and hedonic happiness. Yet their lack of happiness could be due to factors unrelated to work, such as Taub's materialism and marriage troubles or Dr. Miller's health problems. Although Dr. Miller is currently engaging in the very activities that are likely to promote happiness (such as strengthening friendships and developing new skills), her desire for fulfillment may ultimately lead her back to a career devoted to helping others. To achieve long-term well-being, Dr. Miller cannot neglect her desire for purpose and meaning.

If the doctors at Princeton-Plainsboro are successful in their quests to be happier, then their coworkers and patients will reap the rewards. Employees who enjoy frequent positive moods tend to get more favorable evaluations from others, including higher evaluations for the quality of their work and for their productivity, dependability, and creativity. In addition, research indicates that happy people are more satisfied with their jobs than are their less happy peers. Satisfied workers are, in turn, more likely to perform good deeds that extend beyond the requirements of the job. For example, satisfied employees help their coworkers, protect the organization, and aspire to further develop their abilities within the organization. They are less likely to disregard workplace policies, as House regularly does, or to take a colleague's ideas as their own, as Foreman does to Cameron without remorse.

Yet House still has it all wrong. He does not want his team to be happy because he is convinced that "miserable people save more lives. If your life has meaning, your job doesn't have to have meaning" ("Adverse Events"). Yes, House saves lives, and yes, House is miserable, but he has no proof that his misery makes him a better doctor. To test this, he would need to compare his job performance when he is miserable to his job performance when he is happy. (The problem is, he is never happy!) House's unmatched ability to save patients is due, in large part, to his creativity. Rest assured, happiness would not restrict House's creativity or diagnostic prowess. Decades of research demonstrate that people induced to feel positive are more flexible, innovative, and efficient in their problem solving than are those induced to feel neutral or sad. One study found that physicians in a positive mood were relatively more likely to consider the correct diagnosis of a disease earlier and to show flexibility in their diagnostic thinking. These physicians were also less inclined to jump to premature conclusions without sufficient evidence—one of House's major flaws. In sum, House should reconsider his belief that "nothing we do has any lasting meaning" ("Living the Dream") and permit himself to feel good once in a while. Only then could he be really, *really* good at his job.

Flow

Contrary to Thirteen's and Dr. Miller's views, it is entirely possible to experience the "feel-good," hedonic shade of happiness at work. The secret is to work in *flow*, a state of complete absorption in the present moment. House likely experiences flow when he is sitting for hours in his office, staring at the whiteboard, bouncing a ball, and focusing intensely on solving a diagnostic puzzle. He loses track of time and is unaware of himself, the pain in his leg, hunger, or any other physiological discomfort. Like a musician composing a masterpiece or an artist creating a painting, his experience is challenging enough to require the peak of his abilities but not overwhelmingly difficult. After House is finished solving the puzzle, he would probably report that the whole process felt good. He felt alert, in control, and capable, like a natural high.

Anyone—young or old, from chess players to dancers to surgeons—can experience a state of flow. The task at hand should stretch the person's abilities by establishing an optimal balance between skill and challenge. Otherwise, if the task is too easy, the individual can become bored, and if the task exceeds his or her skills, then the person is likely to feel frustrated or anxious. House's team is often assigned to engage in risky tasks that require unwavering concentration, such as surgery. These challenging activities are probably more enjoyable than clinic duty or team meetings, precisely because they induce flow.

Other doctors, as well as patients, think less of House because he is more concerned with solving diagnostic puzzles than with his patients' welfare. Wilson sees the real motivation behind House's decisions to run risky medical procedures in "Informed Consent": "This has nothing to do with saving a life. You just can't bear the thought of a patient dying before you've been able to figure out why." Yet the doctors and the patients at Princeton-Plainsboro recognize that this is a win-win situation: House gets to solve puzzle after puzzle, and patients get to live. Everyone is happy . . . except maybe Cuddy, who has to deal with the paperwork and the legal ramifications.

Spirituality

If you are invited as an overnight guest in Wilson's home, do not be alarmed when you hear voices. House thinks he is having auditory hallucinations, but what he actually hears is Wilson speaking to his dead girlfriend. Wilson has no proof that Amber's spirit listens to him—or that her spirit even exists—yet his nightly ritual comforts him and makes him happy.

Like the vast majority of Americans, Wilson is *spiritual*, meaning that he believes in something divine and greater than himself. Spirituality takes many forms, including faith in a higher being or God, fate, karma, and forces that guide life and death. Religion—that is, spirituality practiced in an institutional context—offers a framework for individuals to understand their role in the world and to imbue their lives with meaning. Furthermore, religion offers people a sense of identity and connects them to a community of supportive and like-minded individuals.

To say that House is not spiritual would be a drastic understatement. House is notoriously disrespectful and intolerant of others' spiritual and religious beliefs because "faith isn't based on logic and experience" ("Damned If You Do"). He does not care how much hope, contentment, and meaning spirituality provides, nor does he care that spirituality can inspire believers to become better people. House is concerned only with the fact that individuals who endorse spiritual beliefs—and who disregard the lack of scientific proof for those beliefs—must somehow be weak, stupid, or incapable of thinking for themselves. In "House vs. God," he greets Boyd, an adolescent faith healer, with the following statement: "Faith. That's another word for ignorance, isn't it? I never understood how people could be so proud of believing in something with no proof at all. Like that's an achievement." Although the divine cannot be proved or disproved, House is determined to seek evidence that *this* life is the only life. House arranges for Wilson to come to his office, "safely" kills himself just before Wilson arrives, and—fortunately for him—is revived. House's experiment confirms that there is no bright light or life beyond death, and it actually saddens him that his recently deceased patient had nothing to look forward to.

House is not the only atheist doctor in the hospital, but he likely sets himself apart from the others (such as Cameron) as the only doctor who is unwilling to accept the benefits of spirituality. The benefits are plentiful, based on a growing body of research evidence. Religious people are happier than those who are nonreligious, particularly if they report having a strong relationship with the divine and engage in religious behaviors, such as attending services. People who regularly participate in religious services have many friends and acquaintances, and these social bonds can be immensely valuable because they provide emotional and tangible support. Finally, religious folks tend to live longer than their nonreligious counterparts, have superior mental and physical health, cope better with hardships, and have more satisfying marriages.

Should Everyone Strive for Happiness?

People commonly argue that happy folks are content with the status quo and therefore do not care to make improvements in their own lives or in society. As House puts it in "Forever," "Yeah, if we're all just satisfied with what we have, what a beautiful world it would be. We'd all slowly starve to death in our own filth, but at least we'd be happy." House's statement is a tad extreme and quite incorrect. The truth is (according to research), happy people possess the very qualities that are necessary to make substantial changes in society: social skills, energy, perseverance, optimism, creativity, altruism, and productivity, to name a few. Happy individuals are more likely than those who are unhappy to set high goals and work persistently to achieve those goals. Anyhow, being satisfied with one's life is distinct from being satisfied with one's society, the government, or the world at large.

Another popular misconception is that happy people never feel negative emotions. This is far from the truth—in reality, happy individuals experience a wide range of both positive and negative emotions. They just spend more of their time on the positive end of the emotional continuum. When faced with a significant negative event, such as a threat or a loss, happy people react appropriately—they become cautious and vigilant, withdraw, avoid harm, and experience negative moods. Yet happier individuals are more resilient than those who are less happy; they cope better (for instance, by relying on their social networks for support) and hence recover more rapidly from adversity.

Is There Hope for House?

House deserves some credit. After all, not many of us would have the guts to commit ourselves to a psychiatric hospital or save a friend from delivering a career-destroying speech (by drugging the friend, but that's beside the point). House has made tremendous progress in the years that we have known him, but is he a likely candidate for happiness? Based on his copious maladaptive behaviors and views (e.g., "Half the people I save don't deserve a second chance," "Living the Dream"), the answer is "probably not." At least, not yet.

Rather than striving for happiness, House is better off working on his depressive tendencies. House is unlikely to be clinically depressed—he still gets out of bed in the morning, goes to work, and finds pleasure in solving diagnostic cases—but he does show some symptoms of low-level depression. In particular, he is often in a sad or irritable mood, has little interest in interacting with other people, and holds negative and distorted beliefs about the world. Although House does not have a self-esteem problem (as Wilson says in "Need to Know," "You don't like yourself, but you do admire yourself"), he does not entirely feel that life is worthwhile.

The process of becoming less depressed is both different and similar to the process of becoming happier. House may try therapy and medication for depression—both of which have proved helpful to him in the past. The cognitive and behavioral exercises that he can practice to lift his depression—for example, thinking optimistically, engaging in social activities, and exploring hobbies that he used to enjoy—are also likely to help enhance his happiness. It has been quite a while since we have seen House playing air guitar on his cane. We hope to see it again soon.

Final Diagnosis: Happiness Has Many Sources

For a hospital full of sick and dying patients, Princeton-Plainsboro produces a surprising amount of happiness. A doctor walks down the hallway, feeling fulfilled because she has made a patient's life better; meanwhile, in an adjacent wing, surgeons are deeply engrossed in their craft and feel as if everything else in the world is temporarily suspended. In the cafeteria, colleagues are savoring their meals and enjoying one another's company. In the hospital administrator's office, a crippled genius is amused and proud of the latest prank he has pulled. As you can see, happiness has many sources—sometimes joy and ecstasy from a spiritual insight, at times awe and amazement at resolving a complex riddle, oftentimes contentment and satisfaction that arise from human connection, and for House and his team, a sense of purpose and meaning in their life's work.

Many of us look for happiness in the wrong places. We may take a job mainly because it pays more, passing up an opportunity to work in an otherwise more fulfilling but lower-paying occupation. People get married and cannot imagine the marital bliss ever fading, and most of us believe that having children is essential to our lasting happiness. A compelling amount of research, however, says that we are wrong. Scientific evidence suggests that if we want to be lastingly happier, we would be better off focusing our efforts on building and maintaining friendships; seeking purpose, meaning, and flow in our work; and, for those who are so inclined, nurturing our spirituality. Remarkably, those who succeed in enhancing their long-term happiness will be more likely to achieve financial prosperity, as well as to get married and stay happily married, at a later time.

Stay Tuned for the Next Diagnosis

Sometimes, the diagnostic process ultimately fails. Patients may die before doctors correctly diagnose and treat them, or doctors miss something and make the wrong diagnosis. House and his team certainly fail in the case of Kutner. He seems to be the happiest doctor in the department before his sudden suicide. Kutner is friendly and sociable, has avid interests outside of work, has loving and supportive adoptive parents, and holds a Guinness World Record for crawling twenty miles. He appears to have a zest for life and even says that because he had a horrible childhood (due to witnessing the murder of his biological parents and being in foster care), he had nowhere to go hedonically but up. The other doctors fail to notice any signs of distress that Kutner is exhibiting. Or, maybe Kutner is so good at covering up his unhappiness that not even House—the most gifted diagnostician in the United States—or Lucas, a private investigator, can guess that something is amiss.

Nevertheless, House demonstrates that the diagnostic process is frequently successful. We have uncovered in this chapter that House, his team, and his colleagues are not quite as miserable as they initially appear. In fact, they can be fairly happy at times. Ruling out money, marriage, and parenthood as their primary sources of long-lasting happiness, we discover that it is likely their work that makes them happy—the friendships formed, the intrinsic rewards inherent in their jobs, the flow experiences, and the spiritual issues raised by their work. Indeed, the various sources of happiness experienced by the team may be the driving force behind their diagnostic triumphs.

SUGGESTED READINGS

Csikszentmihalyi, M. (1990). *Flow: The Psychology of Optimal Experience.* New York: Harper & Row.

Cohen, A., and T. A. Wills (1985). Stress, social support, and the buffering hypothesis. *Psychological Bulletin, 98,* 310–357.

Dunn, E. W., L. Aknin, and M. I. Norton (2008). Spending money on others promotes happiness. *Science, 319,* 1687–1688.

George, J. M., and A. P. Brief (1992). Feeling good—doing good: A conceptual analysis of the mood at work—organizational spontaneity relationship. *Psychological Bulletin, 112,* 310–329.

Isen, A. M. (1993). Positive affect and decision making. In M. Lewis and J. M. Haviland-Jones (eds.), *Handbook of Emotions,* 1st ed. (pp. 261–277). New York: Guilford Press.

Lucas, R. E., A. E. Clark, Y. Georgellis, and E. Diener (2003). Reexamining adaptation and the set point model of happiness: Reactions to changes in marital status. *Journal of Personality and Social Psychology, 84,* 527–539.

Lyubomirsky, S. (2008). *The How of Happiness: A Scientific Approach to Getting the Life You Want.* New York: Penguin Press.

Lyubomirsky, S., L. A. King, and E. Diener (2005). The benefits of frequent positive affect: Does happiness lead to success? *Psychological Bulletin, 131,* 803–855.

Pinquart, M., and S. Sörensen (2000). Influences of socioeconomic status, social network, and competence on subjective well-being in later life: A meta-analysis. *Psychology and Aging, 15,* 187–224.

Pollner, M. (1989). Divine relations, social relations, and well-being. *Journal of Health and Social Behavior, 30,* 92–104.

Ryan, R. M., and E. L. Deci (2001). On happiness and human potentials: A review of research on hedonic and eudaimonic well-being. *Annual Review of Psychology, 52,* 141–166.

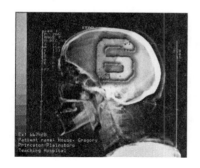

Not Even Gregory House Is an Island

The Role of Social Support in *House*

MEGAN L. KNOWLES

"What would you want, a doctor who holds your hand while you die, or a doctor who ignores you while you get better?"
—House, "Occam's Razor"

As it turns out, House didn't give hand-holding enough credit. Hugs and reassurances alone will not cure the sick, but social support isn't something to shake a metaphorical cane at, either. When friends, family, coworkers, and communities provide social support to the ailing, the grieving, or the detoxing, they often cope more effectively with these stressors. Social support can even improve the health and well-being of individuals on ordinary days when they aren't under stress. Does this mean that House should emulate Cameron and Wilson with their sympathetic smiles and reassuring arm pats? Not so fast. Social support does not always produce positive outcomes. Unwanted support or the wrong type of support may actually exacerbate individuals' stress. So, what is the answer—is social support beneficial or not?

Social scientists and epidemiologists have been studying this question for decades, and their research suggests that people benefit from social support under *some*, but not all, circumstances. This chapter reveals the situations in which people benefit from others' support and examines the nature of social support within the confines of Princeton-Plainsboro Teaching Hospital (PPTH). Specifically, we'll investigate four questions central to the study of social support: (1) What types of support attenuate life's stressors? (2) Is it better to give social support than to receive it? (3) Do perceptions of support matter more than the support you actually receive? (4) How much social support is enough to reap its benefits? This chapter provides insight into these core questions about social support. It will do so in the context of the staff and the patients on *House*, but the insights apply to the real world as well. Reading this chapter will help you gain interesting knowledge about social support, as well as practical knowledge about how best to obtain and confer social support in your own life.

Let's start by defining social support. *Social support* refers to the resources you receive from members of your social network or the resources you provide to them. These resources range from concrete goods and services to advice and information to comfort and compassion. Each of these consists of a distinct type of social support. This leads us to our first question.

Optimal Types of Social Support: Comfort, Cash, or Counsel?

What types of social support do the PPTH staff and patients receive? If these types serve particular functions, which most effectively mitigates the effects of stress? The most common types of social support observed among the staff and the patients are tangible support, informational support, and emotional support.

Tangible support refers to material aid or help that diminishes or resolves a problem. Time and time again, Wilson provides House with tangible support—whether it's thousands of dollars to buy a motorcycle or his half sandwich to quell House's boredom and hunger. In addition to his money and his lunch, Wilson often sacrifices much more—sometimes risking his own livelihood to put out one of House's fires. Wilson jumps in front of the proverbial train at least twice in order to save House. By lying to Vogler and Tritter, Wilson shows that he is willing to give up his own job and freedom so that House can keep his. Wilson's self-sacrificing behavior extends beyond his relationship with House to his relationships with his patients. He goes so far as to donate part of his liver to a patient in "Wilson."

Wilson: I want to donate a lobe of my liver to Tucker.
Cuddy: That's insane.
Wilson: I'm donating a small portion of—
Cuddy: You have hundreds of patients.
Wilson: And until I run out of excess organs, why shouldn't I
     do everything I can to help them?

The tangible social support Wilson provides House and his patients is undoubtedly beneficial because it serves to mitigate the stressor itself. Notably, tangible social support is most effective when the stressor is controllable. If Wilson's patient had a terminal illness, his liver donation would have done little good. If House's conviction was assured, Wilson's lies to Tritter would have served no function. Under uncontrollable circumstances, tangible support loses its value.

In ambiguous situations, another type of social support can be helpful. *Informational support* refers to advice, information, or guidance that can serve to clarify a situation or a problem. Members of the PPTH staff frequently give informational support to one another and their patients. On some occasions, staff members go beyond the call of duty to provide the information their colleagues and patients require for diagnosis and treatment. For instance, House undergoes deep brain stimulation in order to trigger memories of Amber and the bus accident in "Wilson's Heart."

> House: Everything's in black and white.
> Wilson: Who was talking? Is Amber there?
> House: [*To Chase*] You're supposed to be jolting my hypo-thalamus, not petting it.
> Chase: We don't want to overload it.
> House: As long as I'm risking my life, I might as well be watching a talkie.
> Wilson: Increasing from three to five volts.

Undergoing this risky procedure could be characterized as informational support because, ultimately, House is trying to provide his diagnostic team with information to save Amber. Unfortunately, the memories unearthed do not yield any information that can save the life of his best friend's girlfriend.

In less risky and dramatic ways, doctors frequently provide informational support to their patients by giving them advice or guidance. Often, this helps patients who are struggling to understand or deal with their illnesses. Of course, stressors can take forms other than illness. Individuals dealing with problems in the home or the workplace may benefit from bouncing ideas and potential solutions off a friend or getting his input about a worrisome situation. In "Sex Kills," Wilson reaches out to House for informational support but is rebuffed.

> Wilson: Does it occur to you that maybe there's some deeper guidance than keep your mouth shut? That maybe a friend might value concern over glibness? That maybe . . . maybe I'm going through something that I need to have an actual conversation about?

Like tangible support, informational support may help individuals resolve problems or mitigate stress in controllable situations. When a stressor is controllable, tangible and informational support may be most effective at reducing anxiety because such support deals with the stressor directly. Receiving a liver transplant from Wilson relieves his patient's anxiety because the transplant saves his life. Sadly, House is unable to save Amber's life, but he is able to recover sufficient information to provide a diagnosis and allow Wilson and Amber to say good-bye. Less helpful is House in "Sex Kills." If he had actually listened to Wilson and provided him with thoughtful advice about his marriage, Wilson might have been able to save it.

Even if Wilson were unable to salvage his marriage, a conversation with House might have benefited him in other ways. Wilson may have been seeking not only informational support from House but emotional support as well. *Emotional support* refers to expressions of caring and comfort. In this instance, House does little to provide Wilson with reassurance or comfort. Wilson may or may not be seeking advice from House, but he is surely looking for reassurance and relief from what may be an uncontrollable situation. Indeed, when individuals feel as if they have no control over a stressor, they may not seek tangible or informational support but warmth and connection. In "Airborne," Wilson intuits that his patient Fran would benefit from having company as she deals with her undiagnosed illness. He asks her acquaintance, Robin, to provide her with the emotional support she needs.

> Wilson: I know I'm throwing a lot at you. She just has no family in town. And I really think she could use a friend right now.
> Fran: You don't have to stay.
> Robin: No, it's . . . no problem.
> Fran: But why? You don't even know me.
> Robin: You've gotta be scared.

Like most frightened, sick people, Fran is comforted by the presence of a friend or, rather, a stranger. Fran's smiling response to her compassionate friend diverges from House's typical response to his patients—avoidance. Unlike his more caring colleagues, Cameron and Wilson, House rarely provides emotional support. He does not like to receive it, either. Believing House to be stricken with brain cancer in "Half-Wit," the Cottages try to provide him with tangible support by finding an experimental treatment. Chase, in particular, tries to provide emotional support as well. When Chase attempts to comfort his presumably ailing boss, he reaches out—quite literally—to support House with a warm, sympathetic embrace: "I'm sorry you're dying. I'm going to hug you."

If House were a normal person suffering from cancer, this gesture might provide emotional support and comfort. In light of research showing that physical touch attenuates stress responses and improves therapeutic outcomes, this intimate display of caring and affection would have bolstered the spirits of most patients—but not House. From his perspective, compassion is overrated, handholding is useless, and hugs are advantageous only if he can cop a feel in the process. Here, House is unequivocally wrong. Emotional support often reduces anxiety among people who are in uncontrollable situations.

In sum, members of the PPTH staff provide and receive tangible, informational, and emotional support. Most commonly, they give advice and other informational support to their patients and to one another. Some provide an abundance of emotional support as well. Wilson and Cameron seem to be unlimited sources of empathy and caring. Both Cameron and Thirteen seem unduly concerned with the terminally ill, for different reasons. Chase and Foreman typically display compassion, unless their patients are obese or homeless, respectively. House provides no emotional support to his patients or his colleagues. Among the staff, tangible support is typically provided within strong relationships—between Foreman and Thirteen and Wilson and House. Wilson provides House with much more tangible support than he receives, an imbalance that does not bode well for their friendship. Keep in mind that no one type of social support is inherently better than another. All types of social support attenuate stress in some circumstances. Ultimately, the most effective type of social support is matched to the situation and the needs of the person. Thus, the PPTH staff and we, alike, should take into account the controllability of the situation and the particular needs of the individual when providing others with social support.

So far, we've established that House rarely provides substantial social support—especially in the form of comfort and concern. He mocks his more compassionate colleagues and sees them as weak or squishy for caring about their patients, rather than simply diagnosing them dispassionately. Yet despite his derision of social support, House is often the willing recipient of help (unless it is imposed on him). As Wilson's ex-wife Bonnie says to House in "House Training," "You always needed him. And he was always there for you." Implicit in her statement is the reality that House is not always there for Wilson. Given the value of reciprocity in relationships, we should consider the costs and benefits of giving versus receiving support.

Giving and Receiving Social Support: The Importance of Reciprocity

Among the PPTH staff, who are the givers and the receivers of social support? Wilson lavishes social support on his cancer patients and willingly sacrifices his money, time, and well-being to help out House, the "long distance runner of neediness" (according to Cuddy in "Don't Ever Change"). Like Wilson, Cameron is also incredibly self-sacrificing. In "Acceptance," she reveals that she is willing to not only befriend terminal patients but marry them.

> Cameron: She's terminal.
> Wilson: Yeah. So, I take it you were in there informing her?
> Cameron: Well, I—I hadn't exactly gotten around to that, but I was just—
> Wilson: Doing what? Making friends?
> Cameron: Cindy's divorced. She doesn't have any kids, no siblings, both her parents are gone—
> Wilson: It's not your job to be her friend. Do you understand? And it's not worth it. She feels better her few final days, and you're not the same, maybe for years.
> Cameron: You don't think it's worth it.
> Wilson: I know it's not worth it.

> Cameron: My husband—I met him just after he was diagnosed with terminal brain cancer. If I hadn't married him—he was alone. When a good person dies, there should be an impact on the world. Somebody should notice. Somebody should be upset.

Thus, Cameron and Wilson give more support than they receive, whereas House receives more support than he gives. In contrast to these three, the remaining staff members seem to give and receive support to equal degrees. Foreman and Thirteen had a reciprocally supportive relationship, for example.

Who is doing it right? In other words, is it better to give support or to receive support? As it turns out, there are substantial drawbacks to both. A person such as House who typically receives more support than he provides may have recurring health, psychological, or social problems that require support over the long term. If his problems are legitimate (House's chronic pain), he probably benefits from others' help (access to Vicodin), but he would be a drag on his social network. Over time, people would become less and less likely to provide the support desired. In House's case, Cuddy and Wilson eventually refuse to write any more prescriptions for him, hoping he will tackle his addiction instead. If the requests of a needy person are not considered legitimate, then he is viewed in a negative light—as a selfish and inconsiderate person. Certainly, people make such attributions for House's behavior. House counters others' doubts about the legitimacy of his injury with the regular refrain, "I'm in pain!"

People who give more social support than they receive may feel generous and charitable, initially. Over time, though, they start to feel taken advantage of, if the social support they provide to another is not reciprocated. Unable to receive sufficient support, these individuals have more trouble coping with life stressors. Worse yet, conferring too much social support would drain individuals' capacity to help themselves. In "Dying Changes Everything," Wilson acknowledges a similar exhaustion. He feels so used by House that he decides to "break up" with him and get a new job elsewhere.

Wilson: You spread misery because you can't feel anything else. You manipulate people because you can't handle any kind of real relationship. And I've enabled it. For years. The games, the binges, the middle-of-the-night phone calls. I should have been the one on the bus, not . . . You should have been alone on the bus. If I've learned anything from Amber, it's that I have to take care of myself. We're not friends anymore, House. I'm not sure we ever were.

Thus, it is not better simply to give support or to receive support, but to do both. The Cottages, who engage in reciprocal supportive relationships, as do Foreman and Thirteen, are most likely to reap the benefits of social support. This raises the question: Does an individual have to give or receive support in order to benefit from it, or is the simple knowledge that it is available sufficient? In other words, do we benefit from others' help, or do we benefit from knowing their help is available?

Perceived Availability of Social Support: It's the Thought That Counts

Do perceptions of support matter more than the support you actually receive? You might expect the availability of support to be highly correlated with the amount of support received, but this association is surprisingly weak. Taub, for instance, might recognize that his wife and the other Cottages will be there for him if he ever needs their help, yet he may receive support from only his wife on a regular basis. In other words, there may be a disconnect between the availability of support and the actual support received. There are at least three causes and associated consequences of this incongruence.

First, even if people have a large, complex social network that could provide sufficient social support, they may be hesitant to request support, in order to maintain feelings of self-sufficiency, independence, and competence. Some people may feel that requests for help would be burdensome on loved ones, or they may feel inadequate and ineffectual if they accept others' help. House surely feels ineffectual in asking Wilson for help in "Under My Skin."

> House: I'm hallucinating. . . . I need you to sit in on my differentials, double-check everything I do.
> Wilson: You can't treat patients.

House takes pride in his diagnostic skills, so his ego likely takes a blow in making such a request. Such an outcome would be consistent with research showing that individuals who receive help show subsequent drops in self-esteem. Individuals who recognize that they need help, especially in domains important to them, feel incompetent in that domain and more negatively about themselves in general. In the language of a famous game show, once you choose to phone a friend, you concede that you don't know the answer yourself. Consequently, a person might try to maintain a sense of competency and self-esteem by persevering on a difficult task and eventually resolving it without help. Thus, recognizing that support is available without actually using it would be beneficial. Or, at the very least, persevering on the task alone would not be as detrimental to his or her self-esteem as admitting defeat and requesting help.

Second, you might have many friends and colleagues who could provide support, but in some situations, they may not know how to provide support effectively. They may provide unsolicited advice when emotional support is needed, or they may display concern and warmth, rather than the tangible support that is desired. Imagine Cameron going around the hospital, hugging and sympathizing with all of her patients, even an undiagnosed patient in need of a test. This patient would probably grow impatient and wish Cameron would just get on with the test. Conversely, imagine House ordering an array of tests for a terminal patient with hours to live. I doubt that this terminal patient would appreciate these useless tests. These patients would benefit more from knowing support is available, than from receiving support that is ineffective or fails to meet their needs.

Third, your support network may exacerbate your stress, rather than serve as a source of support and comfort. Watching friends and family awkwardly try to say or do the "right thing" in response to your pain, suffering, or loss can be exasperating. Some support providers may be overbearing and demanding of your attention when you are already under stress. Carrying out the social niceties associated with social interactions may further deplete people under stress. For example, in "Painless," a patient finds his family to be more draining than comforting when dealing with his chronic pain.

> Jeff [*Speaking to House*]: You're alone. That's why you can handle your pain. No need to put up a front, to be what anyone else wants you to be.

In line with Jeff's experience, research done in natural settings often shows that received support predicts worse coping and exacerbates personal distress. Often, received support is negatively associated with health and well-being because individuals report receiving more support when they are under severe stress than under normal circumstances. Again, people would benefit from knowing support is available but not necessarily receiving it.

Altogether, this research suggests that perceiving social support to be available is more beneficial than actually receiving social support. That is not to say, however, that receiving social support is detrimental in all situations. In controlled environments, with everything being equal, individuals who receive support on difficult tasks outperform those who do not receive support. Having others off of which to bounce ideas, the Cottages are more likely to successfully diagnose a patient as a group than anyone attempting a diagnosis on his or her own. Also, individuals who receive tangible support but are unaware of it (that is, invisible support) may reap the benefits of that support without suffering blows to their self-esteem or coping abilities. For instance, family members may take care of a patient's home, pets, or bills while he is in the hospital with an illness or an injury. Even though the patient is unaware of the help he is receiving, having these things taken care of will minimize his stress down the road. Similarly, in "Big Baby," Thirteen would have benefited *unknowingly* from Foreman's decision to switch her from the placebo group to the treatment group if the drug trial had been successful.

> Foreman: She's on the placebo.
> Chase: You can't possibly know that.
> Foreman: Accidents happen. I found out.
> Chase: You cannot tell her. You'd be compromising the trial. She knows she had a 50/50 chance of not being on the drug. If you feel like you're lying to her, too bad.
> Foreman: I don't want to tell her. I want to put her on the real drug.

Whereas received support is often associated with negative outcomes and occasionally associated with positive outcomes, studies pertaining to the availability of support yield more uniformly positive findings. Consequently, I would argue that there is truth in the idiom "It's the thought that counts." Knowing you have supportive others who could come to your aid should you need them effectively attenuates stress and improves well-being across a variety of situations. If we acknowledge that social support availability is an important predictor of physical and psychological health, we have to consider two additional questions. How do we know how much social support is available to a person? When is it "enough"? To address these related questions, we now turn to a discussion of social networks.

Social Networks: One (Overburdened) Friend Is Not Enough

How much social support is "enough"? One way to objectively measure the amount of social support available to individuals is to assess the nature of their social networks. To do so, we have to consider a number of factors. How many people are in their social networks? How frequently are they in contact with each of those people? What kinds of relationships do they have with all of the people in their networks? Do the people in their networks play a variety of roles? Are their social networks interconnected, with members having relationships with one another? Are their social ties strong and stable, or are they weak and wavering? Are their relationships reciprocal or one-sided? Taken together, these factors paint a portrait of a person's social network.

Let's look at the intersecting social networks of the PPTH staff. House's social network does not include many social ties with whom he has substantial contact. He rarely interacts with family members. He tries to get out of dinner with his parents and uses a variety of delay tactics to avoid his father's funeral. He does seek out information about his biological father but makes no attempt to contact him. House has regular contact with Cuddy and the Cottages, but those interactions are usually within the context of a case. House interacts with Wilson, the only person he consistently calls a friend (Lucas is disqualified, due to the inconsistency of their relationship). House's absence of friends is made apparent in "Sports Medicine":

> House: What, you're saying I've only got one friend?
> Wilson: Uh, and who . . .?
> House: Kevin, in Bookkeeping.
> Wilson: Okay, well, first of all, his name's Carl.
> House: I call him Kevin. It's his secret "friendship club" name.

House, Wilson, and the rest of the PPTH staff have small social networks in comparison to real-world standards. Yet their social networks are populated by a variety of relationship types—working relationships, friendships, and romantic relationships. This variety can be attributed to role multiplicity, or each person's taking on of multiple roles within a social network. In addition to being House's sole friend, Wilson is also his trusted colleague. Cuddy takes on multiple roles in House's social network as well. She plays the role of exasperated boss and the slow-burning love interest. Similarly, Chase and Cameron and Thirteen and Foreman are not only colleagues but were romantic partners as well.

PPTH staff members take on different roles within each others' social networks throughout the years, just as the nature of relationships changes in the real world. What sets *House* apart from the real world is the highly interconnected nature of the staff's social networks. Members of the PPTH staff form and dissolve almost all of their relationships within the hospital's walls. Consequently, their social networks greatly overlap and interconnect. You and I, on the other hand, do not have such boundaries or a limited cast to draw on to form relationships. Our less interconnected social networks are more compartmentalized with coworkers, friends, and family members who may not know one another.

What difference does it make if a social network is dense and interconnected? Dense social networks can be helpful in transmitting information, which may be beneficial in some situations and detrimental in others. Word of House's (faked) brain cancer spreads quickly among the Cottages, Wilson, and Cuddy. In response to this news, they mobilize their resources quickly to come to House's aid. If House were actually suffering from cancer, this support would benefit him, but instead, their actions backfire. House is no longer eligible for the experimental treatment that would have relieved his pain. Gossip and bad blood between individuals can strain social relationships within dense social networks as well. Falling out with a friend might create tension in other relationships within a dense social network, given the friend's ties with others. House is hurt to find out that Wilson was in contact with his PPTH colleagues during their "breakup" in "Not Cancer."

> Wilson: Don't do this. I'm trying to move on.
> House: By hanging out with Cameron, talking to Cuddy, Foreman, but not me?

People's social interactions reverberate in dense social networks. House's firing of Chase in "Human Error" affects not only Chase but also people connected to him. Cameron, for instance, quits shortly thereafter and, in doing so, alters House's social network. When it comes to the density of social networks, a moderate amount of interconnection between social ties appears to be best.

Moderately dense social networks benefit individuals if they also include multiple strong ties. Some ties, such as the relationships between Cameron and Chase and Foreman and Thirteen and the friendship between House and Wilson, are considered strong because they are voluntary, relatively intimate, and pervasive across contexts. People who have small, dense social networks usually have strong ties within that network, but this does not appear to be true for House. House has a tenuous relationship with Cuddy and working relationships with the Cottages, but these relationships are weak and ephemeral. His only important, long-lasting relationship is his friendship with Wilson. House doesn't normally discuss his feelings or relationships with others, but he clearly values his friendship with Wilson. During their "breakup" in season 5, House tries to convince Wilson to stay at PPTH, makes up excuses to visit his apartment, and even goes full-on stalker by enlisting Lucas to follow him. House eventually acknowledges the importance of their friendship in not only actions but also words in "Birthmarks."

> You're scared to death of losing anyone that matters. So you drop the person who matters the most to you!

Why is this friendship worth fighting for? Well, having only one strong, long-lasting relationship, House is dependent on Wilson and not only for the errant french fry or sandwich. Even though House mocks his friend's compassion and support on multiple occasions ("I can hear you in there caring!" in "Need to Know"), he wouldn't have it any other way. Once Wilson agrees to return to PPTH and presumably resume their friendship, all becomes right in House's world.

> If you're coming back just because you're attracted to the shine of my neediness . . . I'd be okay with that.

House may be joking in "Birthmarks," but that doesn't belie the fact that he really is needy. Usually, he needs people such as Wilson to clean up his messes, often a result of his interactions with patients or authority figures such as Tritter and Vogler. What is worse than being needy? Being needy and not reciprocating when others need help. A degree of reciprocity exists within each of the staff members' social networks, with the exception of House. House typically participates in inequitable exchanges—often asking Wilson, in particular, for favors without providing much in return, as in "You Don't Want to Know."

> Wilson: Of course, you're type AB. Universal recipient, you take from everybody.
> House: Of course, you're type O. Universal donor. No wonder you're paying three alimonies.

The lack of reciprocity within House's relationships is the most problematic aspect of his social network. Over time, failure to support his best friend will erode their relationship, even if it is communal or need-based. House helps Wilson a few times (for example, letting Wilson stay with him), but these occasions are outnumbered by the times Wilson sacrifices for House.

In sum, the staff members' social networks can be considered very small, unusually dense, and interconnected, with regular contact among most members. Generally, the relationships within these networks are neither equitable nor stable because the nature of their relationships changes throughout the course of the series. House, in particular, has only one close relationship, with Wilson, whom he overburdens. By his own choice and admission, House is pretty socially isolated. Yet House is not totally "alone" in this respect. None of the PPTH staff seems to have robust social networks. On the whole, they are a pretty lonely, unsociable group.

Escaping the Island: Expanding Social Networks to Maximize Support

How could House and colleagues improve their social networks in order to reap the benefits of social support? They could form more social connections with people outside the hospital, thus making their networks larger and less dense. They need not join a dozen book groups and gain a dozen new BFFs because such additions would require too much relationship maintenance. Moderation is key. Also, they could acquire more than one important relationship and, as a result, be confident in their ability to procure support when necessary. Again, they need not care passionately for everyone in their social network, but they need to have more than one close social bond. By having more than a single strong relationship, they would be less reliant on one individual, who may or may not always be available in times of stress. This is analogous to research showing that widows live longer than widowers after their spouses' death because they have close friends to draw on for support. Widowers typically report being close only to their wives, leaving them without close companionship after their wives' passing. An important change for House, in particular, would be to respond to Wilson's support with gratitude and to offer help in return. Given their unusually small, dense social networks populated by very few strong, reciprocal relationships, the PPTH staff should focus on growing their social networks by adding new, unrelated people and generating more close, reciprocal relationships. This would bring the staff's social networks more in line with those found in the real world.

What about us? How can we improve our social networks in order to reap the benefits of social support? Assuming that we are not as isolated as House and his colleagues, the answer is a bit more difficult. In fact, the answer depends, in part, on the nature of the stressor we are trying to overcome. Someone diagnosed with a terminal illness would benefit from a small social network with strong ties and high density because this person needs emotional support from caring, close others. If an individual needs to follow a strict health regimen in order to extend his life, he is more likely to do so if he has close family and friends who give his life meaning and give him a reason to take care of himself. On the other hand, certain stressors, such as divorce, may require individuals to change their identities in some way or otherwise turn over a new leaf. A divorcee with a large social network with weak ties and low density may find it easier to cope with this life change. She would have more avenues for meeting new people and figuring herself out as a newly single person. Conversely, a divorcee who finds herself in a small, closely knit group in which everyone knows one another—including her ex-husband—would have more difficulty coping with her divorce. In short, the "best" social support network is dependent on the situation, but across situations, networks that include more than one strong relationship and are characterized by reciprocity are most predictive of health and well-being. Everything being equal, it is better to have more than one friend.

The Value of Social Support

"It's not the dying that gets to people. It's the dying alone. The patients with family, with friends . . . They tend to do okay."
—Wilson, "Half-Wit"

As expressed in "Half-Wit," Wilson's sentiment is consistent with research conducted with tens of thousands of participants in the last thirty-five years. Under most circumstances, social support mitigates stress and improves health and well-being. In comparison with the socially isolated, those who have adequate social support are less likely to suffer from depression, fatigue, upper respiratory infections, poor immune function, and many other ailments. Unfortunately, we don't know how beneficial social support is for individuals diagnosed with lupus, amyloidosis, or sarcoidosis, but we do know that social support predicts the survival of cancer and HIV patients. So, social support is beneficial. What else should we take from this chapter?

This chapter addressed a series of questions about the nature of support and provided suggestions to the PPTH staff (and readers!) in order to maximize the benefits of social support. We can draw four definitive conclusions:

1. *Tangible, informational, and emotional support are effective in alleviating stress but not under all circumstances.* The type of support provided must match the situation and the needs of the patient. Consequently, the PPTH staff needs to take into account the controllability of the situation and the particular

needs of the patient in order to provide them with an effective type of support.

2. *Reciprocity is paramount in supportive relationships.* Members of the PPTH staff who provide support without receiving any in return (Wilson) and those who receive support without providing any in return (House) should strive to achieve a balance between giving and receiving support.

3. *Perceiving social support to be available is more important than actually receiving support.* Receiving support is beneficial under some circumstances (see the first point), but support availability is more predictive of health and well-being across a variety of situations. Perhaps the PPTH staff should focus on expanding their social networks in order to acquire more available social resources, rather than simply asking for more help.

4. *The extent to which a support network is "enough" to alleviate stress depends on the stressor you are trying to overcome.* In all circumstances, however, it is helpful to have more than one close other in your social network so that you do not become overly reliant on a single person.

Members of the PPTH staff would benefit from expanding their social networks somewhat, reducing the density of their social networks, and forming an additional close relationship with a friend, a colleague, or a private investigator. If the PI can dig up dirt for you, while simultaneously giving relationship advice and holding your hand, all the better.

SUGGESTED READINGS

Cohen, S., and W. A. Wills (1985). Stress, social support, and the buffering hypothesis. *Psychological Bulletin*, 98, 310–357.

Stroebe, W., and M. Stroebe (1996). The social psychology of social support. In E. T. Higgins and A. E. Kruglanski (eds.), *Social Psychology: Handbook of Basic Principles* (pp. 597–621). New York: Guilford Press.

Uchino, B. N. (2004). *Social Support and Physical Health: Understanding the Health Consequences of Relationships.* New Haven, CT: Yale University Press.

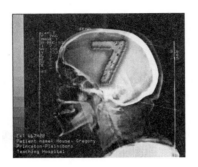

The Psychology of Humor in *House*

ARNIE CANN AND ADAM T. CANN

Princeton-Plainsboro Teaching Hospital, a prestigious hospital in a small New Jersey town, is a place where serious, life-changing decisions are made every few minutes (at least, during the one hour we watch each week). Even when the medical issue is relatively minor, the doctors dutifully take turns seeing patients with aches, pains, rashes, runny noses, and other common ailments. At times the job is monotonous, but the work is always done with a seriousness of purpose. Well, almost always.

> Wilson: Twenty-nine-year-old female, first seizure one month ago, lost the ability to speak. Babbled like a baby. Presents deterioration of mental status.
> House: See that? [*Reacting to stares from passersby*] They all assume I'm a patient because of the cane.
> Wilson: So put on a white coat like the rest of us.

House: I don't want them to think I'm a doctor.

Wilson: You see where the administration might have a problem with that attitude.

House: People don't want a sick doctor.

Wilson: Fair enough. I don't like healthy patients. The twenty-nine-year-old female . . .

House: The one who can't talk. I liked that part.

—"Pilot"

What Is Humor?

Humor takes many forms and plays many roles in our lives. Stand-up comedians try to build careers by making us laugh, a friend tells us a joke when we feel low, a sleeping cat falls off a windowsill. In each situation, humor is at work. House, his colleagues, and his team use humor to deal with the incredible stress of their jobs. When the team sarcastically debates a diagnosis in "The Down Low," Foreman reminds them to be doctors, not comedians. To which House whines, "But we're doctors all the time. It's so boring." It's easy to see the humor here, but why is it funny?

Humor, in most cases, is based on social incongruity. Irony, overstatement, double entendres, puns, sarcasm, and many more—they all share the aspect of nonserious incongruity or surprise. Good humor tells a story that builds to a climax, but the ending catches us off-guard.

House: Lift up your arms. You have a parasite.

Jill: Like a tapeworm or something?

House: Lie back and lift up your sweater. You can put your arms down.

Jill: Can you do anything about it?

House: Only for about a month or so. After that it becomes illegal to remove, except in a couple of states.

Jill: Illegal?

House: Don't worry. Many women learn to embrace this parasite. They name it, dress it up in tiny clothes, arrange play
dates with other parasites . . .
Jill: Play dates . . .
House: [*Showing her a sonogram*] It has your eyes.

—"Maternity"

Admittedly, there is incongruity in the study of humor itself. After
all, in order to study what is funny, you have to take it seriously. The
psychology of humor has been an area of research for more than a
century, but it has seen significant growth only in the last few decades.
Humor organizations such as the International Society for Humor
Studies and journals (for example, *Humor: International Journal
of Humor Research*) testify to the development of the field. In this
chapter, we will reveal what has been learned about humor and will
explore the many potential benefits of appropriate humor, looking for
examples in the lives of our medical heroes. We will also acknowledge
the dark side of humor: humor that hurts. Finally, we will begin to
profile the characters based on their dominant humor styles.

House can be one of the funniest characters on television, but
he presents an interesting paradox, in that he can be both funny
and mean at the same time. In "Paternity," House's reaction to a
young mother who doesn't believe in vaccination says a lot about his
character.

Mother: We're not vaccinating. [*Holds toy frog up to the
baby*] Ribbit, ribbit.
House: Think they don't work?
Mother: I think some multinational pharmaceutical company
wants me to think they work. Pad their bottom line.
House: Hmmm. May I? [*House takes the frog*]
Mother: Sure.
House: Ribbit, ribbit. [*Baby laughs, House looks at frog*] All
natural, no dyes. That's a good business; all natural children's toys. Those toy companies, they don't arbitrarily
mark up their frogs. They don't lie about how much they

spend in research and development. The worst a toy company can be accused of is making a really boring frog! [*Mother and House both laugh*] Ribbit, ribbit. You know another really good business? Teeny, tiny baby coffins. You can get them in frog green or fire engine red. Really. The antibodies in yummy mummy only protect the kid for six months, which is why those companies think they can gouge you. They think that you'll spend whatever they ask to keep your kid alive. Want to change things? Prove them wrong. A few hundred parents like you decide they'd rather let their kids die than cough up forty bucks for a vaccination, believe me, the prices will drop really fast. Ribbit, ribbit.
Mother: Tell me what she has!
House: A cold.

The idea of a "really boring frog" is a novel, unexpected twist. Also funny—although maybe not to the mother—are the "teeny, tiny baby coffins." Again a twist, albeit a gloomier one. While House often deals in dark forms of humor, he has other uses for it. We see the lighthearted House when he first meets Foreman's father, Rodney, in "Euphoria."

House: I've started your son on a new course of treatment. If it works, he'll get better. If it doesn't, he won't. While he's not getting better, he's going to experience so much pain that we'll have to put him in a chemically induced coma while we figure out what to do next.
Rodney: My son says you're a manipulative bastard.
House: It's a pet name. I call him Dr. Bling.

House uses the unexpected, and slightly silly "Dr. Bling" to deflect Rodney's potential anger. Rather than be insulted by the less-than-flattering description Rodney mentions, House responds with the seemingly ridiculous notion of "manipulative bastard" as a pet name. The quip is still a case of social incongruity but without the dark imagery of baby coffins.

Humor Is Part of Being Human

Laughter, smiling, and humor are essential parts of our "humanness." The first truly social response a baby provides is usually a smile, while laughter is one of the first social vocalizations. Babies are excellent laughers. They do it at appropriate times and before they have other meaningful language skills. Laughter is such an inevitably human response that even children born deaf and blind—who have no chance to see or hear laughter—perform this most basic of human behaviors. Children as young as nineteen months of age respond with laughter to jokes based on the incongruous uses of objects. Show a child an intentional misuse of an object, such as putting your shoe on your hand, and the child recognizes the intent to be funny; he or she gets the joke. Children will also shamelessly steal your material. Young children readily repeat a "joke" to get laughs from others. Yet they also appreciate that not all incorrect uses of objects are funny, and they will correct, rather than repeat, actions they see as mistakes that are not meant to be funny.

Clearly, humor is an important part of healthy social development, and humans are natural and inevitable participants in the humor exchange. Given our natural affinity for humor, we should not be surprised to see it liberally applied in many social interactions. The potential usefulness of humor can be inferred from the fact that laughter as a social signal is also found in other primates. For nonhuman primates, laughter is a reaction most commonly found during social play. Like human children, other primates enjoy a game of chase or a friendly wrestling match, and laughter is used in these episodes as a signal that "we are having fun" so that we are sure the "play" is safe rather than threatening.

In human adults, humor and laughter show up in friendly banter, rather than in physical play. Cuddy and House often do a verbal dance as they talk, each using humor to signal that they are not taking each other too seriously. In "Unfaithful," a conversation that could become awkward becomes much more comfortable when humor is playfully added to the mix.

Cuddy: You doing anything Friday?
House: Taking a lovely young lady to the Philharmonic.

Cuddy: That your way of saying you're having sex with a hooker?

House: Two. Can't create a harmonic with just one.

Cuddy: Well, I was hoping you might be available for Rachel's Simchat Bat. It's a . . .

House: Jewish baby-naming ceremony, a time-honored tradition dating all the way back to the 1960s.

Cuddy: My house at seven. It'll just be the rabbi and a few friends and some family.

House: Nothing like welcoming a baby into the world with a completely naked display of hypocrisy.

Cuddy: There'll be plenty of wine and nice people you can quietly mock.

House: Wish I could, but I already put down a deposit on sixteen crates of Jell-O.

At Princeton-Plainsboro Teaching Hospital, we see regular applications of humor by all of the doctors and even some of the patients. A little bizarre imagery or a gentle pun, and the patient is ready for the next medical procedure.

Foreman: We inject gadolinium into a vein. It distributes itself throughout your brain and acts as a contrast material for the magnetic resonance imagery.

Cameron: Basically, whatever's in your head lights up like a Christmas tree.

Foreman: It might make you feel a little lightheaded.

—"Pilot"

Humor's "Medical" Value

Why is humor so prevalent in the lives of these doctors, and why is its presence of actual medical value? First of all, consider humor's physiological benefits. If the *House* special effects team took us inside the human body to observe the response after a good joke has been told, we would see the nervous system respond to the joke and trigger a variety of reactions in the brain. Multiple studies have found that exposure to humor and the resultant smiling and laughter can stimulate the release of biochemicals associated with improved immune response. Just watching a humorous event, such as enjoying a stand-up comedian's act, can help us stay healthy by enhancing our biological response to health threats. The immune system is obviously complex, but there are many examples of medically desirable biochemical changes associated with exposure to humor. Evidence also reveals that negative emotions have the opposite effects, suppressing desirable physiological responses to stress and infection by stimulating the release of other, less desirable biochemicals. No one is yet ready to declare that humor become a central element in medical treatments, but there will be benefits, and the lack of any evidence that humor can do harm makes it a reasonable supplement. A "healthy laugh" is an appropriate phrase, with multiple possible meanings. Whether they realize it or not, House and the team are justified in inserting humor into their treatments. Maybe this is why House can be so whimsical when he talks to a patient whose skull has been cut open so that the brain activity can be monitored. Get a laugh, help a patient endure the test.

> House: Not only will this allow us to clock your brain's processing speed, you'll also get free cable for the first three months. [*House shows her a flash card.*] What's this?
> Sarah: A blue car. Is that part of the test?
> House: Nope, my lease is up next month. You like? [*She smiles wanly.*] I'm gonna ask you a series of questions designed to stimulate left-brain function—logic, reasoning, problem solving. Or as my mentor, Old Ben, liked to call it, "The dark side." If we find slow areas, we know we found damage. We treat. You go home. Ready?
> Sarah: I'd nod yes, but I can't move my head.
>
> —"Big Baby"

Leaving the biochemistry of humor behind, the emotional impact of humor can be a desirable neurological experience on its own. The emotional side of humor—the positive way it makes us feel—has been given the label "mirth." While laughter and smiling are often associated with mirth, people are also capable of fake smiles and laughs, and they often employ them to create the right impression. True smiles and laughs are known as "Duchenne displays," named for the French scientist Guillaume Duchenne, who first identified the differences between the real and the fake versions. Duchenne laughs and smiles activate areas of the brain associated with reward. They provide a pleasant emotional boost, a mirthful neurological experience. Regular doses of mirth keep the reward center stimulated and keep you in a positive state, and this generally positive state has health benefits. People with more positive mood report fewer health complaints, and their bodies are more resistant to attack. Stable positive emotional states have even been shown to make you less susceptible to the common cold. Be happy, be healthy.

Psychological Benefits of Humor

The psychological effects of humor are numerous. Constant stress—even at low levels—can be damaging to your psychological well-being. Within House's team, stress can be a distraction that interferes with creative problem-solving and diagnoses. Humor helps release and lower stress. In fact, research has shown that exposure to humor can serve as a preventative or a cure for stress. Enjoyment of humor prior to a stressful experience leads to less stress being reported. For those times when you didn't know stress was coming, it helps to seek out some humor after the fact. The negative emotions will be reduced and positive emotions elevated. Less stress and fewer negative emotions mean a greater sense of well-being. House's team knows this. In "The Socratic Method," the patient is a police officer who got shot but still is laughing. No reason to take the case too seriously, even as the initial diagnosis begins. Stress is expected, but the disruption it brings can be managed—add some humor to change the tone and improve the mood. Everybody on the team contributes to the humor in this exchange.

House: Cop with a sense of humor. Differential diagnosis.
   Guy's in the ER bleeding on everybody.
Foreman: Drugs?
Chase: He's a cop.
Foreman: Good point, how about . . . drugs?
House: Tox screen was clean; he did, however, get hit by a
   bullet. Just mentioning.
Cameron: He was shot?
House: No, somebody threw it at him.
Chase: I'm thinking trauma; he's got bullet fragments lodged
   in his brain.
Foreman: According to Babyshoes, the cop was laughing
   before he got shot.
Cameron: Babyshoes?
Foreman: The guy who shot him.
Cameron: Reliable witness.
House: His name's Babyshoes, how bad can he be?

In "The Softer Side," Wilson also knows how to look on the lighter
side of life and invokes humor when asked to explain House's odd
behavior.

Kutner: I think there's something wrong with House.
Wilson: Who's he making miserable now?
Kutner: Actually, no one. He okayed an MRI just because the
   parents wanted to look for a blind uterus. There was no
   fighting, no arguing, he just went along.
Wilson: It's a valid medical theory.
Kutner: He doesn't think it is. House . . . decided to humor
   . . . these parents.
Wilson: Maybe he had a great cup of coffee or a tremendous
   bowel movement. Bottom line is, your boss is in a good
   mood, stop analyzing it and just enjoy it.

In the difficult jobs that House's team members face, it is essential that they maintain a positive frame of mind. Negative thinking

and worry will not facilitate the creative thinking that saves lives. Humor, however, enhances creativity. A positive outlook increases "out of the box" creative thinking. Being on House's team requires believing in yourself and the validity of your decisions, even when you feel as if you are careening head first down a blind alley. Good humor, real Duchenne responses, and mirthful experiences create more optimistic, hopeful, and happy people. Stressors no longer seem so threatening when you are having a mirthful moment. The qualities hope, happiness, and optimism are examples of positive personality traits that are associated with greater psychological and physical well-being. Research studies tell us that when we are able to find and enjoy humor, it allows us to build a more resilient and resourceful personal style; then the stress of the job won't drag us down or interfere with our creative potential.

The team members demonstrate their optimism and resilience in case after case. Despite setbacks and misdiagnoses, they persist with the confidence that their next "best guess" will be the right one. They joke with one another and with their patients, they laugh to release stress, and they save lives. Humor helps them individually to be better doctors, but it also helps them bond as a group.

Humor as a Social Facilitator

Gentle, friendly teasing communicates support. Humor has been described as a social lubricant, and even difficult situations are made easier by appropriate doses of humor. The positive emotions generated by humor color our impressions of others and make everyone seem that much nicer. In "Insensitive," when Cameron suggests that she and Chase have sex but without the baggage of any lingering emotional ties, the careful interjection of humor allows an awkward conversation to proceed in a safe and friendly manner.

Chase: Happy Valentine's Day.
Cameron: A holiday that only applies to people who are already paired up. For everyone else it's Wednesday.
Chase: Wow. Thank you for that dash of cold water.

Cameron: Don't get me wrong. I still think true love's out there; it's just very far away. Possibly in another galaxy. We may need to develop faster-than-light travel before we can make contact. So I'm thinking we should have sex.

Chase: That makes sense.

Cameron: Despite the wisdom of pop songs, there's no point in putting our lives on hold 'til love comes along. We're both healthy and busy people. We work together, so it's convenient.

Chase: Like microwave pizza?

Cameron: And of all the people I work with, you're the one I'm least likely to fall in love with.

Chase: Like . . . microwave pizza.

Humor acts as a bonding tool that potential team members are trained to appreciate and embrace. When House is interviewing (or is it tormenting?) potential team members in "You Don't Want to Know," even the oft-dour Foreman showcases his wit.

House: We can all applaud the doctor who's willing to break all the rules. But the real hero is the unsung doctor, toiling in anonymity, because he broke the rules without getting caught. I need to know you have these skills. I need you . . . to bring me the thong of Lisa Cuddy. [*Foreman looks up from his paper, the team applicants all give House a weird look*] Not kidding. [*They remain seated.*] Thong. Cuddy. Go. [*They slowly start to leave, stopping before they pass Foreman.*]

Foreman: It's how I got hired.

House and his team accept only the hardest cases, so potential disagreements and conflict are both expected and extreme. Maintaining a good sense of humor makes the disagreements more bearable and allows the team to maintain a positive state of mind; this is hardly an easy task, considering House's attitude and leadership style. Effective humor among team members acknowledges the stress and conflict in a situation, while deflecting developing tension. Two of Cuddy's most prominent traits are her patience and her sense of humor. In "Pilot," when House sarcastically quotes "philosopher" Mick Jagger's aphorism "You can't always get what you want," Cuddy uses humor to manage a potentially volatile confrontation.

> House: You pulled my authorization.
> Cuddy: Yes, why are you yelling?
> House: No MRIs, no imaging studies, no labs.
> Cuddy: You also can't make long-distance phone calls.
> House: If you're gonna fire me, at least have the guts to face me.
> Cuddy: Or photocopies; you're still yelling.
> House: I'm *angry*! You're risking a patient's life.
> Cuddy: I assume those are two separate points.
> House: You showed me disrespect, you embarrassed me, and
>   as long as I'm still working here you have—
> Cuddy: Is your yelling designed to scare me because I'm not
>   sure what I'm supposed to be scared of. More yelling?
>   That's not scary. That you're gonna hurt me? That's scary,
>   but I'm pretty sure I can outrun ya. Oh, I looked into that
>   philosopher you quoted, Jagger, and you're right, "You
>   can't always get what you want," but, as it turns out, "if you
>   try sometimes you get what you need."

Data based on observing interactions between wives and husbands confirm that couples who care for each other and know how to use humor gently and appropriately have long-lasting and satisfying relationships—such as Cuddy and House. We know the love is there, and the humor helps make serious points without doing any serious harm. Notice how the humor seems absent from Foreman and Thirteen's relationship when she rejoins the team in season 6.

In fact, humor can be used to make potentially inflammatory points without resorting to accusation.

> House: See, this is why I don't waste money on shrinks, 'cause
>   you give me all these really great insights for free.

> Cuddy: Shrink. If you would consider going to a shrink, I
> would pay for it myself. The hospital would hold a bake
> sale, for God's sake.
>
> —"Maternity"

Although it's entertaining to watch House, it's easy to see how working with him could have a long list of drawbacks. Yet despite his flaws, House is able to assemble the team he wants when he returns to work in season 6. Why? He does, at least, have a sense of humor.

People automatically assume that a good sense of humor implies other positive interpersonal qualities. Having a good "sense" of humor is one of the most highly valued qualities we seek in others. When psychologists asked college students to list the qualities they find most attractive in dating partners, both men and women put a good sense of humor at the very top. People with a good sense of humor are expected to be less neurotic, more socially skilled, more open to new experiences, and generally more agreeable. Although these traits don't exactly describe House, they are easy to identify in his team. More than once do Chase and Foreman roll their eyes in response to House's eccentric behavior, instead of reacting angrily. They show that they are agreeable and open, even when frustrated.

Imagine House without his humor—he would be even less likable, if that's possible. Humor is an important skill for our favorite doctor to master, because he spends a lot of time defusing the tension he is so prone to creating. So, just when you start to imagine that House is nothing more than a mean-spirited "manipulative bastard," he reveals his humorous side and becomes at least a little more likable. It's not always the team that is the beneficiary of the "gentle" House, but it does keep the character from becoming too dark. In "Euphoria, Part 2," funny House delights a child, while helping a mother relax just a bit during one of House's brief and usually forced stints in the clinic.

> Mother: The seizures only seem to happen when she's in her
> car seat. She starts to rock and grunt.
> House: She responsive?

Mother: No, no, it's like she's in a zone. And her abdominal muscles become dystonic.

House: Big word. Someone's been on the Interweb.

Mother: I looked up a few articles on epilepsy. You know, there's actually some really great youth soccer leagues that would cater specifically to her special needs, and I think it might explain why she's been having a hard time in preschool.

House: Well, let's confirm your diagnosis before you have her held back. Strobing lights and high-pitched sounds can provoke a seizure. [*Quickly moving a penlight in front of her eyes*] Wooooooooooooooooooooooooooooooo!

Girl: You're a goof!

House: Takes one to know one, loser! Wait, that means I'm a loser. Scratch that. These episodes, she gets sweaty afterward?

Mother: Soaking wet.

House: She seem upset by them or just tired?

Mother: No, she kind of thinks it's funny.

House: You mix rocking, grunting, sweating, and dystonia with concerned parents, and you get an amateur diagnosis of epilepsy. In actuality, all your little girl is doing is saying "yoo hoo" to the hoo-hoo.

Mother: She's what?

House: Marching the penguin. Ya-ya-ing the sisterhood. Finding Nemo.

Girl: That was funny.

House: It's called gratification disorder. Sort of a misnomer— if one was unable to gratify oneself . . . that would be a disorder.

Mother: [*Covering the girl's ears*] Are you saying she's masturbating?

House: I was trying to be discreet—there's a child in the room!

Mother: This is horrifying.

House: Epilepsy is horrifying. Teach your girl about privacy, and she'll be fine. [*He hands the girl a lollipop*] Here you go.

Girl: Thank you.

Humor's Dark Side

Of course, not all humor is good humor. The benefits we have been discussing up to now assumed that humor was used as a positive force for personal or social gain. Yet we acknowledged the dark side of humor when we began this journey, and now it's time to consider situations where humor can do more harm than good. Even the earliest humor theorists, including Freud, recognized that humor could be used as an outlet for aggressive tendencies. *Superiority humor*, as it has been termed, involves belittling or ridiculing others as a way of increasing one's own status. Superiority humor separates people, so that the target of the humor cannot fully enjoy the humorous intent and instead is made to suffer. Those present who are not the target of superiority humor often enjoy it but with trepidation. This type of humor creates tension, because one's turn as a target may be coming soon. Thus, superiority humor directed within a group (such as House's team) can raise tensions, increase stress, and weaken bonds. Superiority humor directed outside the group, though still hurtful, will do less damage to the group's effectiveness. Do we find superiority humor being used to ridicule others in the characters working at Princeton-Plainsboro Teaching Hospital? House, given his own tendencies to belittle others, certainly provides a role model for ridicule.

For House, ridicule is just a part of normal conversation. When you believe most people are morons and that everyone lies, it is easy to see humor at someone else's expense as deserved. In "The Softer Side," House meets the parents of a child who is a genetic mosaic. Given how unusual this condition is, the parents have tried to come to the hospital prepared. House uses humor to remind them that he is a diagnostician, and they, well, are not.

> Melanie [*Mother*]: We think that he has a blind uterus; he should have an MRI.
>
> Joseph [*Father*]: Over the past thirteen years we've educated ourselves.
>
> House: Well, who needs med school when you've got Wi-Fi?

Chase tends to resort to a darker form of humor when he lets his emotions affect his judgment. He has a history with the seminary and often has trouble dealing with religious beliefs. In "Damned if You Do," Chase enters the room of Sister Augustine and finds the other sisters watching television.

Augustine: I hadn't seen television in over twenty years.
Chase: Do you consider it the work of the devil, or do you just
    not get cable where you live?

The comment is sarcastic and humorous, but it also makes Chase's views on religious devotees clear. Superiority humor shows up on a regular basis on *House*, and most of the characters resort to it at some point. Yet even though superiority humor is very common, it can be dangerous as a dominant form of humor.

Humor Styles: Finding Your Humor Profile

When we think of humor as a social quality, the sense of humor we see in ourselves and others, we typically imagine the positive side of humor. In truth, we all tend to demonstrate a variety of humor styles in our behavior, just as we have seen in the characters on *House*. Recent research has demonstrated that our uses of humor can be categorized into four main styles, each of which everybody demonstrates to some degree. Rod Martin, a humor researcher, has developed a model of humor styles that assumes humor can be used either positively, to build relationships and relieve stress, or negatively, to mock others or oneself. Using a questionnaire he developed to assess individual differences in humor styles, he assigned scores to people that represent their tendencies to use each style. The four styles are affiliative humor, self-enhancing humor, aggressive humor, and self-defeating humor.

Affiliative humor entertains others and keeps relationships running smoothly. Self-enhancing humor is used for one's own benefit as a way to help limit the impact of life's many potential stressors. Aggressive humor is the superiority humor that is designed to ridicule or demean others to get a laugh, while self-defeating humor involves making fun of yourself in the hope that others will like you more. Noteworthy is the finding that we inherit from our parents much of our tendency to use the positive styles of humor (it's in our genes), but our environment, the experiences we have growing up, primarily shapes our inclination to use the negative styles. House, clearly, comes from an environment where negative humor was prevalent.

High use of self-enhancing humor and low use of self-defeating humor are related to greater levels of personal well-being and lower levels of perceived stress. Thus, these "self-directed" styles can affect—positively or negatively—your internal state. On the other hand, people who liberally use affiliative humor and avoid aggressive humor have more satisfying relationships with others. Affiliative humor brings people together, whereas aggressive humor drives them apart. With these differences in mind, we could develop profiles of the characters on *House* based on their "humor styles." Let's consider House, and you can construct your own profiles for your other favorite characters.

House's Humor Profile

We know from the examples of superiority humor we've seen that House relies heavily on aggressive humor. He has little tolerance for others and is quick to point out what he perceives as flaws by using sarcasm and ridicule. House also displays self-defeating humor in his occasional quips about his physical limitations. Making fun of personal deficiencies or mistakes to get attention from others is self-defeating and can have negative psychological consequences in the long run. Although it's not his dominant style, House relies on self-defeating humor when it suits his purpose.

> House: If you're dying, suddenly everybody loves you.
> Wilson: You have a cane, nobody even likes you.
> House: I'm not terminal, merely pathetic; you wouldn't believe the crap people let me get away with.
>
> —"Autopsy"

House: The reality is irrelevant. I'll prove it. People who know me see me as an ass, treat me as an ass. People who don't know me see a cripple, treat me as a cripple. What kind of selfish jerk wouldn't take advantage of that fact?

—"TB or Not TB"

House offers the rare glimpse of affiliative humor, but even these moments tend to slip into aggressive humor before they end. As we have seen earlier, when House interacts with children, he can be funny and entertaining, often building a bond. Yet he also tends to turn these interactions into attacks on the parents for their, in his view, misguided beliefs. It's fair to say that House has difficulty maintaining an affiliative style for long.

House does display some self-enhancing humor. He often trivializes threats that could otherwise be sources of stress. This is self-protective and ties into self-enhancing humor's role in coping with problems. For many, being able to laugh a bit when things go wrong is a positive strategy that helps avoid dangerously negative emotions.

Cameron: You're lucky he didn't die.
House: I'm lucky? He's the one who didn't die.

—"Meaning"

Self-enhancing humor is often hard to identify precisely because the person using it is often deflecting stress and trying to find a positive way to deal with a negative situation. One of the most difficult moments in House's life is his father's death in "Birthmarks." Initially, he reacts by aggressively taunting Wilson, but after his best friend breaks a stained-glass window with a liquor bottle, House defuses the tension with humor to help himself deal with the tension and to let Wilson know that despite all of the taunting, their friendship is incredibly important.

Wilson: I'm not afraid.
House: Admit it.
Wilson: I've lost people. It happens.

House: Admit it. Admit it!

Wilson: What are you, five? Stop repeating—

House: Admit it. Admit it. Admit it. Admit it. Admit it. Admit it. Admit it. Come on, admit it. Admit it! [*With a cry, Wilson picks up a liquor bottle and throws it through a stained-glass window; they both stare*]

House: Still not boring.

House's profile: high aggressive humor, high self-enhancing humor, moderate self-defeating humor, and only brief flashes of affiliative humor. His "humor style" should allow him to minimize his personal stressors and gain some favor through mocking himself, but his relationships with others are not helped by his humor. How would you profile your favorite character other than House?

Even though each episode of *House* revolves around a serious medical emergency, there are numerous situations where humor is either useful or necessary. Psychology has discovered many reasons that we all should embrace the inclusion of humor in our lives. Good humor—humor that entertains without causing harm—has many personal and interpersonal benefits: it results in less stress, a more positive outlook on life, biochemical changes that lift our spirits and help our immune systems function more efficiently, and more pleasing interactions with others (both for us and for the others). The doctors at Princeton-Plainsboro Teaching Hospital could probably use more humor, although perhaps less of House's personal brand. Of course, House would not be the character we have come to enjoy if he did not practice his own unique form of humor. House does not want to be likable, but he does like to be funny—even when he is the only one laughing.

SUGGESTED READINGS

Martin, R. A. (2007). *The Psychology of Humor: An Integrative Approach*. Burlington, MA: Elsevier Academic Press.

McGhee, P. (2010). *Humor: The Lighter Path to Resilience and Health*. Bloomington, IN: AuthorHouse.

PART TWO
The Bad: Psychological Malpractice

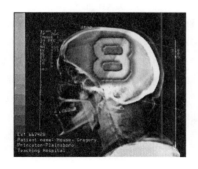

House and Narcissism
Why Are Flawed Heroes Simply Irresistible?

MARK ALICKE

Everybody's good, and everybody's flawed, and House is more good and more flawed than most. He is a pompous, talented ass or a talented pompous ass, but either way, his boorish behavior raises interesting questions about how exceptionally talented people should behave. Cultural prescriptions are divided on this point. The Christian tradition extols modesty and reserve. On the other side of the divide is good old Yankee pride, as represented by the famous quote "It ain't bragging if you can do it." Although nobody really knows who first gave us this morsel of folk wisdom, it has been variously attributed to raconteurs who seem as if they *might* have said it, such as the great baseball pitcher Dizzy Dean and, of course, Muhammad Ali.

The idea that a dose of conceit is tolerable if supportable sounds reasonable on the face of it, and such superficial plausibility has been good enough to launch this and many other cultural truisms. Yet psychologists have shown that cultural truisms, precisely because they are accepted and perpetuated with flimsy support, are easily assailed. The Dizzy Dean-Muhammad Ali truism is no exception. When you think about it, why should smart or talented people have greater license to be obnoxious than ordinary folks do? In fact, House's extraordinary abilities often seem to aggravate his displays of superiority, rather than to palliate them.

Whether House's loutish behavior is tolerated or condemned, there is no doubt that his skills are laudable. Also, as a general rule, people strive desperately to embrace those who possess exceptional talents, unless they happen to live with, work under, or associate with them on a daily basis. Superiority is best appreciated from afar for the simple fact of what it implies, namely, one's own inferiority. Most of us who maintain some grip on reality are aware that we possess certain shortcomings, but it is dispiriting to be repeatedly reminded of them by the presence of friends, acquaintances, and family members who are morally, intellectually, or physically superior.

Research on what is known as *social comparison theory*, however, has shown that the talents of superior others can also be inspiring under two specific conditions: if we believe that we are capable of attaining their performance level, or if their talents are completely unrelated to our own pursuits. For a medical student at the early stages of her training, a diagnostician with House's skills might be extremely inspiring. For someone who was already operating in this profession, however, House's superior talent would most likely have the opposite effect by highlighting the individual's inferior skills.

Yet for those of us who are not physicians and who have no desire to be, House begins with a huge advantage: we want to like him for his prodigious skills as a medical diagnostician, and because we don't know him and we can't (he is, after all, fictional), there is little risk that his abilities will provoke unflattering self-reflections. The problem is that House challenges our ability to admire him at every turn with rude, selfish, inconsiderate, and occasionally malicious behavior—a tension that runs throughout virtually every episode. After each new offense, we dust ourselves off and try to restore our positive feelings, with varying degrees of success. Still, it is doubtful that the show would remain so popular if the main character were completely unredeemable, which suggests that House's positive characteristics manage to compensate, at least partly, for his palpable shortcomings.

In what follows, I consider the feelings and judgments that House is likely to evoke by referring to psychological perspectives on self-enhancement, self-protection, and the personality characteristic of narcissism. House is clearly someone whose confidence in his abilities exceeds even his very high ability level (self-enhancement) and who engages in extreme behaviors to avoid being hurt (self-protection). As we will see, he possesses many characteristics that fit the clinical diagnostic category of narcissism, but he is a unique case, in that his very high self-views are largely supported by his prodigious feats of medical diagnosis. To paint a reasonable facsimile of House, it is necessary to consider the ways in which he deviates from, as well as adheres to, psychological categories such as narcissism. Accordingly, I will try to point out the ways in which House conforms to and diverges from the expectations of psychological theories.

Redemption or Rebuke?

Psychologists don't have many stock explanations for characters such as House, whose shortcomings are so acute as to offset their tremendous abilities. One way to go about analyzing House is to compare him with a real-life character who also has incredible skills and, as his adoring public was stunned to learn, stupendous faults—Tiger Woods. Before his predilections for extramarital sex with porn stars and pancake waitresses became public knowledge, Tiger Woods was one of the most popular humans on the planet. Because he is not terribly witty, funny, or interesting in any other obvious way, one can surmise that it is Woods's phenomenal golf skills that led fans to accept his public image without question. Even though his image has now changed drastically, my guess is that a few more golf championships would restore Tiger Woods's reputation to something like its former status, and if so, the question is, why?

The first thing to consider is the nature of the offense. Adultery is hardly uncommon, and one might conjecture that many tried-and-true marital partners would be sorely tested by the opportunities that present themselves regularly to popular public figures (see Clinton, William J., forty-second United States president). After an initial torrent of condemnation when the infidelities of public figures are revealed, people get over it. Forgiveness may take a little longer in Tiger Woods's case, due to his salacious choice of porn stars for play dates. In legal parlance, this is an aggravating circumstance, but the porn star problem is a minor one. After all, if celebrities are hell-bent on satisfying every possible sexual urge, why confine themselves to rank amateurs? I suspect that the public will soon forget about this colorful addendum to Tiger's extracurricular activities, especially if he restores his athletic dominance and avoids further scandals.

The differences between House's and Tiger Woods's circumstances highlight some of the elements that guide our perceptions of talented people who have conspicuous flaws. The main bond between the two is that they possess extraordinary abilities that make us want to like them and dazzling faults that frustrate the attempt. Perhaps the most obvious difference is that whereas Tiger Woods and his marketers went to great lengths to craft a false persona, House goes to equal lengths not to. One can ask, then, whether it is better to be a private jerk or a public one. Private misconduct seems obviously preferable because nobody knows about it. Once the facts of Tiger Woods's clandestine dealings were exposed, however, the deception and hypocrisy that they revealed augmented his catalog of offenses; in fact, for many fans, the lie that he perpetrated *was* his biggest offense.

Unlike Tiger Woods, House is no hypocrite or deceiver. He takes honesty to its logical limit and beyond. He sets the stage in the pilot episode when he extols the benefits of baby coffins to a mother who refuses to vaccinate her child. Whereas Tiger Woods's shortcomings have virtually no upside (unless one grants him grudging admiration for an Olympian libido), House, at least, is frank and brutally honest. Because House's directness is so far outside the limits of propriety, the rudeness it reveals easily outweighs the honesty it discloses. Still, because honesty is such a valued commodity, observers may allow him some credit for his bluntness. This credit is likely to be extended more readily, of course, by observers of his behavior than by its recipients. Although it may be amusing to watch House irritate others with insensitive remarks, such as when he tells Foreman that if he doesn't "get a rabies shot within three hours, I'll have to make another affirmative action hire" ("Histories"), it would be far less comical to have such remarks directed at oneself.

Another difference between these fictional and authentic cultural icons is that House is unrepentant, whereas Tiger Woods desperately desires to resurrect his public image, although the millions of advertising dollars at stake naturally raise questions about his motives. Nevertheless, Tiger Woods appears to be on firmer ground here: surely, it is better to strive to overcome one's faults than to revel in them, although it would have improved his moral standing to have changed spontaneously, rather than after a four-iron to the noggin and the mass exodus of his sponsors. The *House* writers seem attuned to the value of contrition, because they are apparently attempting to smooth some of House's rough edges as the series progresses. In the episode titled "Open and Shut," he even buys Cuddy an expensive espresso machine in the hopes that doing nice things for people will result in reciprocal benefits. Of course, the reciprocal benefit he hopes for in this case is oral sex, so his offering doesn't exactly qualify as selfless.

Talented individuals with gargantuan flaws probably garner some sympathy if their misdeeds aim at deflecting pain, rather than acquiring pleasure. In the terminology of behavioral psychology, this suggests that people are more understanding of others whose actions are controlled by negative (avoiding pain), rather than positive (acquiring reward), reinforcement contingencies. In Tiger Woods's case, those who believe that he was a victim of sex addiction and that his dalliances were outside his control would presumably sympathize with his struggle to meet the arduous demands of monogamy. Conversely, those who consider sex addiction to be merely an excuse for garden-variety horniness would be more likely to see him as a philandering liar. By contrast, there is no such conundrum regarding House's appalling behavior; acting like a jerk makes him lonelier and more pathetic. House's problems are complicated by the fact that much of his worst behavior is directed toward those who care about him most. In "Control," Cameron asks, "Do you like me? I need to know." After a long pause, House responds, "No." This interchange is typical of House's predilection for gratifying his own need to say what he thinks at the expense of others. Still, one gets the feeling that House would act differently if he could only defeat his demons, whereas Tiger Woods would undoubtedly have added many more amorous admirers if his activities had not come under public scrutiny.

Like diseases and other physical disorders, nasty habits and behavior are detrimental to their owners. Whether these faults arouse sympathy or disdain depends on how people think they evolved. Someone who develops a substance abuse problem after losing his family in a car accident will surely evoke more sympathy than an individual who takes drugs to harmonize with the universe. Likewise, a person whose surly and sarcastic personality can be traced to traumatic life experiences will be indulged more than one who simply enjoys being obnoxious. In short, people with compelling excuses for their shortcomings are treated with more patience than are those with self-inflicted wounds.

Unless Tiger Woods had underlying sexual issues of the sort that would delight a Freudian analyst, his wounds probably reside in the self-inflicted category. House's shortcomings are more difficult to gauge. His psychological problems seem to revolve partly around his leg injury, which caused a permanent limp and a Vicodin habit for the pain. Certainly, his drug addiction is no boon to his personality. But in "Three Stories" Cameron, who by now has been romantically involved with House, asks Stacy what he was like before his crippling injury. Her answer—"pretty much like he is now"—suggests that his injury exacerbated but did not cause his personality flaws.

In a revealing episode, "One Day, One Room," a rape victim intuits House's damaged personality and wants to disclose her ordeal only to him, despite his continual reluctance to help. Eventually, the allure of someone who is suffering more than he is lowers House's guard, and, in a rare moment, he talks about having been abused by his father as a child. This unhappy childhood appears, then, to be the original source of House's bitterness, and his leg injury simply added to his already cynical nature. Still, House is not the only one to have experienced a difficult childhood, and whether he wins sympathy points depends on how difficult people believe it would be for him to alter his objectionable disposition. Social-psychological research on blame and responsibility, for example, has examined the influence of what is called "capacity control" on attributing blame for offensive or harmful behavior. People whose shortcomings or incapacities developed through no fault of their own are blamed less for their unfortunate actions. To illustrate, consider the case of someone whose anxiety disorder was caused by drug and alcohol use, versus one whose disorder was caused by an uncontrollable genetic defect. Now, imagine that the anxiety disorder contributes to the person failing to stop quickly enough at an intersection, which results in a car accident. Which person is likely to be treated more leniently? Research has established clearly that we sympathize more with people who have less control over their quirks and disorders. To me, House seems obstinately unwilling to improve his behavior, but those who believe that his upbringing has damaged him in ways that he cannot control are likely to accord him greater sympathy.

House's ultimate saving grace is that he seems to care a great deal about keeping people alive. He also benefits from a cultural stereotype of the arrogant, temperamental doctor with a god complex, which makes his behavior seem less unusual than it would be for the manager of a grocery store. The category that House occupies—the great man with great flaws—is a familiar one, encompassing notables such as Yahweh, Zeus, Achilles, King Lear, John Rockefeller, George Patton, John F. Kennedy—the list is long. House, in this grand tradition, is permitted far greater latitude for his impudence and impertinence than mere mortals are.

Of course, House is a television character, rather than a real-life hero, and therefore benefits from a willing suspension of disbelief. Any actual physician who behaved as extremely as House would face stronger legal and social sanctions. In "Love Hurts," House tells a young man's estranged parents that their son is dead in order to get them to come to the hospital. Even this pales in comparison to his kidnapping a soap opera star, drugging him, and subjecting him to unwanted diagnostic tests in "Living the Dream." Yet the difference between a fictional character such as House and real people who are known only vicariously is probably not as great as it might seem. The relaxed standards of morality and propriety that House enjoys are experienced as well by sports and entertainment figures who have virtually no direct contact with their adoring fans. While their reputations may suffer temporarily when serious transgressions such as sexual assault, attempted murder, and negligent homicide are brought to light, the need for hero worship is so powerful that fans are almost infinitely forgiving of their idols as long as they continue to perform their uplifting feats. In this sense, House is really not so different from public figures whose transgressions are not only overlooked but occasionally become part of their allure.

One way of looking at the dilemma that House poses is with reference to psychological theories of cognitive consistency. A guiding assumption among many researchers who study attitudes and beliefs is that people prefer belief systems that are consistent and coherent. In other words, it makes good sense for us to like people who are kind, cooperative, and helpful but somewhat less sense to be drawn to people who are often unkind and unhelpful. Certainly, unkindness and unhelpfulness are traits that House frequently displays. Even while working assiduously to arrive at a life-saving diagnosis, he seems primarily motivated by the intellectual challenge, rather than by the burning need to save a patient's life. This would make it easy to conclude something like the following: "House is a major jerk, but I like him anyway because he is so talented." Instead, consistency needs may lead us to deemphasize House's foibles or even to exaggerate his virtues. By minimizing House's shortcomings, we are better able to construct a story that our consistency needs can live with.

The Narcissism Problem

House clearly thinks that he is better than everyone else. Although most people exaggerate their virtues and downplay their vices, House falls into the smaller category of individuals whose self-aggrandizement is largely supported by their actual abilities. No medical diagnosticians are as good as the TV version of House, but if they were, they would face delicate social problems that beset people with extraordinary capabilities, in particular, the problem of being supremely self-assured, while maintaining at least a semblance of humility in the eyes of one's friends and associates.

House is not beleaguered by any need to appear humble. Instead, he takes the opposite tack and delights in trumpeting his superior skills. In "Whatever It Takes," he is ordered to consult on a CIA case in which an agent has incurred life-threatening injuries, including serious burns. An immunologist from Johns Hopkins is also on the case, and House begins by politely mentioning an article the physician wrote and then, in vintage House form, commenting that he uses the journal in which it was published to balance his piano's legs. Of course, House's diagnosis proves to be the correct one, and his finely honed sarcasm adds to the immunologist's chagrin at being outgunned.

Insulting others is just one of House's laundry list of behavioral faults. These faults coalesce in what psychologists might identify as a *narcissistic personality disorder.* In ordinary usage, narcissism means something like excessive self-love. The more technical use of narcissism by psychologists is multifaceted. The clinical definition, as cataloged in the *Diagnostic and Statistical Manual of Mental Disorders*, which is the main classification system for psychiatrists and psychologists, denotes three main characteristics: (1) an exaggerated sense of self-importance, (2) an excessive need for admiration, and (3) a lack of empathy for others.

House certainly scores points on each of these dimensions. His exaggerated sense of self-importance is a consistent narrative theme, as when, after a head injury in "House's Head," Cameron tells him that they are going to have to monitor his head for swelling, and he replies, "How much bigger can it get?" Again, though, when psychologists refer to the extreme self-enhancement that narcissism represents, they usually mean someone whose self-view is way out of touch with reality. The problem with House is that his exalted sense of self has to be viewed in light of the fact that he is usually the one who makes the correct diagnoses and saves lives. If his self-importance is exaggerated, his ability to back it up makes it only slightly so. In this regard, House receives only a barely passing grade on the first criterion for narcissism.

He receives a much higher grade on the second criterion—needing acceptance from others. In "Don't Ever Change," Cuddy calls him the "long-distance runner of neediness." He even describes himself in "House's Head" as a lonely, misanthropic drug addict. House's neediness is ironic because it appears, on the surface, that he couldn't care less what others think about him. In fact, he goes out of his way to alienate people. Yet hurting others before they can hurt you is a time-honored self-protection strategy. House's desperation manifests in many ways: in calling Cuddy at all hours of the night and day and showing up to ruin her dates, in his unwillingness to treat his ex-girlfriend's husband so that either he can have her back or she can suffer, and in his distress at his best friend's resignation from the hospital after Wilson's girlfriend Amber dies. House continually calls Wilson an idiot for leaving but does everything he can think of to convince him to stay. In subsequent episodes he more or less stalks Wilson, even showing up at his house with the excuse of consulting on cases.

One thing that makes *House* a superior television show and his character so compelling is that his personality is nuanced, rather than stereotyped. In one sense, he ranks very high on the third narcissistic criterion, that of lacking empathy. He makes racially and ethnically insensitive comments, tells Cameron that she is only attracted to damaged people because she married a terminal cancer patient, tells a dying patient that there is no God, switches Thirteen's decaffeinated coffee with the caffeinated variety to make her think that her shakiness is due to Huntington's chorea (which her mother died of and for which he wants her to get tested), among other endearments. Nevertheless, there are certain boundaries that House doesn't cross, although his bar for cruelty is obviously set much higher than that of other human beings. When he does clearly cross the line, he recognizes it, such as when he apologizes for mocking a father's questions about his dying son in "Detox."

Usually, when House is berating his friends and colleagues, it is with an eye toward being helpful, even if they explicitly disavow his advice. When he tells Cameron that she is attracted only to damaged people, for example, it is because she is attracted to him, and he believes that he has nothing to offer her. He takes extreme measures with Thirteen because he believes that it is better for her to have an answer about her future (she ultimately tests positive for Huntington's disease, virtually ensuring an early death). He insults his team because he believes he is teaching them to think more carefully about diagnostic criteria, although the effectiveness of his strategy is highly doubtful. It is as though House is playing a verbal game that involves pushing sarcasm and disparagement beyond all boundaries of propriety, and he expects that others will appreciate or at least tolerate this jousting. Those who know him well, especially members of his team and the hospital staff, have either become habituated to his comments or learned to filter them for their underlying intent. Wilson and Foreman in particular, who are coequals, return House's sarcasm in good measure. In "Black Hole," House wants to use a patient's hallucinations to diagnose her illness, to which Foreman comments, "She said she was being sucked into a black hole—does that mean we should look for a tumor in her anus?"—a barb worthy of House himself. In "Birthmarks," when Wilson drives House to his father's funeral, Wilson responds to House's speculation that the person who raised him was not his biological father with "Of course—you were a brilliant, socially isolated twelve-year-old, and you created a parallel universe in which your life didn't suck"—a brutally frank observation of the sort House would convey to others.

Self-Enhancer or Self-Protector?

Except for those who possess very low self-esteem, most individuals strive to maintain favorable self-views. In fact, the tendency to view oneself more favorably than objective reality warrants is a pervasive phenomenon as represented in what psychologists refer to as the *better-than-average effect* and the *optimistic bias.* Research on the better-than-average effect has shown that people consistently overestimate their abilities and virtues in comparison to those of their peers. This effect has been found among undergraduate students' ratings of their leadership skills, athletic prowess, and ability to get along with others; drivers rating their driving skills while in the hospital due to a car accident they had caused; college instructors rating their teaching ability; psychologists rating the quality of their research; students estimating their dating popularity; couples assessing the quality of their marriage; and adults assessing their happiness. Research on the closely allied optimistic bias shows that people underestimate their risk of suffering unfortunate life events, such as disease or divorce, and overestimate their chances of experiencing beneficial events, such as having a happy marriage and becoming wealthy. In addition to these biases, people also tend to believe that they can control random events (part of what is called the "illusion of control"), take more credit than they deserve when good things happen and less credit for bad events (the "self-serving bias"), prefer the letters in their own names to other letters in the alphabet (the "name-letter effect"), and recall past events in a way that puts themselves in a positive light ("selective recall").

The aforementioned tendencies illustrate various strains of self-enhancement. Self-enhancement involves elevating one's actions and characteristics to a level beyond what objective reality warrants. Self-enhancement confers various benefits. It makes people feel good, gives them confidence to persist on difficult tasks, and instills the motivation needed for novel endeavors. Positive self-views can also encourage people to stop spending time on useless tasks and to leave harmful jobs or relationships. Of course, if positive self-views diverge too far from reality, they carry certain risks. People with extremely unrealistic self-images may pursue relationship partners who have no interest in them, might select occupations for which they are poorly suited, and may fail to recognize when they are alienating their friends and acquaintances, among other pitfalls.

House certainly exhibits self-enhancement, particularly when overconfidence in his diagnostic skills leads him to advocate experimental treatments that are unlikely to be effective and in his refusal to show any remorse for his diagnosis when it is erroneous. A more general problem with self-enhancement is that it often has to confront an unwelcome and contradictory reality: We want to see ourselves as devastatingly attractive, but nobody seems to agree; we aspire to brilliance, but those pesky grades, job evaluations, and deflating standardized test scores intrude on our efforts. In everyday life, we receive explicit or implicit negative feedback from friends, romantic partners, and employers. For House, and indeed for any overconfident decision maker, self-enhancement carries the additional danger of leading one into disastrous choices that could have been avoided if all sides of the decision—including opposing viewpoints—had been carefully considered.

To avoid letting our self-views fall too far below their desired levels when reality intrudes, it often becomes necessary to enlist various forms of damage control. Psychologists refer to damage control as self-defense or self-protection. The most famous examples are the Freudian defense mechanisms. Repression, which involves relegating unwanted thoughts and motivations to the unconscious, is the master mechanism and yields offshoots such as denial (claiming that the threatening material is untrue), projection (seeing one's undesirable motives and characteristics in others), reaction formation (adopting characteristics that are opposite to one's motives, such as a person with persistent sexual desires and thoughts becoming extremely prudish), and displacement (transferring emotions from one object to another, such as kicking the dog when you are mad at your spouse). Although the defense mechanisms are usually construed as ways to deflect debilitating anxiety, they can also be viewed, more commonly, as strategies that people routinely employ to prevent their self-views from slipping below a desired level. For example, to avoid viewing ourselves as less intelligent than we would like, we can deny the validity of the grade we obtain in a course, the evaluation we receive from an employer, or the meaning and value of standardized tests (denial). As a defense against accepting that we are selfish or uncooperative people, we can project our own selfishness or uncooperativeness onto others (projection) or even view ourselves as exceptionally selfless (reaction formation). In sum, there are two complementary aspects to maintaining favorable self-views. The first is elevation beyond some objective reality level (self-enhancement), such as viewing oneself as more attractive than a poll of one's peers would indicate. The second component to maintaining positive self-images is to avoid falling below a subjectively acceptable level, for which various defense mechanisms can be deployed (self-defense).

The crux of the narcissistic personality disorder is generally thought to be a defense against feelings of inadequacy. In other words, although the outstanding surface feature of narcissism seems to be self-enhancement—the tendency to promote oneself over others—its ultimate purpose may be to protect the self from unflattering feedback. Put another way, self-enhancement sometimes subserves self-protection. House's case seems to fit this description perfectly. By bullying, disparaging, and belittling others, House keeps them at bay, preventing anyone from hurting or diminishing him. Ultimately, House is a lonely and dispirited character whose fear of friendship or intimacy fosters his rude and obnoxious behavior.

House attending his father's funeral in "Birthmarks" sheds light on his personality development. He never liked his father, and his father's death has done nothing to change that. He has no intention of attending the funeral, but his mother wants him there, and Cuddy and Wilson conspire to have Wilson drive him, kicking and screaming, to Lexington, Kentucky, for the service, where his mother insists on his speaking. He begins in typical House style, by shocking the audience with disparaging comments about his father. Then, in describing his father, he makes the most revealing comments perhaps at any point in the series: "He loved doing what he did. He saw his work as some kind of sacred calling more important than any personal relationship. Maybe if he had been a better father, I'd be a better son. But I am what I am because of him."

So, House is committed to his medical career and invests all of his energy in making correct diagnoses and correspondingly little in his interpersonal relationships. Although many people with high career aspirations are forced to sacrifice some of the time that they would otherwise wish to devote to their friends and family, it seems unlikely that House is making any sacrifice in this regard. Rather, his insecurity in social relationships probably helps focus his efforts on intellectual pursuits in the first place. The irony, of course, is that House's superior abilities make him very appealing to both men and women. Although everyone fears rejection when they entrust their emotional well-being to others, a kinder, gentler House would most likely fare quite well in social and romantic relationships. His fears of rejection, therefore, are not well grounded, as is the case with many insecure people who, from an outsider's perspective, have every reason to enjoy high self-esteem.

At any rate, the barriers he constructs are self-defeating, as amply demonstrated in some of the show's most powerful episodes from the end of season 4. In these episodes, Amber, a physician and a former member of House's diagnostic team who is now dating Wilson, dies from injuries she suffered in a bus crash. The reason that Amber was on the bus was that she came to fetch House, who was drunk in a bar. House had called Wilson for a ride, and Amber, who answered the phone in Wilson's absence, came instead. The bus that they rode in was hit by a truck, and House suffered brain injuries and amnesia, which rendered him unable to recall that Amber was severely injured. House then risks his own life to undergo a (fanciful) procedure that helps him recall the incident. When House fully remembers the event, the physicians realize that they can't save Amber, and she dies in Wilson's arms. Wilson resigns from the hospital, and House tries, unsuccessfully at first, to get him to reconsider.

House cries when he realizes that there is nothing that can be done to save Amber, probably as much for the pain that he knows Wilson will experience as for his regret at not being able to help her. He says that he doesn't want to be miserable and that he doesn't want Wilson to hate him—this is the most vulnerability he expresses during the show's run. Eventually, Wilson returns to the hospital, and House and Wilson repair their relationship and even become roommates. Perhaps inevitably, House begins his antics all over again by trying to break up Wilson's reconciliation with his former wife.

An Antihero for Conflicted Times

House is heroic, pathetic, and consistent. He is driven by the best of motives—to succeed at his profession at the highest level and to save lives—and is hampered by the pettiest of motives: to alienate others before they can reject him. In one sense, he fits the narcissistic personality prototype, in that his exalted self-view belies his extreme insecurity. He is certain beyond doubt that he is a great medical diagnostician but completely unsure that anyone would want to be his friend or romantic partner. In "The Itch," he is as afraid to express his romantic feelings for Cuddy as a schoolboy unable to make a prom date. More poignantly, when he tries to support others, as when he watches a surgery with the patient's family ("Meaning"), he realizes that their appreciation for his support completely fails to arouse any emotions in him.

Despite these shortcomings, the show's ongoing success suggests that a large segment of the viewing audience likes House. This is partly because he is fictional and the worst of his actions don't really hurt anyone, but also because it is difficult to dislike someone who is funny, brilliant, and supremely skilled in a highly respected profession. Cognitive consistency needs are powerful, and they impel us to create a coherent story, making it hard to both like and dislike the same person. Given the choice, House has won by a landslide.

SUGGESTED READINGS

Alicke, M. D., and T. L. Davis (1990). Capacity responsibility in social evaluation. *Personality and Social Psychology Bulletin*, *16*, 465–474.

Alicke, M. D., and O. Govorun (2005). The better-than-average effect. In M. D. Alicke, D. A. Dunning, and J. I. Krueger (eds.), *The Self in Social Judgment* (pp. 85–106). Philadelphia: Psychology Press.

Alicke, M. D., and C. Sedikides (2009). Self-enhancement and self-protection: What they are and what they do. *European Review of Social Psychology*, *20*, 1–48.

——— (2010). *The Handbook of Self-Enhancement and Self-Protection*. New York: Guilford Press.

Brown, J. D. (1998). *The Self*. New York: McGraw-Hill.

Collins, R. L. (1996). For better or worse: The impact of upward social comparison on self-evaluation. *Psychological Bulletin*, *119*, 51–69.

Cooper, J. (2007). *Cognitive Dissonance: 50 Years of a Classic Theory*. London: Sage.

Freud, A. (1946). *The Ego and the Mechanisms of Defense*. New York: International Universities Press.

Koole, S. L., and B. W. Pelham (2003). On the nature of implicit self-esteem: The case of the name letter effect. In S. Spencer, S. Fein, and M. P. Zanna (eds.), *Motivated Social Perception: The Ontario Symposium*, Vol. 9 (pp. 93–166). Hillsdale, NJ: Lawrence Erlbaum Associates.

Morf, C. C., and F. Rhodewalt (2001). Unraveling the paradoxes of narcissism: A dynamic self-regulatory processing model. *Psychological Inquiry, 12,* 177–196.

Sedikides, C., and A. P. Gregg (2003). Portraits of the self. In M. A. Hogg and J. Cooper (eds.), *Sage Handbook of Social Psychology* (pp. 110–138). London: Sage.

Sedikides, C., E. A. Rudich, A. P. Gregg, M. Kumashiro, and C. Rusbult (2004). Are normal narcissists psychologically healthy? Self-esteem matters. *Journal of Personality and Social Psychology, 87,* 400–416.

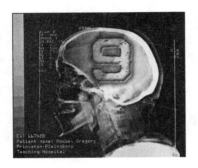

Everybody Lies

BELLA DEPAULO

I love House. I wouldn't want him as a colleague or a friend, and I wouldn't want to lie the way he does, but as a fantasy character—he's the one! With House as my avatar, I can lie guilt-free and with impunity. Identifying as House, I can imagine coming up with brilliant, witty cracks in real time and saying exactly what I think, without caring a whit about how the victim of my barbs might feel. See, House is not only an awesome liar, he is also a take-your-breath-away truth teller.

As one who has for decades studied and taught about the psychology of deceiving and detecting deceit, I savor House for still another reason. He makes it brutally clear just why we so often lie. When we gasp in horror at some searing truth that House has just shot through the heart of his target, we suddenly know exactly why we would never practice such raw, unadorned honesty in our own lives.

Coming Attractions

What is the correspondence between deception in House's world and deception in the real world? Clusters of psychologists are obsessed with lying, so we actually have some answers to that question. We know how often people lie, when they lie, what they lie about, and what they say about why they lie. On the surface, most of the people who have participated in research studies of lying don't look or sound much like House. At first, when I try to analyze House, I'll go along with the impression he is trying to convey. Later in the chapter, though, I'll show how House "leaks" the aspects of himself that he is trying hardest to hide. Along the way, I'll take on the questions of whether House is a good liar and whether he is a good lie detector. Neither question has a one-word answer.

Everybody Lies. House Is Sure of It. Yet Is He Right?

Long before House first limped into our hearts, my colleagues and I set out to investigate his most fundamental belief. Is it really true that everybody lies? We recruited two very different groups of people— seventy-seven college students and a more diverse group of seventy people from the community—to record all of the lies that they told every day for a week. We also asked them to record all of their interactions with other people that lasted at least ten minutes.

Why bother with the social interactions? Because, as House would no doubt agree, every interaction is an opportunity to lie! To understand what kinds of people are the biggest liars, we needed to know how many opportunities each person had to tell lies.

After the week was up, the 147 participants turned in a total of 1,535 lies. On average, the people from the community told about 1 lie a day, and the college students told 2. That amounted to about 1 lie in every 3 of their social interactions for the college students and 1 in every 5 for the people from the community. Of the 70 community members, 6 claimed never to have told a single lie all week. Of the 77 college students, only 1 made such a claim. House would probably call all 7 of those people liars.

I don't know if those seven people really were lying about not telling any lies. My colleagues and I tried to make it easy for participants to 'fess up to their lies. For example, people did not have to put their real names on the forms where they described their lies. In hopes that participants would remember to record all of their lies, we asked them to make a note of each lie as soon as possible after they told it. We also collected their forms several times during the course of the week.

Our findings suggest that House is right: everybody lies. If we had asked people to keep track of their lies for longer than a week, I'll bet that every last person would have had some lies to tell us about. There was one participant in particular whom I was concerned about—she reported so few social interactions that I thought she hadn't taken the study seriously. I decided to interview her myself after the study was over, and I started by asking a very general question: What did you think of the study? She said that taking part in it was a sobering experience—it made her realize that all she did was study and eat. She wasn't much of a liar because she had so few opportunities to lie.

House is a persistent, bald-faced, shameless, matter-of-fact liar. He's center stage in his mendacity. He revels in unearthing the deceits of his patients and laying them bare for all to see. Yet there's something else important about the show, too. Even the characters who are remarkable for their goodness—Wilson and Cameron, for example— are also liars. In fact, only moments into the pilot episode, Wilson has already lied to House, telling him that a patient is his cousin so that House will take the case. In House's world, as in the real world, just about everybody lies.

Okay, Everybody Lies—but Who Lies the Most?

Of the 147 people who kept daily diaries of their lies, the total number of lies they recorded varied greatly. The low end, of course, was anchored by the 7 people who claimed never to have told a lie, and the lie-telling prize went to the person who racked up forty-six lies by the end of the week.

We had an inkling at the beginning of the research that personality might matter, so, before the studies began, we asked each participant to fill out a battery of personality tests. That way, we could know whether certain kinds of people are especially likely to tell lots of lies. We always looked at the *rate* of lying—the number of lies they told relative to the number of opportunities they had to tell lies (their social interactions).

The least surprising result of our personality studies was that Machiavellian or manipulative people lie more than other people do. That's House. He'll manipulate other people to get his way, even scaring them silly in the process. Remember the "Airborne" episode, in which House and Cuddy are on a flight back from a professional meeting in Singapore when one passenger after another becomes wretchedly ill? The two doctors work through the range of possible explanations, then Cuddy falls ill as well. House to the rescue!

House: [*Over PA system*] As soon as you start feeling symptoms, we need to isolate you in the first-class cabin.
[*Some people start coughing.*]
House: [*Over PA system, rattling off the symptoms*] Fever, rash, . . .
[*Some passengers start looking for rashes on their bodies.*]
House: [*Over PA system, continuing*] . . . nausea, and in the late stages . . .
[*He waits a beat. The passengers brace for the last symptom.*]
House: [*Over PA system*] . . . tremor in the left hand.
[*People start to panic, their left hands visibly trembling.*]

This is how House diagnoses mass hysteria. Of course, in typical House fashion, he engages in manipulation throughout the trip. When Cuddy complains to House, as they are boarding the flight, about the money he spent on room service, he says he'll "take care of it." Cuddy soon learns how he took care of it—by downgrading her ticket (but not his) from first class to coach. Later, when the passenger next to House in first class becomes grossly ill, he goes back to Cuddy in coach and tells her to go enjoy first class. "Did you really think I was gonna leave you stuck back here for eighteen hours?" he asks.

Some of the other lying personality types were a lot more intriguing than the manipulative type. Stereotypically, we think of liars as people who don't care at all about others, except for how they can manipulate them for their own ends. There is a subset of liars exactly like that, as I just discussed. Yet another group of liars is very attuned to other people and is always trying to figure out what other people are thinking and how they are reacting. The main thing these liars care about is what other people think of *them*. They constantly try to behave in ways that would attract the approval or avoid the disapproval of other people.

House doesn't usually care about what other people think of him—or, at least, he pretends not to care. So Wilson and Chase are curious when they find that hiding inside a Henry James dustcover of a book House is reading is a collection of schmaltzy sermons, in the episode "Private Lives." House reads all sorts of religious tracts, ridiculing them all, so why would he cover up his interest in this one? Wilson finally figures it out when he finds a picture of the minister who wrote the sermons—and it turns out to be House's biological father. House doesn't want anyone to know that he actually cares about how his father's mind worked. That's not the image of himself that he tries so hard to convey.

House's secret is nothing compared to Wilson's. Wilson—nice, clean-cut, straight-arrow, empathy-conveying oncologist—is outed as an actor in a porno movie! He protests that he wore those antlers and put his arms around "Moon Woman's" bare breasts only because he was helping his college roommate who was working on a project for his filmmaking class. Wilson protests that he was assured that no one would ever see the film. He admonishes House, "No one can know about this." Of course, everyone will come to know about it, and their view of Wilson will never be the same.

Another personality trait linked with lying is sociability. People who are extraverted and who like to spend lots of time with other people lie at a greater rate than introverts do. That's not only because they see people more often and therefore have more opportunities to lie—we always control for that. My guess is that sociable types are quick to say whatever it takes to make the social interaction go smoothly, even if that means lying. These people are liars, but they are very un-House-like liars.

House is nobody's extravert, but he gets it about what motivates the lies of people who *are* extraverted and sociable. In "It's a Wonderful Life," Wilson and House are debating the value of honesty. It is clear where Wilson is headed when he says, "When you care about someone . . ." House, though, won't let his friend finish his thought. Instead, he interjects the House conclusion: "You lie to them! You pretend that their constant ponderous musings are interesting. You tell them they're not losing their boyish good looks or becoming worn out."

The Whats and Whys of Lies

One reason my colleagues and I had to work so hard to get our diary study participants to record all of their lies is that lying has a bad reputation. According to the conventional wisdom, we tell lies to advance our own agendas—for example, to get a raise or a grade we really don't deserve, to get a great trade-in price for a car that's actually a clunker, or to manipulate someone else into doing an odious task that should actually be our responsibility.

People do in fact tell these kinds of instrumental lies that serve themselves and that neglect or even exploit others, but in our diary studies of everyday lies, they were not very common at all. Fewer than 20 percent of the lies were told for reasons of personal material advantage or convenience.

Because the lies that people recorded in their journals were mostly just the little lies of everyday life, we also did further studies in which we asked people specifically to tell us about the most serious lies they had ever told anyone else and the most serious lies that were ever told to them. (Many of their stories are recounted in my book *Behind the Door of Deceit: Understanding the Biggest Liars in Our Lives.*) In the domain of serious lies, about 60 percent were told in the pursuit of material advantage or personal convenience.

That leaves about 40 percent of the serious lies and more than 80 percent of the everyday lies that were not told in the quest for something as concrete or materially advantageous as money or grades or as selfish as getting your own way. Most lies are personal. They are psychological and emotional. Many lies are told to create a particular impression—for example, to make us appear kinder or smarter or more discerning than we in fact are. We tell these lies to spare ourselves from conflict or from looking bad or getting our feelings hurt. Most of us care greatly about what other people think of us. If we don't think we measure up to the person we want to be or the person we think someone else wants us to be, then lying might seem like an attractive option.

In "Adverse Events," the patient (Brandon) is an artist who has not sold any of his paintings for years. He hasn't told this to his wife (Heather), though. Secretly, he makes money by volunteering for numerous medical experiments, often simultaneously, and that's what brought on his disturbing symptoms. By the end of the episode, Heather has learned about the lie.

> Heather: Why did you lie to me?
> Brandon: I wanna be, uh . . . The way you look at me. The way it makes me feel. Uh, I wanna be . . . what you see . . . when you look at me.

That yearning to be seen in a flattering way and to feel good about the image of yourself that is reflected back to you—in our everyday lives, that sort of wish motivates our lies far more often than does the desire to have more money or material things.

An exchange that takes place earlier in that episode highlights other common reasons (or excuses) for telling lies. Brandon has just been told that he will need dialysis.

> Brandon: Dialysis. Use that for kidney failure, right?
> Thirteen: Don't worry. Your kidneys are fine.
> Taub: He's not worried about his kidneys. He's worried about how he's going to explain the dialysis to his girlfriend.
> Brandon: I just don't want her to worry.
> Thirteen: You mean you don't want her to leave you?
> Brandon: What's wrong with that? I love her. It's not like I've lied to her about anything important. I am an artist. I've

> sold plenty of paintings in the past. It's just . . . I've hit a
> bit of a dry spell lately, is all.
>
> Thirteen: So tell her that.
>
> Taub: He can't. He wants her to be happy, too. He's telling her
> what she wants to hear.

In that brief exchange, we can see the core psychological dynamics at the heart of so many lies. Brandon wants to think he is lying to spare Heather and not himself. He says he just doesn't want her to worry. He claims, improbably, that there was nothing important about hiding from Heather his dangerous involvement in several medical studies simultaneously and the two-year failure to sell his paintings that motivated his stints as a medical guinea pig. Taub believes Brandon is concerned not only with Heather's happiness, but with what Heather will think of Brandon if he tells the truth. Thirteen ups the ante—she thinks Brandon's most fundamental fear is that Heather will leave him.

Most likely, all of these considerations were in play. In the lies my colleagues and I collected during years of research, we saw those sorts of concerns play out over and over again.

Telling Them What They Want to Hear

I don't have any kids, but I like them. Some I even love. Even when kids are being annoying in public places, I often feel at least an initial twinge of empathy for the parents. After a while, though, I fantasize about saying what only House would actually say. To the mother of a whining child in an airplane, for example, House advises, "Give her twenty milligrams of antihistamine. Could save her life. 'Cause if she doesn't shut up, I'll kill her" ("Airborne").

That's House telling a brutal truth, rather than a kinder lie that is far more commonplace. There are many times in our lives when we sense that another person does not want to know what we really think—especially if our honest opinions would be deflating or hurtful. So we lie. Maybe we don't tell outright lies, but we mislead.

I'm not guessing about that. My friend Kathy Bell and I have studied the phenomenon in a series of studies. We set up our lab room to look like a little museum, with paintings hanging on the walls. Participants would come into the room one at a time and pick out their favorite and least favorite paintings. Then they'd record their evaluations of each painting. That way, we had them on the record. We knew what they really did think.

Only then did we introduce the participant to another person—an artist—who hadn't seen the participants' critiques. The key moment, psychologically, comes when the artist points to one of the paintings the participant hates the most and says, "That's one of my own. I painted it myself. What do you think of it?"

When we first did a study like this, the "artists" weren't real artists—they were just claiming to be. That's because we were concerned that hearing honest feedback about their own work could potentially be too painful for actual artists.

We learned right away that there was little to worry about. Only 40 percent of the participants admitted to the artist that they disliked the painting of hers that they actually detested. Instead, in that touchy situation, participants often tried to get off on technicalities. So, rather than explicitly saying that they disliked the painting, they would instead amass misleading evidence. When asked directly what they specifically disliked about the painting, they would mention only one or two minor things and keep the rest of their distaste to themselves. In contrast, when asked what they specifically liked, they were a bit too good at generating lots of answers. The result was that the artists got their feelings spared, because the participants managed to convey the misleading impression that they mostly liked the painting. At the same time, the participants could tell themselves that they were telling the truth, because they admitted to at least one of the things they really did dislike about the painting.

In "Knight Fall," Wilson and his ex-wife, Sam, are trying out the process of being together again. Their marriage ended terribly, and Wilson's road to recovery was not pretty. Now he wants Cuddy's approval for his encore romance. We viewers already know, from Cuddy's recent conversation with House, that she, too, is worried that Wilson could get hurt again, but she doesn't have the appetite for intrusion, interference, and manipulation that House does. Notice how her conversation with Wilson unfolds:

Wilson [*Describing House meeting Sam*]: First time, he was naked. Second time, he brought a transvestite prostitute to dinner. Overall, it could have been worse.

Cuddy: Great.

Wilson: That's your reaction?

Cuddy: What? . . . Sorry, preoccupied.

Wilson: House said something to you, didn't he?

Cuddy: Nope. He didn't.

Wilson: It's a little crazy, though . . . isn't it? . . . Things seem to be going great. But they seemed to be going great twelve years ago. The good things are still good. She's smart, funny, gets me. And she's less competitive. Either she's changed, or I've changed. Am I out of my mind?

Cuddy: You never know what can happen. You might as well give it a chance.

Wilson: Yeah.

Wilson is practically begging for Cuddy's blessing. She, in turn, tries giving a mindless one-word response ("Great"), feigns being preoccupied, doesn't say much. When Wilson persists, though, she offers her grudging go-ahead ("You never know what can happen. You might as well give it a chance"). She's telling Wilson what he wants to hear to satisfy him, yet she does it in a way that she can defend to herself as truthful (it is true that you never know what can happen). With this conversational maneuvering, Cuddy behaves like so many of the participants in our art studies. She does not say what she really thinks, honestly and explicitly—Yes, you are crazy! Stay away from that woman! Instead, she leaves it up to Wilson to choose what to take away from the interaction. He can notice the hesitation and realize that Cuddy is hardly enthusiastic, or he can simply latch onto her last words ("You might as well give it a chance") and consider himself supported.

In the art studies, our participants' lie telling and truth telling were sensitive to all sorts of considerations. For example, some of the participants especially liked the artists. The more they liked the artists, the more they lied to them about the paintings of theirs that they hated. Also, sometimes an artist described paintings as her favorites or least favorites (rather than as paintings she had created herself). Participants told the artist more kindhearted lies when she was more invested in the paintings—that is, when they were her own work, rather than merely her favorite paintings in the gallery.

Ordinary humans try not to tell hurtful truths. When the truth might hurt, they lie—or at least mislead. The more they like someone and the more that someone is invested in the work being discussed, the more they lie and mislead. What our studies showed is that sometimes we lie the most to the ones we like the most and to those who care the most about our opinions.

House, of course, doesn't bother with any such niceties or nuances. Mostly, he just says what he thinks. While Wilson and Sam are rekindling their relationship in "Knight Fall," House ends up with only Sam at the dinner table when Wilson excuses himself to go to the bathroom. This is what House says to Sam about her involvement with Wilson: "You're a cold-hearted bitch who ripped his heart out. I watched him struggle for years to overcome the damage you did. And there's no way I'm going to just let you wheel him back in so you can do it all over again."

Subtle, huh? House does, though, wait for Wilson to leave the table before launching into his rant. He realizes that his friend is invested in this renewed relationship, and he isn't ready to be quite so nasty to Sam in front of Wilson. House actually does care about Wilson, so he will keep at least some of his scathing honesty in check to protect him.

Is House a Good Liar?

Sometimes it is enough to be a good liar in the moment. Right then and there, when you are interacting with another person, does that other person believe you? And does that person know *when* to believe you and when not to?

Great liars seem so sincere that the question of whether they may be lying never even comes up. They just seem so obviously genuine.

As House puts it, "If you can fake sincerity, you can fake pretty much anything" ("Honeymoon").

By that first criterion, House is not a good liar at all. Everyone who has spent any time with him knows that he has a very cavalier attitude toward lying, and that he will lie for just about any reason, big or small. This means people can never totally count on him to tell the truth. Whether House is lying is always an issue.

Yet there is another way in which House is a very good liar, indeed. Although the people around House always wonder whether he might be lying, he doesn't give them much help in figuring out *when* he is lying and when he is telling the truth. He just doesn't behave all that differently when he is lying.

Telling lies is more of a challenge to ordinary humans than it is to House. They often experience emotions about lying that become apparent and threaten to give away their lies. If you believe, as most humans do, that lying is wrong and should be used only as a last resort (if at all), then you may feel guilty when you lie. If that guilt shows in your demeanor and your actions, then you will come across differently to others when you lie than when you tell the truth.

The same goes for anxiety and fear. If you decide to lie even though you feel badly about it, you are probably going to be worried about getting caught. Being exposed as a liar would ruin the reputation you have and want to have as an honest person. That worry can potentially show up in the way you look and act. The implication is that you might create a different impression when you are lying—an impression that you are worried about something—than when you are telling the truth.

House doesn't have either of these problems. He doesn't feel guilty about lying or worry about getting caught and ruining his reputation. (He is already known by the people around him as a liar.) Those feelings of guilt or apprehensiveness won't give him away because he doesn't experience them.

Telling lies can be challenging to ordinary humans for another reason—often, you need to think harder to come up with a good lie than to simply tell the truth. You need to keep your story straight, so that everything about the story makes sense and does not collide with what the other person might already know or find out. People can come across differently when they are thinking hard than when they are talking in routine, usually truthful, ways. House triumphs here, too. He is just *so* smart and can think so quickly that he won't look or act much differently when he is lying than when he is telling the truth.

In situations where the truth might hurt (as modeled in the art studies described previously), our first inclination is to lie. In those instances, telling the truth takes more thought. Again, though, House is an exception. He doesn't mull over the emotional implications of what he's about to say—he simply says it.

Skilled liars don't just focus on the moment when they tell their lies. They also monitor other evidence that could reveal their secrets. The stashes of illegal drugs that House keeps in his home, for example, are well hidden.

The online world complicates House's efforts, though, as it does everyone else's. In one of his wild, manipulative plots, House produces a yearbook picture of himself as a cheerleader with an attractive woman sitting on his shoulders. He claims it is a doctored photo. His detective friend, however, does some online research and discovers that the photo is real. Busted!

Is House a Good Lie Detector?

To be a good lie detector, it is not enough to recognize a lie when you hear one. You also have to recognize truths and tell the difference between lies and truths. The risk for someone like House, who expects so much deception from other people, is that he will see lies not only when people are lying but also when they are telling the truth. That's not accuracy—it is a bias toward seeing people as liars.

On a television show, as in everyday life, you can never really know how good of a lie detector anyone is, overall. That's because we often never know when we've been fooled by another person. Even for House, there are many things his colleagues and patients tell him that he does not question. Maybe he is being fooled again and again without ever realizing it.

We can, though, get a sense from the show about how House tries to learn whether someone is lying. Early on in "Adverse Events," House taunts his team by mentioning little nuggets of information he's learned about them, such as the interest rate that Thirteen paid on her car loan and that Kutner crawled twenty miles to make it into the *Guinness Book of World Records*. When asked what he has on Taub, House pushes Taub's buttons with the reply: "I got nothing on Taub . . . Taub's wife, on the other hand . . ."

Taub tries not to take the bait, but by the end of the day, he can't stand it anymore and asks House what he found out.

> House: Your wife has a separate bank account in her name only. She's been making weekly cash deposits for about a year now. No withdrawals . . . yet.
> Taub: That's it? A bank account?
> House: A secret bank account.
> Taub: What makes you think it's a secret?
> House: Because if it wasn't, you'd call it "the" bank account.

By zeroing in on the tiniest part of speech, House has discovered that Taub is just pretending to know about the account. House describes his talent this way (in the episode "Alone"): "I have a gift for observation. For reading people in situations."

Both parts are important—the observation and the context. One question I'm asked most often by people who learn that I study deception is, "What are the cues that tell me when someone is lying?" They are hoping I will give them a Pinocchio's nose sort of answer— that when people lie, their noses will grow, each and every time, and will never grow when they tell the truth. I've been studying cues to deception for decades, and I can tell you this: there is no cue that is like Pinocchio's nose.

Certain behaviors are *sometimes* associated with lying. For example, people occasionally look and sound more nervous when they lie than when they tell the truth. Yet very confident liars might not seem any more nervous when they are lying. Plus, simply because people are nervous does not mean that they are lying. Maybe they are just afraid of being suspected of lying, even though they are actually telling the truth. Or maybe they are anxious for some other reason entirely.

House understands that context matters and is not searching for the perfectly reliable cue to deception. He does not assume, for instance, that whenever his colleagues use the article "a" instead of "the," they are lying.

As perceptive and cocky as House is, he still does not rely solely on his in-the-moment observational skills. He likes evidence. That's why he likes to rummage through people's belongings and sends his team to snoop in his patients' homes. Sure, they are looking for possible clues to the patients' mystery illnesses, but they are also looking for clues to deception.

House's fondness for evidence saves him from potential perils of trying to tell when people are lying, such as the false assumption that if you feel really sure that someone is lying, you are probably right. My colleagues and I reviewed dozens of studies on the link between confidence and accuracy and found that there is simply no relationship between the two. This means that if you are *sure* that someone is lying, the person is actually no more likely to be lying than to be telling the truth. When it comes to lie detection, you really can't let confidence be your guide.

House the Untouchable?

After my colleagues and I finished collecting people's stories about their most serious lies, we had hours of recordings. I was going on a long car trip, so I thought I'd start to study the lies by listening to the stories along the way. I couldn't do it. After the first ten or twelve, I was just too bummed out.

In recounting the biggest lies in their lives, people told stories about infidelities that had lasted more than a decade; about lies told during wartime that cost dozens of lives, about money a spouse promised to save and then squandered in the stock market, and much more. Yet among all of those tales of woe, one really got to me in an odd sort of way. It was hardly one of the most dire of the serious lies.

It lasted only a very short time, but I thought the liar was just so mean. The college student who was the butt of the lie (I'll call him Tom) told the story of his roommate (Jerry) who had just gotten back from a doctor's visit. Jerry somberly confided that he just learned that he had cancer. Tom was a bit wary but also shaken. He sympathized with Jerry for a while. Then Jerry burst into a loud laugh and admitted that he made up the whole thing.

What struck me as so cruel was that Tom was totally boxed in. He suspected that Jerry might be pulling a fast one, but he could not express anything but sympathy and concern, lest the sad tale turn out to be true. Tom was manipulated in a heartless way, so that Jerry could have a little fun.

In an episode reminiscent of Tom and Jerry's real-life experience, Cameron and Foreman and Chase, and then Cuddy and Wilson, come to believe that House has fatal brain cancer. House doesn't initially tell his colleagues he has a deadly diagnosis, but once he realizes what they surmise, he lets them continue to believe it. He rebuffs or ridicules their attempts to help and comfort him, refuses to disclose this turn of events to Wilson (the man who is not only his best friend but also an oncologist), and generally acts like his usual untouchable self.

Then, at the very end, the tide turns toward the truth. House's staff show up at his place in the middle of the night to tell him that he actually doesn't have cancer. House is not ecstatic or even relieved; instead, he asks whether they have told the doctors at Mass General (where he was planning to go for treatment) and is angry and exasperated when he learns that they have.

There is something House wants to hide from all of his colleagues and friends, but it isn't cancer. It is his own emotional pain. House wants no one to know that he faked cancer in order to qualify for an experimental trial for a drug to treat depression in terminal cancer patients.

In the end, House is vulnerable, just like the rest of us, and that vulnerability motivates him to keep secrets and to lie. He isn't really an emotionally untouchable fantasy character—he just plays one on TV.

SUGGESTED READINGS

Albrechtsen, J. S., C. A. Meissner, and K. J. Susa (2009). Can intuition improve deception detection performance? *Journal of Experimental Social Psychology*, *45*, 1052–1055.

DePaulo, B. (2009). *Behind the Door of Deceit: Understanding the Biggest Liars in Our Lives.* Charleston, SC: CreateSpace.

——— (2010). *The Hows and Whys of Lies.* Charleston, SC: CreateSpace.

Hartwig, M., P. A. Granhag, and L. A. Stromwall (2007). Guilty and innocent suspects' strategies during police interrogations. *Psychology, Crime, and Law*, *13*, 213–227.

Nyberg, D. (1995). *The Varnished Truth: Truth Telling and Deceiving in Ordinary Life.* Chicago: University of Chicago Press.

The Global Deception Team. (2006). A world of lies. *Journal of Cross-Cultural Psychology*, *37*, 60–74.

Vrij, A., P. A. Granhag, and S. Porter (2010). Pitfalls and opportunities in non-verbal and verbal lie detection. *Psychological Science in the Public Interest*, *11*, 89–121.

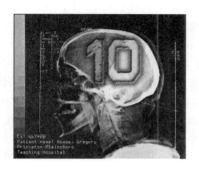

"An Addict Is an Addict Is an . . ."
Defining Addiction

HARAN SIVAPALAN

We are all familiar with the pervasive image of House knocking back some Vicodin pills: in consultations with patients, after making a harsh witticism about Cuddy's cleavage, or in the solitude of his apartment after solving a case. Such behavior is symptomatic of a deeper disorder . . . and no, it's not lupus.

To Foreman, in the episode "Deception," the diagnosis of House's behavior is far less enigmatic than the medical mysteries his team must solve at Princeton-Plainsboro: "The man's an addict." A "crippled, irresponsible addict," Wilson specifies. Even the medically unqualified Vogler, who later attempts to fire House, has no hesitation in branding House an addict in the episode "Babies and Bathwater": "He is a drug addict who flaunts his addiction and refuses to get treatment."

Yet what exactly constitutes an addiction? In the episode "Hunting," Cameron gets high off her patient's drug stash and sleeps with Chase; does that make her addicted to crystal meth? At what point does an indulgence become an addiction?

Precisely defining addiction remains difficult and not without criticism, and there is much variation in the definitions circulating in the fields of neuroscience, psychology, and psychiatry. Common to all of these definitions is a sense of repeated and compulsive drug use—a continued, uncontrolled urge to take drugs. This notion is neatly conveyed by Foreman in the episode "Poison," during a debate with Cameron over House's penchant for pills. We'll overlook the irony that such a debate took place after both characters broke into a teenage patient's house in search of a drug stash:

Cameron: He's not addicted, he has to take drugs.
Foreman: The definition of addiction!

A clearer term that describes House's relationship with Vicodin is that of *dependence.* In fact, in 1964, the World Health Organization coined this term to replace the term *addiction. Dependence*, or *substance dependence*, is also the term used in the *Diagnostic and Statistical Manual of Mental Disorders (DSM)*—a big book of criteria used by U.S. psychiatrists and psychologists to diagnose mental illness. Although going by the book may not be in House's nature, we'll use the most recent version of this manual (*DSM-IV-Text Revision*) and its criteria for *substance dependence* to diagnose this brilliant diagnostician. Incidentally, the term *substance* in this case refers to both illicit drugs and prescription medications, thus including the painkiller Vicodin.

"How Many Pills Are You Taking?": Tolerance

One point of concern for House's colleagues and patients is the amount of Vicodin he takes. In the episode "DNR," the jazz musician John Henry Giles inquires how many pills House is taking. As time goes by, the amount of Vicodin House uses increases insidiously. In fact, Cuddy's recognition of this in the episode "Detox" leads her to make a bet with House that he can't go a week without pills:

> Cuddy: You wanna get high. You're doing, what, eighty mil-
> ligrams a day?
> House: Oh, that's way too much, moderation is the key. Unless
> there's pain.
> Cuddy: It's double what you were taking when I hired you.

Essentially, what we are observing here is the phenomenon of *tolerance*: "a need for a markedly increased amount of the substance to achieve intoxication or desired effect"—which, in House's case, is relieving the chronic pain in his leg. *Tolerance* is one of the physiological hallmarks of substance dependence in the *DSM* and occurs with repeated use of alcohol, sedatives (including drugs such as Valium), and opioids—drugs structurally related to opium from the *Papaver somniferum* poppy plant. The object of House's vice, Vicodin, falls into this last class of drugs, as do heroin and morphine.

The active opioid in Vicodin is hydrocodone, itself a compound of two other opioids—codeine and thebaine. Opioid drugs exert their rewarding effects, such as pain relief and the feeling of euphoria, by binding to specific receptors that are scattered in parts of the brain and in the spinal cord. One of the most important classes of these receptors is called *μ-opioid receptors*. These receptors, once bound, send several further signals and activate special reward circuits in the brain, ultimately resulting in pain relief and pleasure. Such reward circuits, which may be stimulated by other drugs, money, and even humor, are the same pleasure centers Foreman refers to in the episode "Deception": "Drug abuse, drinking, gambling: they all fire up the same pleasure centers in the brain."

If somebody continuously takes Vicodin, cells or neurons in the brain will start to change structure and function differently, a process known as *neuroadaptation*. In the episode "Painless," House is essentially explaining a form of neuroadaptation that has occurred in Jeff, the patient with chronic intractable pain, when he says, "Pain and the drugs that treat pain work by changing brain chemistry, sometimes to the point where pain receptors read painkillers as killer pain."

Tolerance also results from a process of neuroadaptation. The classical view is that continuous exposure to an opioid causes a reduction in the number of μ-opioid receptors on the surface of cells. The net effect of this is that there will be fewer and less sensitive receptors for Vicodin to bind to, in order to produce a sufficient signal that gives rise to pain relief. As such, more and more Vicodin is needed to assuage House's thigh pain. As with a lot of neuroscience, however, this classical view of receptor internalization is unlikely to wholly explain the complex phenomenon of tolerance.

"We Can't Take Away His Vicodin. He'll Start to Detox": Withdrawal

You may ask why these neuroadaptations occur, from a teleological perspective; in other words, what is the purpose of these brain changes in response to drugs? One theory is that your brain is like a thermostat in a heating system. If the temperature rises above a desired set point, the thermostat will record this and initiate feedback mechanisms such as switching off any heaters and turning on any coolers. Similarly, sustained drug use may alter your brain's natural equilibrium, so opposing neuroadaptations occur in an effort to return this equilibrium back to normal. This is an example of a process seen all over the biological world: *homeostasis*—maintaining an organism's internal environment in equilibrium.

Unfortunately, in the event you take up your exasperating-yet-attractive boss's wager that "You can't go a week without your drugs," this equilibrium becomes disrupted. Instead of being in a stable balance between drug and feedback neuroadaptations, abstinence from the drug causes these opposing neuroadaptations to take over. What ensues is a syndrome that produces, in effect, symptoms that are opposite to taking the drug. This is known as *withdrawal* and is brilliantly illustrated by House in "Detox," in the Tritter saga of season 3, and in the illusory events of "Under My

Skin" before "kissing" Cuddy. Along with *tolerance*, withdrawal on cessation of a drug is the *DSM*'s second physiological criterion of substance dependence.

Clinically, withdrawal from opioids such as Vicodin gives rise to a characteristic syndrome of symptoms. In fact, in "Detox," both Foreman and Cuddy individually warn House about several of these:

> Cuddy: If you're detoxing, you'll have chills, nausea, your pain will magnify five, ten times.
> Foreman: There's gonna be side effects: insomnia, depression, tachycardia.

Yawning, sweating, muscle aches, and, in advanced stages, fever and piloerection (goose bumps) are all part of the opioid withdrawal syndrome. As mentioned earlier, withdrawal presents with the inverse effects of taking a specific drug. So, if I were to tell you that one effect of taking Vicodin is constipation (as a result of binding to μ-opioid receptors in the gut), you may be able to predict what happens to House in withdrawal: "I hope this is me detoxing; otherwise, I soiled a perfectly good pair of underwear last night for nothing."

Indeed, as House puts it so eloquently in the episode "Words and Deeds," diarrhea is another symptom of opioid withdrawal. The obvious way to avoid such unpalatable symptoms of withdrawal is to take more drugs. In this manner, House's desire to take Vicodin may be partly construed as an attempt to avoid these withdrawal symptoms. This is known in psychological terms as *negative reinforcement*. This is because the behavior (popping Vicodin pills) results in the *removal* or avoidance of an aversive state (the insomnia, the depression, and the soiled underwear of withdrawal). The term was put forward by the eminent behavioral psychologist B. F. Skinner to describe the behavior of rats that pressed levers in order to avoid getting an electric shock—an aversive stimulus to a nonmasochistic rat!

Returning to the thermostat analogy, House's repeatedly taking Vicodin is like leaving an oven on in a kitchen. In an effort to maintain the normal temperature, the thermostat system will boost the power to the room's cooling system while reducing the power to the heating system. This is akin to neuroadaptation in the brain. If you suddenly remove this oven from the kitchen (take away House's Vicodin), the activated cooling system persists, making the room go cold (House goes into withdrawal). Note that this is opposite to the warming effect of the oven. Because you dislike the cold, you try to raise the temperature again by getting a new oven (House craves more Vicodin).

The heating system in this analogy can be compared to the brain's reward circuits, which are proposed to have decreased long-term function in addiction. Conversely, the cooling system may intriguingly represent so-called antireward circuits in the brain, which are in place to limit the reward from drugs. Neuroscientists George F. Koob and Michel Le Moal refer to this notion of weakened reward circuits and strengthened antireward circuits as the dark side of addiction. They call it this because it leads to an unpleasant brain state that drives addicts to take more drugs or possibly because they're avid *Star Wars* fans!

"Gimme the Script": Compulsive Use

Many drugs fail to or only rarely cause the physiological effects of tolerance and withdrawal, yet may still give rise to substance dependence. Cannabis is one example of such a substance. In the absence of tolerance and withdrawal, people may still be classified as "addicts" if their control over the intake of a drug is impaired to the point where considerable time, money, and effort are dedicated to obtaining and using the drug, and they continue to use the drug despite negative consequences for their health and well-being. Sound familiar? In addition to tolerance and withdrawal, House fits at least three of the four remaining *DSM-IV-TR* criteria that describe this "compulsive use."

Having previously pictured House's diarrhea, I'll assume you have no qualms about casting your minds back to the end of "Merry Little Christmas," with House passed out on the floor next to a puddle of his own vomit. Because House had just taken a cocktail of painkillers and alcohol, you may argue that he intended to pass out as part of a self-destructive, nihilistic bent. Alternatively, House may have taken more painkillers than he intended. In this alternative analysis, House's actions are an example of addictive behavior, in that the substance is often taken in larger amounts or over a longer period than was intended. As opposed to avoiding withdrawal symptoms (negative reinforcement), bingeing on drugs in this way is probably more related to the drug's positive, pleasurable effects. Comparing this to B. F. Skinner's aforementioned rats, instead of pressing a lever to avoid an electric shock, rats would press levers to obtain a reward of food. We refer to this as *positive reinforcement*, because the behavior (taking copious amounts of Vicodin) results in the *addition* of a rewarding stimulus (becoming "too stoned to tell").

A related *DSM-IV-TR* criterion for substance dependence is *a persistent desire or unsuccessful efforts to cut down or control substance use.* In "Words and Deeds," House checks into rehab to appease Tritter, but he also stresses the sincerity in his endeavor: "unless it's real, there is no show." It eventually transpires, however, that House, unable to abstain from Vicodin, bribes his rehab coordinator (dubbed Voldemort) and receives his fix. Even after successfully resisting Vicodin for a week in "Detox," House insists on *not stopping*, deluding himself into thinking he doesn't have a problem.

Clearly, House does have a problem. Owing to intense cravings, coupled with the need to get rid of the unpleasant feelings associated with withdrawal and the "dark side of addiction," addicts often go to great lengths to obtain and use substances. House is exemplary in this regard. During the Tritter saga when Cuddy regulates House's Vicodin intake, he attempts to separately manipulate Chase, Cameron, and Foreman for drugs; visits another doctor, pretending to be injured in a car crash; and even tries "stealing oxy from a dead man." Spending considerable time chasing drugs, using them, and subsequently recovering from their effects are key aspects of substance dependence.

At the end of "Detox," House admits that he's an addict from a physiological perspective—he's just suffered through a week of excruciating withdrawal symptoms. Nevertheless, he remains in denial about Vicodin affecting his life: "I pay my bills, I make my meals, I function." On the surface, this appears to be true, until Wilson interjects, "Is that all you want? You have no relationships. . . . You've changed. You're miserable, and you're afraid to face yourself."

Even at this stage, House's social functioning has suffered at the expense of Vicodin. By the finale of season 5, hallucinations of a post-humous Amber also hamper his ability to practice medicine. Clearly, House's habit, like those of other addicts, has taken a stranglehold of his social, occupational, and recreational well-being.

The final *DSM-IV* criterion for substance dependence stipulates that an addict may continue to take a drug despite acknowledging that this may worsen a recurrent psychological or physical problem. When it comes to continued hallucinations of Amber and, in one instance, Kutner, House draws the line and checks into Mayfield Psychiatric Hospital. Despite not convincingly fitting this last criterion, House's tolerance, withdrawal, and other markers of compulsive use warrant a *DSM* diagnosis of substance dependence.

Contrast this with Cameron's onetime use of Kalvin's drug stash that I mentioned earlier. After recovering from her high, she shows no more compulsion to take the drug and no cravings: her life isn't adversely affected. Her behavior cannot be classified as an addiction.

You may argue that this system of defining substance dependence seems rather subjective and overly contrived. Indeed, this criticism has been leveled at the *DSM* and at psychiatry in general. A new man-ual, the *DSM-V*, is due to be released in May 2013 and aims to take on some of these criticisms. For instance, craving, a symptom seen in many addicts, is likely to be added as another criterion. Even with *DSM* guidelines, psychiatric diagnoses rely heavily on a practitioner's clinical judgment, as, too, is the case with House's field of diagnostic medicine.

"What's Life without the Ability to Make Stupid Choices?": The Neuroeconomics of Drug Addiction

Having examined the detrimental effects of addiction on House's physical, social, and occupational well-being, we may ask the ques-tion "Why does House continue to take Vicodin? Why is it that an accomplished doctor, trained in the calculated, scientific, and rational art of medicine, seems to make an irrational choice when it comes to Vicodin?" It's not solely his pain meds; add Scotch, computer games, Internet pornography, and melodramatic television soaps to the list of unhealthy indulgences. House consistently chooses these things in the face of dire consequences for his health and career (or, at the very least, a stern talking-to from Cuddy).

At the opposite end of the spectrum we have the more controlled and cautious constitutions of Cuddy, Cameron, and Foreman. In the episode "House Training," the patient Lupe dies following Foreman's decision to start radiotherapy for autoimmune disease. In an effort to soothe Foreman's resultant culpability, Chase asks, "You want to go get drunk?" Instead of drowning his sorrows, Foreman shows restraint and replies, "No, thanks, I've got paperwork."

Contrast this with Thirteen in "Lucky Thirteen." Despite being warned (by House, of all people!) about the potential "downward spiral of destruction" from drug use, she is seen continuing her risky behavior at the end of the episode. Such differing choices regarding drugs actually may emanate from two competing systems in the brain.

The dominant system that mediated Foreman's more prudent decision is called the *reflective* or *executive* system. It is composed of structures in the front part of the brain (frontal lobes), with one of the most important of these termed the *prefrontal cortex* (PFC). The PFC is involved in many of our higher cognitive functions, such as planning, focusing attention, and decision making but also in inhibiting more impulsive, automatic, or so-called prepotent behaviors. When Foreman decides not to get drunk despite Chase's offer, his prefrontal cortex and executive system weighed the pros and cons of the offer and inhibited the more impulsive urge to binge drink. Moreover, the PFC is fundamental in connoting the future consequences of a decision. Arguably, Foreman has juxtaposed the short-term soothing of pain against the slippery slope of using alcohol as a coping strategy in the long term and resolves that the former is not worth it.

On the other hand, Thirteen's decision to take the instant reward of drugs and a one-night stand, despite the negative consequences, is dominated by a different brain system—the impulsive system.

Central to this system is an almond-shaped structure situated in the temporal lobes (at either side of the brain): the amygdala. It plays a major role in human emotion and in signaling an immediate reward to various stimuli: drugs, money, even strippers named Caramel at bachelor parties.

On making a decision, the executive and impulsive systems interact and compete with each other in a manner analogous to Cuddy and House deliberating over a patient's treatment. In the same way that Cuddy sensibly tempers calls from House to perform an inherently risky brain biopsy in the episode "Let Them Eat Cake," the executive system may exert top-down control over the impulsive system. In this case, a decision will depend more on its future outcomes, as opposed to its immediate outcomes. If, however, the impulsive system becomes hyperactive, or if the top-down control from the executive system is weakened, the impulsive system will dominate a decision, biasing it toward immediate, short-term outcomes. Continuing the analogy, if House becomes particularly impelling or Cuddy's authority is undermined, then House may decide on the patient's treatment.

The study of the brain behavior that underlies decision making is fundamental to the academic field of neuroeconomics. Incorporating aspects of psychology, neuroscience, and economics and using a variety of experimental techniques from MRI scans to card games, research in neuroeconomics may shed some light on why people with substance dependence take drugs despite run-ins with the law, adverse health effects, and the destruction of relationships.

Now cast your minds back to the episode "The Social Contract" and the brash, tell-it-like-it-is audacity of patient Nick Greenwald. The cause of this patient's disinhibited behavior is damage to the patient's frontal lobe. As Kutner points out, Nick's behavior bears great resemblance to that observed in the historic patient Phineas Gage, a man who, in 1848, survived a railroad blasting accident whereby a 43-inch-long iron bar (more precisely, a tamping iron) was propelled through his skull and out the other side. As Thirteen remarks, "Gage was a different person after the spike; argumentative, impulsive."

In fact, Thirteen is echoing the observations of Gage's own physician, Dr. John Harlow:

> The equilibrium or balance, so to speak, between his intellectual faculties and animal propensities, seems to have been destroyed. He is . . . impatient of restraint or advice when it conflicts with his desires.

After Gage died, approximately twelve years after his injury, Harlow exhumed his body and examined his skull, which is now on display in the Warren Anatomical Museum at Harvard Medical School. More than a century later, in 1994, neurologist Hanna Damasio and colleagues took X-ray images and measurements of Gage's skull to ascertain the trajectory of the tamping iron through his brain. Like the patient Nick Greenwald, Gage's impulsive behavior was a result of damage to his frontal lobes, including what is thought to be part of the prefrontal cortex, the *ventromedial prefrontal cortex* (vm-PFC).

Interestingly, research shows that drug addicts such as House exhibit the same decision-making behavior as patients with damage to the ventromedial prefrontal cortex, such as Gage and Greenwald. One of these behavioral similarities is that they adopt the same strategy in a card game called the Iowa Gambling Task. The game involves four decks of cards from which a player must turn one card at a time. Each card carries a monetary reward, but scattered unpredictably in these decks are cards carrying a penalty. Two of these decks are so-called bad decks. The monetary reward of each card is larger, but the penalty cards are also larger. In one setup of the game, if you were to pick ten cards in succession from these bad decks, you would gain $100 for each reward card but would lose $1,250 in total penalties, giving you an overall loss of $250. The other two decks are termed *good decks*. Although the monetary reward is smaller—$50 for each reward card, using the aforementioned setup—the penalty cards are also smaller, incurring a loss of $250 per ten cards. Therefore, over ten cards you stand to make a net gain of $250. Normal subjects soon learn to avoid the bad decks and pick mainly from the good decks. Strikingly, drug addicts and those with vm-PFC damage opt for the higher immediate rewards of the "bad decks," despite the larger losses awaiting them.

This likeness extends deeper than only strategies in card games. Using a technique called *functional magnetic resonance imaging* (fMRI) to measure activity in various brain areas, drug addicts have been found to show lower activity in the vm-PFC. Whereas in Phineas Gage the cause of this low activity was a tamping iron shot through his skull, in addicts the culprit is long-term use of drugs. This is another example of neuroadaptation, mentioned earlier. As you'll also remember, the vmPFC (a specific part of the PFC) belongs to the wider executive system. In simplistic terms, reduced activity in the PFC resulting from repeated exposure to drugs will lead to less top-down control by the executive system over the impulsive system. Accordingly, the impulsive system will take over and will favor decisions with high immediate gain. In the episode "The Softer Side," the implications of this for House are that the short-term rewards of methadone outweigh the long-term emotional and financial consequences of losing his job.

Wilson: You're choosing methadone over this job.

Such seemingly irrational choices may also stem from an impulsive system that is hyperactive, thus overwhelming the executive system. As opposed to top-down control by the executive system, the case in addicts is more akin to bottom-up control by the impulsive system, predisposing one to make a decision with an immediate reward. As alluded to earlier, a key component of the impulsive system is a brain structure called the amygdala. Researchers, with the aid of another imaging technique termed *positron emission tomography* (PET) that allows them to measure blood flow to different parts of the brain, revealed that activity in the amygdala is higher in drug addicts. This may reflect a state whereby drug addicts are actually oversensitive to immediate rewards. Perhaps Tritter accurately summarizes the nature of this in the episode "Merry Little Christmas" when he remarks, "The thing about addicts, no matter how smart they are, they are dumb when it comes to drugs."

Now consider the following proposition: I will give you $20 today or, if you wait until tomorrow, I will give you $40. Ignoring several variables, I'm guessing that you opted for the latter. If I alter this proposition so that I either give you $20 today or $40 if you wait a year (again ignoring factors such as inflation, interest, etc.), the latter amount suddenly becomes less attractive, despite objectively being of equal value. This phenomenon is known as *temporal discounting* and denotes the reduction in the subjective value of a reward over a period of time. Drug addicts tend to exhibit higher rates of temporal discounting, so that future rewards are more quickly devalued than they are by normal subjects.

Heightened temporal discounting may arise from drug-induced changes in both brain systems. A culmination of a hyperactive impulsive system and an underactive executive system will lead to greater salience granted to immediate rewards and poorer consideration of future rewards, respectively. Maybe now, armed with a basic knowledge of neuroeconomics, we can partly excuse House the next time he's "sprawled naked on [his] floor with an empty bottle of Vicodin or collapsed naked in front of [his] computer with an empty bottle of Viagra" (Wilson describing House in "Whatever It Takes").

"Drugs Don't Make Me High, They Make Me Neutral": Addiction as Self-Medication

Essentially, the competing *executive* and *impulsive* systems perform a type of cost-benefit analysis on taking drugs, but what exactly are these benefits? On the surface, for vivacious patients such as HIV-positive Kalvin in the episode "Hunting" and punk-rocker Jimmy Quidd in "Games," the reason for drug use seems obvious: to have fun, get high, and savor the euphoria. Yet as Thirteen states in reference to Quidd, "Drugs are always a mask for something else." Such a realization also dawns on Cameron, when she reveals a deeper reason behind Kalvin's recreational drug use, albeit through experimenting with his stash herself: "Drugs are great, HIV freed you, your dad hates you, you're so happy. Everything's a lie! You blame yourself for your mom's death. You're not trying to have fun, you're trying to self-destruct. You wanna kill yourself? Fine, but stop recruiting!"

You may also remember that in our previous examples, both Foreman and Thirteen consider taking drugs in times of stress, frustration, and emotional upheaval. Foreman is coping with the guilt of having "killed" a patient, while Thirteen is coming to grips with her own Huntington's-afflicted mortality. Returning to the notion of possible benefits of taking drugs, some of their allure is their temporary ability to ease emotional pain and get rid of unwanted feelings, such as anxiety, anger, or depression. Indeed, the need to soothe such mental anguish may be a greater drive to take drugs than the desire for intense pleasure. This concept is elegantly put forward by House to Thirteen in the episode "Joy," while they are discussing the reason for their sleepwalking patient's use of cocaine:

Thirteen: But if you can't feel pleasure, what's with the cocaine?

House: Really? Is that why you do drugs? Because you're happy? Most people do 'em because they want to be happy. His subconscious craved it, needed it.

Therefore, in the same way you might take an aspirin tablet to ease a headache, you might drink alcohol to relieve anxiety, say, from donating part of your liver to a patient who happens to also be your friend (using Wilson as an example). This idea of drugs being taken to alleviate psychological disturbances forms the basis of the aptly named *self-medication hypothesis* of drug addiction. The brainchild of psychoanalysts and clinicians, notably Edward J. Khantzian, it was borne from observations of heroin and cocaine users who cited relief from feelings such as rage or depression as reasons for their drug habits.

As may be gleaned from the often complicated lives of patients at Princeton-Plainsboro, people can suffer from a diverse range of negative emotions or *affects*: anger, loneliness, and boredom, to name but three. Just as there is a large variety of such emotions, drug dealer Mickey, of the episode "The Down Low," could also tell you about a huge range of available drugs, both within and outside of the law. Furthermore, some classes of drugs are better than others at medicating various types of negative emotions. Over time and after experimenting with several drugs, addicts may then settle for one specific drug that they most frequently use—a drug of choice. Having smoked cigarettes at Mayfield Psychiatric Hospital, passed out drunk in front of the TV, and even tripped on LSD, House's drug of choice is clearly the opiate Vicodin.

As laid out by the self-medication hypothesis, the exact drug of choice someone chooses is contingent on three main factors: the personal constitution of the user, including his or her personality; the biochemical action of the drug; and the type of psychological symptoms that the user seeks to medicate. Even accounting for those personal differences, evidence shows that certain drugs of choice seem to be chosen for specific psychological symptoms. For instance, psychostimulant drugs such as cocaine tend to be preferred by people troubled by inattention and hyperactivity. The drugs of choice chosen by characters in *House M.D.* also reflect their predominant psychological struggles.

In "Brave Heart," it is apparent that Chase suffers from flashbacks to the death of African dictator Dibala, a death in which he is complicit by doctoring (oh, the irony) a set of blood results. The intrusive, relived images of blood emerging from Dibala's mouth and the defibrillator noisily discharging are clearly sources of anxiety for Chase. These flashbacks are distressing to the extent that he pretends to forget his watch in order to avoid the ICU where Dibala died. To cope with the psychological pain, he turns to an easily available drug—alcohol:

> Cameron: It's two in the morning. Where were you? Ooh, you're drunk.
> Chase: I needed to get wasted. I did, and now I'm better.

The symptoms with which Chase presents are similar to those seen in people with an anxiety disorder known as *post-traumatic stress disorder* (PTSD). Sufferers of PTSD characteristically reexperience a traumatic event to which they were directly or indirectly exposed: events such as being sexually assaulted, witnessing a natural disaster, or learning that a loved one is terminally ill. Consequently, as with Chase and the ICU, these people make great efforts to avoid any places, people, or even conversations associated with these traumatic events. Also like Chase, PTSD patients may become shut off from the world after their experience, no longer partaking in once-enjoyable activities and being unable to show emotion. This phenomenon is known as *psychic numbing.*

Studies of specific sets of patients with PTSD, such as Vietnam War veterans, firefighters, and female prisoners, have shown alcohol to be their drug of choice. One attraction of alcohol is its ability to counteract this process of psychic numbing, allowing patients to express themselves more freely. Unfortunately, a downside is that such alcohol-induced disinhibition may lead to the expression of feelings such as rage—a downside literally felt by House after Chase punches him in "Ignorance Is Bliss"! That said, PTSD patients may paradoxically self-medicate with high doses of alcohol in order to drown out overwhelming emotions associated with the traumatic events.

As we have seen, the self-medication hypothesis works on a symptomatic level to explain Chase's motive to drink alcohol: to assuage his PTSD-like symptoms following the Dibala incident. Yet what happens if we probe deeper? Are we able to understand Chase's alcohol use in terms of his brain structure? PTSD patients also show signs of increased arousal, manifesting as heightened vigilance, difficulty in sleeping, and being easily startled. This may emanate from overactivity in a part of the brain called the *locus coeruleus*, a structure involved in the human body's fight-or-flight response to stressors. It turns out that alcohol may be particularly effective at dampening the activity of the locus coeruleus in PTSD patients, explaining its attraction as a drug of choice.

Alcohol's effect on the biochemistry of the brain differs from that of opioids such as Vicodin. It is thus unsurprising that opiate addicts such as House seek to control different sets of symptoms from alcohol abusers such as Chase. On a physical level, House's dependence on Vicodin is conspicuously explainable: he's in pain from an infarction in his leg, dead muscle, and nerve damage. Yet as Cuddy proclaims in

"Detox," House's addiction is more recondite than this: "It's not just your leg. You wanna get high."

While in agreement with Cuddy that House's Vicodin dependence is more complex than simple leg pain, the self-medication hypothesis would suggest that instead of purely wanting to get high, House pops his pills to cope with issues of rage and aggression. Indeed, aside from "genius," most descriptions of House by his colleagues and patients involve the disparaging words "miserable," "misanthropic," or "ass." In the episode "Heavy," Cameron intimates her own psychoanalysis of House: "Because I'm not insanely insecure. And because I can actually trust in another human being and I am not an angry, misanthropic son of a bitch."

Yet what is causing this insecurity and anger in House? Clinical interviews with opiate addicts have shown that several have suffered from or been exposed to violence or aggression in early family life. Although it's a latent theme in the show, House also seems to have suffered from aggression: at the hands of his father. When House's parents visit from New Jersey, in "Daddy's Boy," his resentment toward his father becomes apparent: "Not the caring 'til your eyes pop out part, just the insane moral compass that won't let you lie to anybody about anything. It's a great quality for boy scouts and police witnesses. Crappy quality for a dad."

At this point, it seems that House's father engaged in what is termed *punitive parenting*: dishing out punishments, put-downs, and strict discipline. This discipline, in fact, was tantamount to child abuse. Fast-forward to season 3 and the pathos of "One Day, One Room," where House actually exhibits an empathetic side toward rape victim Eve. At first, House concedes being abused by his grandmother: "I hardly ever screwed up when she was around. Too scared of being forced to sleep in the yard or take a bath in ice."

At the end of the episode, House admits that it was, in reality, his father who was his abuser.

It is not solely being a victim of aggression that predisposes someone to opiate dependence. Another major factor is being psychologically unable or underdeveloped to cope with these feelings. Psychoanalysts sometimes refer to the process of *self-regulation*, which, in simple terms, refers to the ability to consciously acknowledge and control one's emotions. Opiate addicts are thought to have defects in self-regulation, making it difficult to deal with the feelings of rage and aggression. Instead, these emotions may be directed at other people and may erode interpersonal relationships, just as is observed between House and Stacey in season 2. In fact, personality analysis of drug addicts has shown that cynicism, anger, and negative feelings toward oneself and others are predictors of using heroin (another opiate) as a drug of choice. In "Role Model," Senator Wright identifies these traits in House, branding him "hiply cynical" and accusing him of making "easy, snide remarks."

The calming and mellowing effects of opiates are thought to counter such aggressive emotions, thus making them the drug of choice for these symptoms. Notice how after pushing Stacey away in the episode "Need to Know," House goes to the rooftop and takes Vicodin? Linking to this, you may also recall that House is frequently on his own when taking Vicodin. Problems with self-regulation may mean that loneliness and separation also drive opiate addiction. The genius patient James Sidas cites relief from such feelings as a motive to take drugs in "Ignorance Is Bliss": "When I was in the hospital they put me on narcotics, and suddenly, everything was just better. I didn't feel isolated or lonely."

Not everyone in solitude or with anger issues will self-medicate with opiates (unless Cutthroat Bitch is secretly a junkie?). Similarly, many people take drugs without becoming addicted: consider the case of Cameron and crystal methamphetamine. It is perhaps better to think of drug addiction as a complex, multifactorial process with several risk factors. In reality, behaviors I have discussed, such as increased temporal discounting, and their neurological correlates, such as a hyperactive impulsive system, confer vulnerability to drug addiction, rather than cause it, per se. Unfortunately, for someone who has been abused by his father, suffers from severe leg pain, and has virtually unlimited access to Vicodin, this vulnerability becomes magnified, and substance dependence ensues.

Now that you've read this chapter, I hope that, if nothing else, I've impressed on you the diverse range of subjects that psychology encompasses; from broader philosophical issues in defining mental illness to the intricacies of how individual neurons work. Here's hoping you become "addicted" to this fascinating subject!

SUGGESTED READINGS

American Psychiatric Association (2000). *Diagnostic and Statistical Manual of Mental Disorders*, 4th ed.—text revision: *DSM-IV-TR*. Arlington, VA: American Psychiatric Publishing.

Glimcher, P. W. (2003). *Decisions, Uncertainty and the Brain: The Science of Neuroeconomics*. Cambridge, MA: MIT Press.

Khantzian, E. J., and M. J. Albanese (2008). *Understanding Addiction as Self Medication: Finding Hope behind the Pain*. New York: Rowman & Littlefield.

Koob, G. F., and M. Le Moal (2005). *Neurobiology of Addiction*. London: Academic Press.

RELATED ACADEMIC PAPERS

Bechara, A. (2005). Decision making, impulse control and loss of willpower to resist drugs: A neurocognitive perspective. *Nature Neuroscience, 8*, 1458–1463.

Bechara, A., H. Damasio, D. Tranel, and A. R. Damasio (2005). The Iowa Gambling Task and the somatic marker hypothesis: Some questions and answers. *Trends in Cognitive Sciences, 9*, 159–162.

Bickel, W. K., M. L. Miller, R. Yi, B. P. Kowal, D. M. Lindquist, and J. A. Pitcock (2007). Behavioural and neuroeconomics of drug addiction: Competing neural systems and temporal discounting processes. *Drug and Alcohol Dependence, 90* (1), S85–S91.

Damasio, H., T. Gabrowski, R. Frank, A. M. Galaburda, and A. R. Damasio (1994). The return of Phineas Gage: Clues about the brain from the skull of a famous patient. *Science, 264*, 1102–1105.

Harlow, J. M. (1868). Recovery from the passage of an iron bar through the head. *Publications of the Massachusetts Medical Society, 2*, 327.

Himmelsbach, C. K. (1941). The morphine abstinence syndrome, its nature and treatment. *Annals of Internal Medicine, 15*, 829–843.

Koob, G. F., and M. Le Moal (2005). Plasticity of reward neurocircuitry and the "dark side" of drug addiction. *Nature Neuroscience, 8*, 1142–1444.

Khantzian, E. J. (1985). The self medication hypothesis of addictive disorders: Focus on heroin and cocaine dependence. *American Journal of Psychiatry, 142*, 1259–1264.

———— (1997). The self medication hypothesis of substance use disorders: A reconsideration and recent applications. *Harvard Review of Psychiatry, 4,* 231–244.

McFarlane, A. C. (1998). Epidemiological evidence about the relationship between PTSD and alcohol abuse: The nature of association. *Addictive Behaviours, 23,* 813–825.

Suh, J. J., S. Ruffins, C. E. Robbins, M. J. Albanese, and E. J. Khantzian (2008). Self medication hypothesis: Connecting affective experience and drug choice. *Psychoanalytic Psychology, 25,* 518–532.

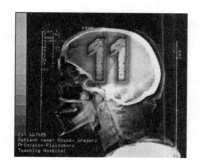

Rebellion at Princeton-Plainsboro
House and Conformity

JOLANDA JETTEN AND FIONA KATE BARLOW

"I have issues with authority."

—House, "The Softer Side"

Imagine that you are invited to a theme party and have been asked to dress up as your favorite movie star. You decide that no ne of the other guests are likely to wear costumes, and you arrive in your normal clothes. On arrival, however, you notice that you are the only one who is not dressed up as James Bond, Inspector Clouseau, Marilyn Monroe, or other celebrities. How would you feel? It is likely that most of us would feel anxious, uncertain, and out of place. Some of us might even feel so embarrassed that we would turn around and rush home to quickly find an appropriate costume.

Not House, though. In "Known Unknowns," House attends an '80s-themed party. Everyone is dressed as if they were back in the 1980s, wearing leggings, colorful clothes, and wacky hairdos. House attends the party in fancy dress, but his costume is from the 1780s— he wears a waistcoat and a powdered wig. House is profoundly unconcerned about being the odd one out. As the fellow guests dance, he walks up and greets Cuddy, who says,

Cuddy: House . . . 1980s.
House: You sure? They weren't specific.

House does not feel uncomfortable being different. In fact, it is clear that he purposely dressed in a way that did not conform to the party's dress code. This example captures what House is all about: he goes through life without any concern about not fitting in. He does not appear to feel pressure to adhere to social norms and stands firm in what he believes is the right thing to do.

As viewers, we cannot help but admire House's nonconformity, rebellion, and refusal to follow hospital rules and social norms more generally. Indeed, and in particular in Western culture, we tend to have enormous respect for people who are able to resist the pressure to conform and who appear to act as individuals. This admiration is reflected in popular media: many of our movie and book heroes are mavericks, rebels, and strong individuals who do not compromise their views or behavior just to fit in. The classic cowboy archetype is perpetually alone. He rides off into the sunset on his horse, metaphorically and literally leaving others in his wake. Likewise, Batman is a tormented loner, unable to share core components of his personality with friends and family—often retreating solo to the bat cave to ruminate. Sherlock Holmes, James Dean, the list goes on. Like House, many of our heroes adhere only to their own rules and shun the societies from which they sprang.

In this chapter, we will start with a definition of conformity and then move on to discuss why people conform. It will very quickly become clear that it is not that easy to tell whether someone is conforming or rebelling. We will also consider whether conformity is good or bad and whether we like people who conform to others. Consider Cameron, for example. She is the one most likely to go along with the others, and people sometimes see this as a weakness. What about House? He is admired for his skills, but he is not necessarily liked as a person. By the end of the chapter, you will have a better sense of what conformity is, what the consequences of conformity are, and how you can overcome bad types of conformity.

How Do We Even Know If We Are Conforming?

Social psychologists define conformity as a process whereby we copy others' behaviors or adopt their beliefs or values as our own. The acceptance of influence from other people, groups, or society at large can occur consciously, as well as unconsciously, whereby we do not seem to be aware that we are following the crowd. Furthermore, conformity may be a reflection of compliance, whereby we feel pressured into adopting an individual's or a group's opinion publicly, but we reject it privately. In contrast to this coerced type, conformity may also involve true internalization, whereby we conform both publicly and privately. Not surprisingly, conformity that is due to mere compliance is rather short-lived, and individuals may express another opinion as soon as they feel that the pressure to conform publicly has subsided. Effects of internalized conformity are much longer lasting, and we may not even notice that we are conforming to others. In such cases, our views are completely aligned with those of others and are taken on unquestioningly as appropriate and right rules for conduct.

Chase, Cameron, and Foreman engage in both types of conformity. At times, it is clear that they are not convinced of House's diagnosis, and they only grudgingly follow House's prescribed treatment. At other times, however, they blindly follow House and defend his diagnosis to patients and hospital staff alike. This occurs to such an extent that in the first season of the show, they openly wonder whether their continued commitment to House is the result of "Stockholm syndrome"—that is, the tendency for hostages to develop positive feelings and emotional attachment to their captors and to blindly follow their orders.

It is not always easy, however, to determine whether behavior involves conformity or nonconformity. Consider the episode "Kids," where in the middle of a hospital epidemic, House interviews a young applicant named Dr. Spain for a position on his team. At the outset of the interview, everything is looking good for the hopeful candidate, and we naturally assume that this has something to do with House's perception of him as somewhat of a rebel and a nonconformist. Not all is as it seems, though.

> Dr. Spain: You know, I really admire the way you don't care what anyone thinks. You just do what you want, the way you want.
>
> Wilson: So, you went to Hopkins for both undergrad and med school?
>
> Dr. Spain: That's right.
>
> House: He's in a band.
>
> Dr. Spain: You into music?
>
> House: Totally. What kind of music do you play?
>
> Dr. Spain: Um, mostly blues, you know. James Cotton, some original stuff.
>
> House: Oh, dude. You are so hired.
>
> Dr. Spain: Really?
>
> House: Not a chance.
>
> Dr. Spain: Why?
>
> House: Tattoo. [*Dr. Spain turns his right arm to reveal a kanji symbol on his forearm.*]
>
> Dr. Spain: Wow. I thought you'd be the last person to have a problem with nonconformity.
>
> House: Nonconformity, right. I can't remember the last time I saw a twenty-something kid with a tattoo of an Asian letter on his wrist. You are one wicked free thinker. You want to be a rebel? Stop being cool. Wear a pocket protector like he [*gestures to Wilson*] does and get a haircut. Like the Asian kids who don't leave the library for twenty-hour

stretches, they're the ones who don't care what you think. Sayonara.

As we can see, conformity and nonconformity can sometimes be difficult to tell apart. Think of punks, emos, hippies, and those joining other subcultures whose main motto appears to be trying to be different from the mainstream. Paradoxically, their rebellion against society is marked by conformity to their subcultures' norms about appropriate dress, hairstyle, and music preference. Emos or Goths, for example, who do not conform to their subcultures' mode of dress or behavior may be excluded from their group, just as mainstream society may exclude their group as a whole.

What about House? Surely, he is a nonconformist in the truest sense of the word. Not according to Foreman in "Deception," who interprets House's behavior as ruthlessness, rather than as nonconformist: "All he stands for is the right for everyone to grab whatever they want, whenever they want." So, how can we tell whether people are truly going their own way or whether their behavior is otherwise motivated?

Part of the problem is that we often do not have a clear sense of what the norms are to which we are conforming. Most norms are not set in stone, and individuals may debate what is appropriate and therefore who is conforming and who is not. There are many norms, however, that are very obvious and that we consensually agree on. They are so obvious that we do not even articulate them as being norms that should not be broken: "do not stare at people," "do not tell people that they are not as smart as they think they are," or "do not spit at someone with whom you disagree." Although we may fantasize about breaking these unspoken rules, we rarely do. If we do break them accidentally, we are highly embarrassed and feel personally exposed.

Again, not House, though. He must be aware of these norms, yet he takes pleasure in breaking them and can in that sense be labeled a true nonconformist. He frequently comments on Cuddy's breasts and body, asks his team in public about their most personal secrets, and makes rude comments to patients and fellow doctors. By breaking these unspoken social norms, House brings them to light. It's also important to note that even though we ourselves may not have the courage to follow suit, we love House for not feeling constrained and for acting out our fantasies.

Diagnosis = Conformity
Prognosis = Not So Good

Why should we care about conformity and nonconformity? Because every day, many times a day, most of us have to decide whether to go along with others or to go our own way. If we make the wrong decision, we and others around us can end up paying a price. Imagine this meeting at Princeton-Plainsboro: House limps over to the whiteboard and picks up his marker. Chase, Foreman, Taub, and Thirteen are sprawled around the room, waiting. A new patient has just been admitted to the hospital, and House begins to list the patient's symptoms: fatigue, fever, shortness of breath, hair loss, chest pain, dry eyes, and easy bruising (which we know because House intentionally bumped the patient with his cane). Before asking for a diagnosis from the group, House laments out loud, "Why did they waste our time with this one? This is an open-and-shut case of lupus." Everyone around the table quickly agrees. There is little discussion. Just a few questions to confirm the diagnosis. Hair loss? Yes. Depression? Yes. This is followed by a few "Damn, we're good" looks spread around the room and a recommendation that the patient begins on doses of hydroxychloroquine. Next.

Something potentially bad has just happened here. Not the diagnosis (unless it is early in the show). What was wrong was the actual process by which the decision was made. House and crew considered only one diagnosis, discussed only the evidence that favored that diagnosis, and were so confident in their initial diagnosis that they made no contingency plans in case they were wrong. The problem more generally is that there was too little critical thinking. This problem is known as *groupthink*, and it frequently occurs in long-standing, highly cohesive groups. Members of such groups often have such a strong desire to stay together and support the group that they suspend their critical thinking and reality testing. In short, they conform too much, too quickly, and too easily.

What is even stranger about groupthink is that it has a certain sort of self-inflicted quality about it. Because the members of the group are so highly motivated to get along, they may engage in self-censorship. They may keep their concerns to themselves. After all, no one wants to rock the boat. Yet this only makes things worse. If all of the members in the group keep their concerns to themselves, then it will appear that everyone agrees, even if he or she does not. This is called the illusion of unanimity. If everyone agrees (or at least seems to), then the decision must be a good one.

The illusion of unanimity can give rise to another illusion that works something like this: "we are an extremely competent group of doctors, we have made lots of amazing diagnoses in the past, and we all agree on this latest diagnosis. How can we possibly be wrong?" This is called the illusion of invulnerability. The group convinces itself that it cannot be wrong.

If that is not enough, yet another problem stems from all of this. If your group is good and competent and the decisions its members make are right, then it is easy to feel morally superior. You might even force your treatment onto patients who have explicitly refused that treatment. All of these symptoms of groupthink (and more) start with a simple case of too much conformity.

We do not see many symptoms of groupthink displayed in the differential room at Princeton-Plainsboro because House is really good at encouraging divisive—and often acrimonious—debate. He forces everyone to speak his or her mind, and he generally does not allow his group to get along (i.e., cohere) well enough to allow groupthink to take hold. Of course, that does not prevent House from adopting a "Damn, I'm good" mentality himself. This is not a symptom of groupthink but rather House's vigorous and often excessive self-confidence—perhaps because his (and the group's) diagnoses are often correct. Cuddy raises concerns about House's illusions of invulnerability right from the beginning in "Pilot":

Cuddy: How is it that you always assume you're right?
House: I don't, I just find it hard to operate on the opposite assumption.

By keeping groupthink in check, House makes it likely that any overconfidence he and the staff members experience is earned—not a symptom of inappropriate conformity.

The Cure for Costly Conformity

So, how do we avoid making poor or even faulty decisions? In short, how do we refuse to conform when we know we shouldn't? It turns out that House may have the answer! House and his team appear to do all of the things that social psychologists recommend we do to avoid groupthink that results in bad decisions. For example, psychologists encourage all members of groups to question facts, to avoid committing to a single plan, and to actively seek alternative courses of action.

In managing his team, House excels precisely by doing these things. He actively encourages people to speak out within his team and attempts to create an environment of creativity and critical thinking. He forces his team to argue points and think outside the box when it comes to determining diagnoses for patients. House never allows an environment to emerge that promotes groupthink. Instead, he concentrates on the issues at hand, pointing out the danger of using faulty heuristics to diagnose people, as evidenced in "Occam's Razor":

> Foreman: Occam's razor. The simplest explanation is always the best.
> House: And you think one is simpler than two?
> Cameron: I'm pretty sure it is, yeah.
> House: Baby shows up. Chase tells you that two people exchange fluids to create this being. I tell you that one stork dropped the little tyke off in a diaper. Are you going to go with the two or the one?
> Foreman: I think your argument is specious.
> House: I think your tie is ugly. Why is one simpler than two? It's lower, it's lonelier, but is it simpler? Each one of these conditions is about a thousand-to-one shot; that means

that any two of them happening at the same time is a million-to-one shot. Chase says the cardiac infection is a ten-million-to-one shot, which makes my idea ten times better than yours.

The brainstorm sessions wherein House challenges his team typically lead to discussions with House taking on the role of devil's advocate, shooting down others' ideas. Even though, for members of his team, being told publicly why the proposed diagnosis cannot be right may be a humiliating experience, it is clear that it forces everyone who works with House not to overlook important symptoms. House's leadership prevents the team from settling for an easy or obvious diagnosis that might not be right. He encourages his team to withstand the pressure to find a quick solution when diagnosing patients by reminding them on a regular basis that "we are missing something."

The structure of House's team also helps them to avoid groupthink. The meetings are informal, relaxed, and slightly chaotic. Everyone brings lunch or coffee, with some members getting comfortable enough to put their feet on the table. The absence of a formal structure or agenda in a context that encourages brainstorming has been found to reduce the occurrence of groupthink.

Although this suggests that House is the main driver in keeping groupthink in check, it is also clear that House needs his team just as much as they need him to perform optimally. That is, while faulty decision making can occur in teams because they become vulnerable to groupthink and too much conformity, the best ideas also emerge from teamwork. It is teams or groups that stimulate discussion and increase creative thinking, thereby enhancing the quality of decisions. The importance of a team becomes apparent when House finds himself without one. Both Wilson and Cuddy realize the value of having others with House in "Alone." Cuddy suggests to House that "You need someone to bounce ideas off." Later she explains that this is because "Foreman would have done anything to prove you wrong, and Chase would have tried to prove you right." This is probably the very reason that House's nonconformity leads to superior diagnostic performance. It is by having others around him who engage with his ideas that House functions well.

Conforming for Clarity

If conformity can lead to poor decision making, and if we generally do not like conformers, then why do we conform so often? One reason is uncertainty. When we do not know the answer ourselves, other people can be a good source of information. Is that new movie any good? Ask someone who has seen it. Where is a relaxing place to take a vacation? Ask someone who travels a lot. Do these pants make my butt look big? Ask a friend. When we are not sure of the answer ourselves, we can look to others for clarification.

Here's how this might work at Princeton-Plainsboro. You are attending your first staff meeting with House, Chase, Cameron, Foreman, Taub, and Thirteen. Their reputations have preceded them. You know they are good. House starts the meeting with a question: What is the cut-off point for a healthy glucose peak one hour postprandial?

Before you even finish translating the question, Chase blurts out, "180 milligrams per deciliter." You should have known this, but you are having trouble thinking. In fact, even now you do not know for certain that Chase got the answer right. Then Thirteen speaks up: "180 milligrams per deciliter." That must be right. As if to remove any doubt, Foreman, Taub, and Cameron in quick succession all provide the same answer. Now everyone looks at you. What is the cut-off point for a healthy glucose peak one hour postprandial? You know the answer now, don't you? Or at least you can be pretty confident that you know the answer. "180 milligrams per deciliter."

Why did you go along with the group? The answer seems fairly straightforward. You did not know the answer, so you turned to the other members of the staff as a source of information. We call conformity that emerges from this type of process *informational influence*. Even House does this when faced with a difficult diagnosis. In "Ugly," the CIA "borrows" House to help out on a top-secret case. House is asked to consult with Dr. Terzi, a female CIA doctor who also happens to be very attractive; attractive enough, in fact, that without considering the other applicants being interviewed,

House offers her a job on his team. He brings her in to interview but assures her that she should consider the whole process a mere formality. He finds out quickly, however, that her brains do not match her beauty:

> House: I think she might be an idiot.
> Wilson: Who?
> House: But she can't be an idiot. She's in the CIA, for God's sake.
> Wilson: The Bay of Pigs was a daring triumph.

Even worse, her stupidity seems to act as kryptonite to House's intelligence! As House puts it, "She said something idiotic again, and I didn't even notice it. It took Foreman to point out that it was idiotic. She's making *me* an idiot." Eventually, this forces House to doubt himself and lean more heavily on the judgments of his staff, in this case, Foreman and Thirteen:

> Dr. Terzi: Heart block plus liver failure could mean autoimmune. Maybe scleroderma.
> House: [*Out of the corner of his mouth*] Foreman? Does that make sense?
> Foreman: Not without tight skin on the hands, muscle weakness, and a thirty-year-old patient.
> Thirteen: Liver failure plus heart block could be a mitochondrial disorder.

To explain this, we need to take the accuracy motivation into account. Sometimes we are genuinely unsure about what to do or think in a given situation, and we look at others to inform us and help us make up our minds. Yet as soon as we are certain of our own views, for example, when the situation becomes less ambiguous and provides us with clear clues about the right answer (e.g., a sign indicating how we may get to the nearest exit), conformity levels drop because we feel that we no longer have to rely on others to help us make up our minds.

Conforming for Comfort

We know that people may conform when they are uncertain, but what if they are certain? What if they are 100 percent confident they know the answer? Then there would be no conformity, right? No. They may still conform but for a different reason.

Imagine that it is your first day at Princeton-Plainsboro Teaching Hospital, and House starts the meeting with this question: What is the normal resting temperature of the human body? Oh, that's easy. You know that one. Everyone does. It is 98.6 degrees. Just as you are thinking this, though, something unusual happens. Thirteen blurts out, "96.8." And just as surprisingly House responds, "Right. Anyone else?" Then Kutner answers: "96.8." They seem so sure in their answers, but they are giving the wrong answer. The normal resting temperature of a human body is 98.6. Everyone knows that. What am I missing here? Finally, Taub says, "96.8."

Now it is your turn to answer. Everyone turns toward you, expecting an answer. "What is the normal resting temperature of the average human body?" You know the answer is 98.6, but if you give that answer, you will be going against everyone in the room. What will they think? Will you have to defend yourself? It's your first day here. Should you rock the boat this early? Should you just go along with the group?

If you are like most people, you'll go along with the group. A classic study by Solomon Asch in the 1950s shows us that when all eight people before you clearly give the wrong answer, it is fairly difficult to withstand conforming in such a context, even though it is clear that the majority is wrong. Asch found that 76 percent of participants conformed at least once to the wrong majority answer. After the study, many of these participants spontaneously mentioned that they knew that they were giving the wrong answer but went along with the group because they did not want to appear foolish or be the odd one out. That is precisely why you would give the wrong answer, even though you would know very well that all of the others were wrong. This type of conformity is due to *normative influence*—we go along with what we see as normative by those around us (even if that is inconsistent with what we think or see).

House, however, would not conform. He would be relatively immune to pressures for conformity that emanate from wanting to fit in or avoid trouble or ridicule. This makes him an easy target for powerful individuals who are used to having others blindly follow their at times unreasonable and silly orders. Recall, for example, the situation where Vogler, the hospital's rich benefactor in season 1, donates large amounts of money to the hospital. In return for this generosity, Vogler feels entitled to dictate to others how the hospital should be run. Although most employees in the hospital understand they will have to conform (at least publicly) to Vogler's wishes to avoid repercussions and punishment, House does not give an inch. Wilson foresees trouble in "Control" when he tries to talk House into doing what Cuddy and Vogler want.

> Wilson: Oh, come on. You know how good you have it here.
> House: Yes, I'm the big pooh-bah, the big cheese, the go-to guy.
> Wilson: You do the cases you want to do, when you want to do them. You're not going to get that anywhere else.
> House: Relax, I've been through three regime changes in this hospital. Every time, same story.
> Wilson: Just keep your head down, that's all I'm saying. And put on your coat.

Of course, even after Wilson's warning, it is not in House's nature to keep his head down, so House does not yield to the pressure because he does not care about being the odd one out. As a result, in a special committee meeting, Vogler threatens to withdraw his financial support for the hospital if the committee does not fire House. Even though everyone on the committee knows privately that it is the wrong decision to fire an excellent doctor like House, all except one committee member (Wilson) vote to sack House. Their conformity probably reflects a fear of Vogler's disapproval and a fear that their own jobs will be on the line if they do not conform to Vogler's proposal.

Although Wilson's nonconformity may have been difficult for him because he was facing a unanimous committee who all went along with Vogler, research also tells us that dissent becomes easier once there is another person who resists conforming to the wrong answer. This is also what we see at Princeton-Plainsboro: the very act of Wilson's nonconformity makes it easier for other committee members to resist conforming afterward. When the committee is reconvened, there is more rebellion, and Cuddy refuses to vote in favor of sacking House as well. Asch also found in his follow-up studies that as soon as participants found themselves in the company of one other person who defied the majority (the dissenter was actually a person hired by the experimenter and was instructed to do so), they felt less pressure to conform and thus were more likely to stand up to the majority and give the correct answer.

The Personal Cost of Rebellion

We may admire House because he does not feel held back by pressures to conform, but it does not necessarily follow that we also like him. Indeed, Foreman sums up the attitude of many doctors at Princeton-Plainsboro in "Deception," when he says, "House is not a hero. A person who has the guts to break a bad rule, they're a hero. House doesn't break rules, he ignores them. He's not Rosa Parks, he's an anarchist."

Foreman's observation fits well with social psychological research findings. For example, in a now classic study, Stanley Schachter brought male participants together in a laboratory setting to discuss the case of a young delinquent, Johnny Rocco. In keeping with the attitude of the time, most participants typically agreed that Johnny Rocco should be rehabilitated, rather than punished. Unbeknownst to those taking part in the study, however, Schachter planted his own people in groups, who were instructed to behave in scripted ways. One was a model member (he conformed and agreed with the majority), the second was a slider (he initially disagreed with the majority but eventually came around to their way of thinking), and the third a deviate (who disagreed with the majority for the entire conversation). Members of the group paid a lot of attention to both the slider and the deviate—more comments were addressed to them, than to those who initially conformed. When the slider came around to agree with the majority attitude, however, the group stopped paying attention to him and continued to focus on the deviate.

House, as the classic deviate, also attracts more attention than his less-contentious peers, and accordingly, Cuddy often laments that she spends too much time in her role as hospital director managing House. Even though there may be rewards in being noticed, such attention also comes at a cost. In his study, Schachter measured the degree to which participants indicated that they liked the model member, the slider, and the deviate. He found that participants universally liked the model member and the slider but indicated that they disliked the deviate. Recent research by Benoît Monin, Pamela J. Sawyer, and Matthew J. Marquez corroborates this finding. These researchers show that we do not like deviants *even* when they do the morally right thing. For example, in one of their studies, deviants who refused to make racist comments along with the majority were unpopular. Other research by Floor Rink and Naomi Ellemers shows a similar finding: even though groups perform better when they have a dissenter in their midst, this person is often not liked. This appears to be the fate of dissenters—they provoke debate and critical thinking and draw attention to themselves but are not necessarily liked or appreciated.

House is not the only rebel at Princeton-Plainsboro. In season 5, House secretly hires a private investigator named Lucas, who initially disguises himself as a coffee machine repairman in order to maintain his cover (alas, Lucas is found out almost immediately). Right from the outset, Lucas is disliked by the team for his cheeky, disagreeable temperament. Take, for example, the dialogue between Taub and Lucas in the episode "Not Cancer":

> Taub: Cancer made no sense. The head and heart make less than no sense.
> Lucas: That makes no sense.
> Taub: I know. I was making a point.
> Lucas: Oh, good. I thought you were an idiot.
> Taub: Why are you talking?

Throughout the show, Lucas generally has a difficult time finding acceptance by those other than House, who often genuinely seems to like him. This can be attributed at least in part to Lucas's nonconformity.

All Together Now: "Conformity Is Good"

Conformity is somewhat like a colonoscopy or a root canal. It has a bad reputation, but it can be a force for good. Conformity plays an important role in our social interactions with others. Precisely because people are willing to go along and set aside their own personal views at times, group life is more harmonious and pleasant, and society as a whole functions more smoothly. Just think how difficult it would be to work in a team that would consist only of people like House. Intuitively, we know it would simply not work. That is why teams need people such as Cameron. She is more likely to conform and is not afraid of admitting that she is open to social influence. Cameron is adept at conforming not only to other members of the team but also to social norms concerning kindness and politeness. Take, for example, the episode "Finding Judas," in which the team's bank accounts are being frozen as a result of House's misbehavior. This is understandably frustrating for everyone involved; however, Cameron does not violate social codes, despite considerable provocation.

> Cameron: [*Talking on her cell phone*] Hello? Thank you for your help. [*She hangs up phone*] They froze my accounts.
> Chase: *Thank you for your help?*
> Cameron: It's not her fault.

This is an example of Cameron's skill at conforming to social norms. At times she faces criticism for her conformity, however, and there are allegations that she is weak. We see an example of this in "Deception," where Cameron asks House about her capacity to lead.

> Cameron: How would you describe my leadership skills?
> House: Nonexistent . . . otherwise, excellent.
> Cameron: There's more to being a leader than being a jerk!

Again, however, House and the team more generally need Cameron as much as she needs them. Cameron, as the typical conformist, is the social glue that holds the team together. In addition, her conformity gives House the valuable support that he needs when making contentious or risky decisions, often with the end result that a life is saved. In "Big Baby," House wants to perform a serious (but necessary) operation on a patient's brain. Alone, he does not have the confidence to make the decision, but with Cameron's support as the interim hospital administrator, he takes the risk.

> House: I can't find the proof you want because it's inside her head. And the only way I can get at it is to cut it open and rip it out, which is apparently the *one* test you won't let me run. So either I do this or I do nothing!
> Cameron: What do you want me to do? Say yes just because you're House?
> House: I'd certainly like that, yeah.
> Cameron: [*Pauses*] Yes.

Later, after the patient has been successfully operated on, Cameron discusses her conformity with Cuddy.

> Cameron: I approved an insane procedure with no proof, no evidence, no . . .
> Cuddy: You made the right call.
> [*Cameron sighs*]
> Cuddy: The problem was a brain problem; without the procedure, House never notices the increased left brain function. She'd be dead if you didn't say yes.
> Cameron: I know. . . . But . . . I'll always say yes to House.

Although House may sometimes tease Cameron about her tendency to conform, he also directly benefits from it. In addition, even House seems to occasionally recognize the social good that conformity can bring about. For example, when Vogler threatens to fire either Foreman, Chase, or Cameron if House does not conform to hospital rules and practice, House dons a white coat in an attempt to get on Vogler's good side. It thus appears that House is not being non-normative for the sake of it; he is not taking a public stance and is not out to expose social norms. Rather, in the absence of a good reason to conform, he does what he likes and questions the usefulness of rules and norms.

A Question of Balance

Should we envy House for not being worried about being the odd one out, or should we conclude that he is a fool for always sticking his neck out (at times for no apparent reason)? In particular, in the early episodes, House appears to strike a balance between the costs of his nonconformity (i.e., consistently offending those closest to him, such as Wilson, Cuddy, and his team) and the benefits (i.e., each week solving new puzzles and providing solutions that others do not think of). At least, it appeared to be a balance that House himself is happy with. We see him eschewing personal relationships and maintaining a disdain for human connections. In the long run, however, this is not a satisfactory balance, and in later episodes, House seeks out connections and even a romantic relationship.

By that time, however, the costs of his nonconformity have become too much to bear for some who are close to him. For example, Cuddy, who becomes the target of his affection, quickly realizes that a life with House would be marked by conflict and distress. That is, the very nonconformity that makes him an excellent diagnostician also makes him unattractive as a life partner.

A House Is Not a Home: The Costs and Benefits of Nonconformity

Conformity and nonconformity are two sides of the same coin—House's nonconformity can only exist insofar as others' conformity does. Nonconformists help change norms and provide creative solutions that conforming masses may not be able to see. Because he takes on the role of a medical maverick and a diagnostic cowboy, House is indispensable as a doctor—a true genius. Yet conformists have vital roles to play, too: they maintain harmony in teams and groups and, in this way, provide a background of certainty and stability against which nonconforming individuals can excel. Without Cameron's and Wilson's social competence, Chase's obsequiousness, and Foreman's adherence to the rules, House's brash rudeness and nonconformity would not be possible, let alone lead to excellence in diagnostics.

Although this makes clear that conformists and nonconformists need each other, their life paths are likely to be very different. Conformists are community members, with families and friends. In contrast, nonconformists, although essential in our society, are alone. Like all media and real-life dissenters, House pays a price for ignoring norms. He has a drug addiction, many broken relationships, and a lonely home life. House himself sums up his fate in "The Right Stuff," when he is walking down the corridor with the applicants for the positions he created by firing his team. On arrival at the elevator, the applicants want to get in with House. He, however, stops them and says, "I ride alone."

SUGGESTED READINGS

Asch, S. E. (1951). Effects of group pressure upon the modification and distortion of judgment. In H. Guetzkow (ed.), *Groups, Leadership, and Men*. Pittsburgh: Carnegie Press.

Bellah, R. N., R. Madsen, W. M. Sullivan, A. Swidler, and S. M. Tipton (1985). *Habits of the Heart: Individualism and Commitment in American Life*. New York: Harper & Row.

Janis, I. L. (1972). *Victims of Groupthink: A Psychological Study of Foreign-Policy Decisions and Fiascoes*. Boston: Houghton Mifflin.

Jetten, J., and M. J. Hornsey (eds.) (2011). *Rebels in Groups: Dissent, Deviance, Difference and Defiance*. Hoboken, NJ: Wiley-Blackwell.

Monin, B., P. Sawyer, and M. Marquez (2008). The rejection of moral rebels: Resenting those who do the right thing. *Journal of Personality and Social Psychology*, 95, 76–93.

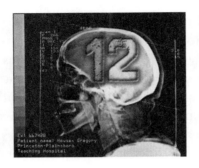

Values Matter

Casting the *House* Characters onto the Interpersonal Circumplex

DELROY L. PAULHUS AND MIRANDA L. ABILD

House: You like me. Why?

Cameron: That's kind of a sad question.

House: Just trying to figure out what makes you tick. I am not warm and fuzzy and you are basically a stuffed animal made by grandma.

—"Role Model"

Part of why we sense that House and Cameron are two very different people is their wildly divergent values. Our values define who we are as human beings. If House, for example, valued being loved over being respected (which he certainly does not), then he would not be the character we have come to know. These value differences play out in terms of the personalities, attitudes, and behavior of the

Princeton-Plainsboro staff, as well as the interpersonal tensions that develop among them. Yet there are so many different values people can hold. Where do we even begin?

Fortunately, the otherwise unmanageable diversity of human values can be organized around two central themes—*agency* and *communion*. Agentic values emphasize attributes that draw respect from others (e.g., achievement, intelligence, competence, power) and make the individual stand out. Communal values emphasize benefits to others, including society at large (e.g., harmony, nurturance, loyalty). They help the individual fit in and make the individual more likable. These two values are ideal for organizing social behavior because they reflect the two fundamental human motives: getting ahead and getting along.

Note that agentic and communal values are not necessarily in opposition. An individual can value both, value neither, or value one but not the other. These combinations of values yield four types of individuals with unique value profiles.

In the first part of this chapter, we will map the characters of *House* onto these value profiles. In the latter part, we will flesh out our analysis of House by considering whether his personality maps onto any of the so-called dark triad, three traits that ensue from a value system that is overly agentic and insufficiently communal.

Because the primary characters in *House* are all high achievers working in a helping profession, they all must value both agency and communion. Relative to one another, however, clear differences are evident. Whereas House appears to value agency more than communion, several other personalities found within the walls of Princeton-Plainsboro (e.g., Cuddy, Wilson, Chase, Cameron) provide foils against which House stands out. For a visual representation of their contrasting value profiles, we turn to the *interpersonal circumplex*.

The illustration shows how the interpersonal circumplex is formed when agency and communion are displayed as the axes of a two-dimensional space. Based on their values, individuals can be projected to a specific location on the resulting circle. Those with similar values are located close to one another—most likely in the same quadrant. For example, people who value both agency and communion highly

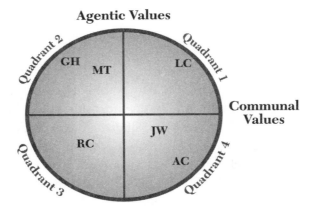

Where the doctors of Princeton-Plainsboro stand on interpersonal values. GH = Gregory House; JW = James Wilson; LC = Lisa Cuddy; RC = Robert Chase; MT = Michael Tritter; AC = Allison Cameron

would be placed in quadrant 1. By contrast, those in quadrant 3 value neither. Those who favor one value over the other fall in either quadrant 2 or 4. Thus, the circumplex provides a quick visual comparison of the value profiles of several individuals.

Interpersonal Dynamics

Our effort to locate these familiar characters on the circumplex seems to imply that personalities are fixed and, on their own, sufficient to predict how people will behave in social encounters. Instead, a wealth of research on interpersonal processes has determined that social interactions are more dynamic in nature (see Horowitz and Strack, 2010). People "pull" behavior from one another. For example, an exasperating individual may repeatedly provoke anger in an otherwise docile partner. A more domineering individual may eventually induce submission in an otherwise assertive partner.

As they continue over time, unique social interactions can stabilize even though they are actually created by, and unique to, the situation. As a result, one cannot make a general statement about the success or failure of a person's relationships or interactions based on the quadrant that he or she inhabits. Instead, different personality combinations can clash or they can flourish. Much research on the circumplex has addressed the fate of various combinations of characteristics. For example, which ones encourage attraction and which ones endure over time? Such interpersonal dynamics include notions of similarity and complementarity.

The effects of partner similarity are most evident on the communion dimension. It stands to reason that those sharing similar values are more likely to get along. Altruists will find each other's value system attractive, and their relationship will endure. The same goes for a pair of cynics. As a couple, the altruist and the cynic are doomed. This phenomenon is reflected in the familiar aphorism "birds of a feather flock together."

Complementarity, on the other hand, is most evident on the agency dimension. Couples are more likely to get along when one of them prefers to lead, while the other prefers to follow. Here a different aphorism—"opposites attract"—is apropos. In more saccharine terms, they complete each other. Similarity is actually an impediment on this dimension. Two individuals with agentic traits are more likely to clash, whereas two individuals lacking agency might never get anything started ("I dunno; what do you want to do?"). Most appealing and durable are relationships with one agentic and one communal individual.

To summarize, we have offered the interpersonal circumplex as a handy framework for locating each of the series' characters in the appropriate value quadrant. We have also introduced the concepts of similarity and complementarity to help explain why relationships often depend on the combination of the two partners' value profiles. Keeping the quadrant illustration in mind, we will now walk you through each value profile, explaining where they belong on the circumplex and the dynamics of their relationships with House.

Quadrant 2: When Agency Supersedes Communion

We begin with the quadrant epitomized by our protagonist, House. Individuals with this value profile believe that agentic goals should not be compromised by insipid socialization. Hence, the profile is sometimes referred to as *unmitigated agency*. House is more than willing to sacrifice interpersonal warmth for personal triumph—at least,

when he is publicly proclaiming his values. Traditional moral impera-
tives take a backseat to those that advance more concrete objectives—
in this case, curing patients. When colleagues are repulsed by his
behavior, House often voices outright disdain for social niceties. This
disdain is made abundantly clear when he feigns envy for an autistic
child in "Lines in the Sand."

> Why would you feel sorry for someone who gets to opt out of
> the inane courteous formalities which are utterly meaningless,
> insincere, and therefore degrading? This kid doesn't have to
> pretend to be interested in your back pain or your excretions
> or your grandma's itchy place. Can you imagine how liberating
> it would be to live a life free of all the mind-numbing social
> niceties? I don't pity this kid, I envy him.

Despite his position as a health professional, House looks out for
his interests and is rarely seen doing or saying anything that doesn't
somehow express his own personal values. To him, saving lives is more
like an incidental—and downright annoying—side effect of achieving his personal goals. In fact, there are times when House exhibits
agency so extreme that he borders on being antisocial or immoral. In
"Insensitive," he is willing to breach the Hippocratic oath in order to
harvest nerve cells from a young girl who has congenital insensitivity
to pain. The possibility of resolving his personal health concerns (his
bad leg, in this case) outweighs the potential harm to his patient.

The rare individuals who manage to put House's bullying at risk
come from the *same* value quadrant. Two in particular—Vogler and
Tritter—turn out to be his nemeses. The physically and financially
powerful Edward Vogler threatens the hospital administration with
closure unless they fire House. In "Finding Judas," the vengeful
police officer Michael Tritter takes House to court and forces him to
enter rehabilitation.

> Cuddy: You think Dr. Wilson deserved to have his assets
> seized? His entire practice ruined?

Tritter: No.

Cuddy: So, you just don't care?

Tritter: This is how I get what I want. I put pressure . . . on people.

When House confronts Tritter (or Vogler), it is the similarity of their values that ensures a clash. With both competitors incapable of communal compromise, the pair is destined to have an extended war. No one emerges unscarred from a battle of unmitigated agentics.

Quadrant 4: When Communion Supersedes Agency

As illustrated, people in quadrant 4 have the reverse value system of those in quadrant 2. They will sacrifice personal achievement to maintain harmonious relationships with others. Allison Cameron immediately comes to mind. Often referred to as "the caring one" on the diagnostic team, Cameron demonstrates her communal values in almost every episode. Although less extreme, Wilson is also located within the same quadrant.

Cameron's position on the circumplex helps explain her infatuation with House. We would argue that the relationship quickly turns romantic because House and Cameron complement each other on agency. At their best, both he and she seem to relish his domineering style. Unfortunately, they clash so dramatically on the communal dimension that Cameron eventually calls it off. Rather different is the dynamic between House and his closest friend, Wilson. Of the main characters, Wilson is closest to House in age, status, and leisure pursuits. They are also both divorced and (often) single. Such similarities naturally promote and sustain their friendship.

Inevitably, their value profiles guarantee volatility in their relationship. Wilson's communion allows him to endure House's unrelenting jabs. Up to a point. In "Merry Little Christmas," Wilson is forced to reveal the truth about House's forgeries to obtain drugs. That episode represents one of the most serious challenges to their relationship. On the positive side, their ongoing discussions about male–female relationships may benefit both parties. In conversations about their respective relationship histories, House continually points out the maladaptive side of Wilson's submissive and nurturing tendencies. Wilson eventually acknowledges this insight. At the same time, Wilson is best able to convince House to reconsider (some of) his hurtful behavior.

Quadrant 1: Integrating Agency with Communion

At least one series character helps refute the idea that agency and communion are incompatible. This is Cuddy. She somehow navigates around the juggernaut known as House. She manages to exploit House's genius, while minimizing the interpersonal havoc left in his wake.

Although Cuddy appears to submit to House on many occasions, she is often using his competitive drive to manipulate him. For example, by challenging House to cure his patients without touching them, she disengages him from less productive antics. One could argue that Cuddy's agency ensues from her role as director, rather than from her character. Such a conclusion, we believe, does not give her enough credit. She is clearly capable of running the hospital, overseeing cases, and making difficult decisions on behalf of both the patients and the facility. In "Insensitive," she sacrifices otherwise needed male affection to affirm her individuality. Overall, Cuddy skillfully manages to integrate her agentic and communal values, making her a compassionate but effective leader.

Their communal compatibility eventually leads Cuddy and Wilson into a dating relationship. Largely because of House, that relationship does not survive. Because House is also attracted to Cuddy, he does his best to sabotage her relationship with Wilson. In "House Training," he even goes so far as to stalk their romantic encounters and intervene on their dates.

In sum, the relationships among House, Cameron, Wilson, and Cuddy exemplify both the complementarity and the similarity notions. Relationships are facilitated when the partners are agentically opposite or communally similar.

Quadrant 3: Neither Agency nor Communion Is Worthy

Finally, we turn to quadrant 3 of the interpersonal circumplex. Here neither agency nor communion is valued. As a result, individuals with this profile commonly feel alienated. Because they cannot relate to either of society's primary values, these individuals are likely to disengage from their social environment.

Off the top, it seems unlikely that power players in a teaching hospital would show such a value profile; however, some of the attitudes expressed by Chase suggest that he is the best candidate. Chase is the least likely to challenge House in situations where others might be hurt. Consider Chase's cold-hearted defense of House's failure to protect a sexually abused child in "Skin Deep":

Cameron: She's a child. She needs to be protected.
Chase: Why does she need more protection than some crack whore shivering in the waiting room?
Foreman: I think you're just afraid to piss House off.
Chase: There's that, too.

The core characters in *House* share the values of health professionals in a highly competitive environment. Nonetheless, our protagonist, House, stands out. Compared to him, the other characters fill out different locations on the values circumplex. Whether he is dissecting the corpse of a household cat, inducing a migraine in a coma patient, or conducting an unnecessary postmortem, House will go to any length to satiate his need for unraveling medical mysteries.

The next section delves deeper into House's psyche. It distinguishes several possible characterizations and weighs the relative support for each diagnosis.

The Dark Triad of Personality

"You can be a real bastard."

—Cameron, "Maternity"

In "Maternity," Cameron's characterization of House seems fair enough, but what kind of bastard is he? The most likely suspects are the Machiavellian, the narcissist, and the psychopath—three personalities that share quadrant 2 of the interpersonal circumplex. They all belong in that quadrant because they involve a strong preference for agentic over communal values.

Known as the dark triad (Paulhus and Williams, 2002), all three personalities are socially offensive but for somewhat different reasons: the Machiavellian is manipulative, the narcissist is a self-centered braggart, and the psychopath, an impulsive thrill seeker. They are often evident in the same person but need not be. As opposed to their clinical counterparts, the subclinical versions of these personalities can survive—indeed, flourish—in everyday society.

As detailed earlier, the quadrant 2 value profile (unmitigated agency) allows individuals to exploit others without concern for shame, guilt, or anxiety. At the same time, they are vulnerable to slipping into a full-blown personality disorder. Even those who currently flourish may show signs of breaking down under conditions of chronic stress. This edgy quality certainly characterizes House.

Is he a narcissist? Typical symptoms are exaggerated self-confidence, continual mocking of others, and a sense of entitlement to special privileges. All of these apply to House in large doses. Although he rarely brags in an overt fashion, he makes his sense of superiority clear by demeaning others who make any claim for success.

Clinicians typically attribute such overt grandiosity to an underlying insecurity. Their rationale is that the narcissist's need to stand out represents a compensation for raging self-doubt. That diagnosis seems to be supported in the season 6 finale, "Help Me." In a rare fit of self-pity and no longer numbed by his opiate of choice, House states, "I'm the most screwed up person in the world."

Is House a Machiavellian? Indeed, he provides a prototypical example. Master manipulators achieve their ends in strategic, long-term fashion. Social intelligence and cognitive complexity are essential for this personality type. Consider his rather elaborate setup of Cuddy in "Games." His goal of retaining three trainees requires that he officially choose two males over a (better-qualified) female candidate. He knows that Cuddy will then add on the female candidate, and the master plan will be consummated.

The potential for widespread havoc is greatest for the Machiavellian. The real-life example of Bernie Madoff is illuminating. You'll recognize the name of this stockbroker, currently serving 150 years in prison for his enactment of history's grandest financial fraud. Madoff was able to hide his scheming from most experts long enough to have purloined up to $65 billion. Instead of financial gain, House employs his strategies to indulge his fascination for solving medical puzzles. Pleasing people and—it must be said—even saving lives are secondary to the process of peeling away layers of the onion.

Finally, we consider the possibility that House is a subclinical psychopath, that is, an impulsive thrill seeker with no conscience. Despite his strategic manipulations, there is some reason to believe that House gives in to impulsivity from time to time. He overreacts, lashes out, and generally provokes others in ways that greatly undermine his self-interest. In "Finding Judas," House punches Chase, insults Cuddy, and steals drugs. His impulsivity leads to gross misdiagnoses. Only his formidable intellect and medical acumen allow House to recover from such self-destructive malfunctions.

At first blush, such impulsive episodes seem to refute our claim that House is a prototypical Machiavellian, that is, a master strategist. The reconciliation, we suggest, lies in his addiction to Vicodin. Irritability and volatility are inevitable without continually increasing dosages.

Master of the Dark Triad: A Hollywood Fiction?

We wrote this chapter because of our fascination with the character of House. He looms large among a cast of less remarkable personalities. By locating all of them on the interpersonal circumplex, we have offered a concrete graphical depiction of four different value systems.

All who come into contact with House concede his status as the consummate unraveler of medical mysteries, but what is the role of his dark value system? Undoubtedly, House would not be the same person without a value system that favored agency over communion. Does the possession of a character resembling a Machiavellian, narcissistic psychopath actually promote his success? Or would he be even more successful with a sunnier personality?

We were recently informed that the series episodes are actually pure fiction, so we will have to wait for the series writers to reveal what becomes of our potent protagonist. If we can extract a psychological lesson from our own ambivalent reactions to his portrayal, it's the following: don't confuse brilliance with eccentricity. It would be foolhardy to emulate or even admire House's character, especially the darker side, simply because he is successful. Yes, characters on the series afford him many liberties because of his genius, but it's hard to imagine this happening in the real world. Only in fiction can this perfect balancing act continue, week after week, without blowing up. In real life, House's Vicodin addiction would probably send him into a self-destructive trajectory until he lost his job and his ability to practice medicine. Conflicts with other people would tend to escalate, with irrevocable consequences. His narcissistic, Machiavellian, and psychopathic personality traits would alienate other people, which means he would have no loving and supportive "Dream Team" to repeatedly clean up his messes.

As keen observers (and, yes, fans), we found House's brooding genius to be especially appealing, even downright seductive—but God forbid that anyone would see him as a role model. Not unlike other troubled celebrities, House provides the same lesson as a train wreck, that is, a tragedy that is hard to take our eyes off.

SUGGESTED READINGS

Horowitz, L. M., and S. Strack (2010). *Handbook of Interpersonal Psychology: Theory, Research, Assessment, and Therapeutic Interventions*. Hoboken, NJ: John Wiley & Sons.

Paulhus, D. L., and K. M. Williams (2002). The dark triad of personality: Narcissism, Machiavellianism, and psychopathy. *Journal of Research in Personality, 36,* 556–563.

Trapnell, P. D., and D. L. Paulhus (in press). Agentic and communal values: Their scope and measurement. *Journal of Personality Assessment.*

PART THREE
The Ugly: Is *That* My EKG?

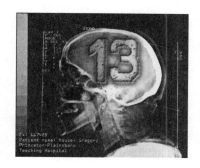

Power in the House

Does Gregory House's Authority over Others Affect His Own Behavior?

JORIS LAMMERS AND ANNE GAST

House: Sorry. You're in the wrong room. My name on the door, my team, my decisions.
Cuddy: My building, my floor, my people!

— "Human Error"

The power struggle between House and Cuddy is one of the most amusing aspects of the series. Cuddy uses many strategies to curtail House and bring him under her control, but however cunning her tricks are, House never fails to take it a step further. For him, no trick is too dirty to maintain or improve his position. This power struggle is not only entertaining; it greatly illustrates social psychological findings on how powerful people behave.

If we think of the powerful, the people who often come to mind are Napoleon, Mao Tse-Tung, President Obama, Donald Trump, Oprah Winfrey, or Bill Gates—dictators, presidents, or influential industrialists. Yet people can obtain power in many ways. They can gain power from their position in a hierarchy. Cuddy, for example, derives a lot of her power from her position as the dean of medicine. Because people respect her authority and acknowledge her rightful position, she can ask or even order them to do things. Power can also flow from more individual sources, however, such as physical strength, charisma, or money. In hospitals, one personal source of power trumps all others: knowledge. There is no one who swims in knowledge as much as House does—medical knowledge, general knowledge, and a unique ability to combine different pieces of information and evidence into a diagnosis. Think, for example, about "Whatever It Takes," in which House is flown to a secret location to diagnose a CIA agent. From hearing a side remark about forty days of carnival, he concludes that the agents lied about where the patient was stationed and therefore mixed up various kinds of nuts:

> House: Whoever knew that John was stationed in Brazil, not in Bolivia.
> Agent Smith: It's the same region, the same parasites.
> House: But not the same language. In Bolivia, chestnuts are chestnuts. In Brazil, on the other hand, it's castanhas-do-Pará, literally "chestnuts from Pará." Because it would be stupid for people from Brazil to call them Brazil nuts!
> Agent Smith: So he ate Brazil nuts. Big deal.
> House: No, he ate a lot of Brazil nuts, which is a big deal because they contain selenium.

Knowledge allows doctors to cure people and save lives. Compare this power with the almost trivial power of a president or an industrialist. Sure, presidents can cause or solve economic crises, industrialists can fire or hire thousands of employees, but no one can stop death. Doctors can. Doctors are godlike, apart from small differences: "God doesn't limp" ("Humpty Dumpty").

Given his abundant medical knowledge and expertise, within the hospital House must feel like God. In the hospital, House is surrounded by people who depend on his knowledge to stay alive. A dramatic example of this can be found in "Locked In," where a patient suffers from locked-in syndrome. The man is conscious and fully aware of his environment but cannot act or react. The doctors naturally assume he is dead and start to prepare to remove his organs for donation. At that moment, House (who due to a motorcycle accident is in the bed next to the patient) realizes that the patient is not brain dead and is conscious. He takes up the case and, together with his team, finds a way to communicate again with the man and finally cure him. This case demonstrates how knowledge can make a doctor powerful, even if he is officially a patient himself.

Medical knowledge also has a less benign face. For example, in one instance in the series, House enters the hospital restaurant and merely suggests that there might be bacteria in the mayonnaise. This has the direct effect that everyone stops eating. If you or I said that the mayonnaise was not good, people would think we were too picky, and they would ignore us. If a doctor says it, people take notice and behave accordingly.

The bottom line is that House's medical knowledge brings him into an extremely powerful position in the universe of Princeton-Plainsboro Hospital. He can change others' behavior, he can save their lives. What does this do to a person? House's behavior is quite peculiar, to say the least, but could it be that this is because he has so much power on a daily basis? Some people might believe that House would still be as strange as he is even if he were a plumber. We do not. We think that House's bizarre behavior is greatly influenced by the fact that he has so much power. Research proves that the experience of power can psychologically change a person. People who feel powerful think and act differently from people without power.

Power Changes a Person

"An anagram for Gregory House? 'Huge ego, sorry.'"
—House, "House Training"

The question of whether power can change a person psychologically has been asked for centuries. Plato already believed that a position of power can transform people, mostly for the worse. The nineteenth-century British politician Lord Acton echoed this idea when he claimed that "power corrupts and absolute power corrupts absolutely." Based on this view, many people have pointed to anecdotes that seem to demonstrate that powerful people, such as Alexander the Great, Nero, or Mao, were indeed corrupted by their power. Yet these anecdotes do not really prove that power corrupts. First, we might believe in our stereotypes about powerful people and simply underestimate how often people without power can also be corrupt. Second, even if we know that powerful people are more immoral or corrupt than average people, we cannot be sure which came first, the chicken or the egg: Does power make people corrupt, or are people with immoral motives particularly interested in power? Or do you perhaps need to be immoral to achieve power?

Psychologists use experiments to answer these questions. In any experiment—whether in medicine or in psychology—a group of people is randomly selected to be treated one way while another group of people is treated in another way. Think of the episodes in season 5 in which Foreman runs clinical trials to test a new medication for Huntington's disease. In these trials, one group of patients is treated with the new medicine and the other is given a placebo (which doesn't contain any active ingredients). If, after a few months, the medicine group has fewer symptoms than the placebo group, Foreman can conclude that the new medicine is more effective than the placebo. Of course, some patients might have had fewer symptoms to start with. For exactly this reason, it is important that the groups are large and that patients are assigned randomly to one of them. In this way, scientists hope to balance out these initial differences. When Foreman finds out that his then girlfriend Thirteen has been assigned to the placebo group, he secretly puts her into the medicine group. This morally motivated act compromises the scientific principle of random assignment and the interpretability of the results, which is why this is unacceptable behavior for the supervisors of the clinical trials.

The same procedure that analyzes the effects of new medicines can also be used to study the effects of power. We can randomly give certain people power and others none and then determine whether these people differ. If we do this with a sufficient number of people, the effects of preexisting personality differences are canceled out against one another. Power can be given to participants in different ways. For example, participants in an experiment can be given the power to control other participants, to monitor their performance, and to administer payment or punishment. Yet feelings of power can also be induced in a more direct manner: by simply asking people to think about an experience of power.

This procedure, which is called *priming*, works in a very straightforward manner. If I ask you to think back and remember a time when you were really happy—for example, when you graduated, when you got married, or when you got a great job—this will also affect you in the present. As you recall this memory, you reexperience the feelings and emotions that you felt at the time. The result is that you will start to feel happy again. Of course, this is not limited to happiness. If you think back to a sad event—a funeral, the time when you were fired, or any other loss—you will again feel sad. This can also be done with power. By remembering a personal episode of power—irrespective of where it was or what happened—you will start to feel a bit powerful again.

These experimental methods and priming manipulations might seem artificial, and some people believe that if you want to study the behavior of powerful people, you have to observe those who are actually powerful. Yet for the previously explained reasons, experiments with priming manipulations are actually a better tool to study power, because they allow us to establish causality. By observing people who are actually powerful, we can conclude only that power is associated with certain behavior. By using priming experiments, we can conclude that power causes behavior. With these experimental methods, researchers have therefore studied the effects that having power and feeling powerful have on people. They have found that Plato and Lord Acton were right: the experience of power does change a person. People who feel powerful behave differently from people who lack power. Interestingly, together these effects read like a very accurate description of House. Let's look at some behaviors that are typical for powerful people and see whether we can find them in House.

Powerful People Focus on Goals

A primary personal characteristic of House is that he is strongly focused on his own goals, whether they are to diagnose an illness, to get a huge flat-screen TV, or to find out whether Cuddy wants to have a baby. To get what he wants, House is willing to do anything. He is not afraid to break rules or protocols, offend people, or commit felonies, as long as this enables him to get what he wants.

> Cuddy: You broke into my files.
> House: I had no choice; personnel files are confidential.
> —"Simple Explanation"

In this, House is a prime example of how powerful people behave. Powerful people are also very strongly goal oriented. In fact, one could say that powerful people are like tigers. Normal people such as ourselves are lambs; we have our eyes on the two sides of our heads. Although this does not make it easy to keep our attention in front of us, on our goals, at least we can easily spot danger lurking at the sides. Tigers have their eyes in the front of their heads. They are focused on their goals, and they ignore whatever happens to their left and right. This allows them to assertively move forward and grab their prey. Powerful people are like that. They know what they want, do anything to get it, and brush away each obstacle on their way to reaching their goals. Cuddy describes House's behavior accurately: "Fifty-one weeks of the year I let you run around like a monkey in a banana factory" ("Living the Dream").

Psychologists discovered that powerful people are more focused on their own goals by running many studies in which they induced a feeling of power in participants and then studied how this changed people's behavior. In one study, Adam Galinsky and his colleagues seated the students participating in their research at a desk in an uncomfortably cold room. On the desk was a table-mounted fan that blew even colder air into their faces. Despite the discomfort, many students were hesitant to do anything about the fan. After all, it might have been put there for a good reason. Those who were primed with power, however, behaved completely differently. Many rotated it so that it no longer blew in their faces, others turned the fan off, and some pulled the plug from the socket, not even bothering to find the switch. House probably would have done the latter.

Many similar studies have been conducted since then, and they all point to the fact that people who feel powerful are more goal-oriented. Powerful people are not distracted by rules or practical problems or important objections. The same goes for House. He simply behaves as if normal rules of working in the hospital do not apply to him:

> Chase: We've got an MRI scheduled in twenty minutes. Earliest Foreman could get the machine.
> House: I teach you to lie and cheat and steal . . . and as soon as my back is turned, you wait in line?
> —"Failure to Communicate"

Other people's central beliefs or motives mean nothing to House. In "Living the Dream," House wants to compare a patient's reaction to alcohol with that of both a drinker and a usually abstinent control drinker. He quickly decides that Jeffrey Cole has to do the control drinking, because he is a Mormon and therefore never drinks. Furthermore, in nearly every episode, House has his team break into a patient's house to search for drugs, bugs, or other secrets. House will do—and will force his team to do—whatever it takes to achieve a goal.

In "Son of a Coma Guy," he even persuades the comatose (but temporarily awake) father of a child who suffers from a heart muscle disease to commit suicide to donate his heart and save his son. These are all examples of a powerful person brushing aside concerns and other people's rights to pursue his goal. Powerful people strongly dislike it if they are hindered in their pursuit of a goal. In "Living the Dream," note the example of House abducting the star of his favorite daytime soap opera, *Prescription: Passion*, because he is convinced that the actor suffers from a dormant but life-threatening disorder. The kidnapping takes place during the exact week that the hospital is being inspected.

> House: You want the star of the hottest daytime drama on TV to die in your hospital?
> Cuddy: I want you to cure him without committing any more felonies.
> House: I can't do my job when you're gonna tie my hands like that!

Powerful People Enjoy Risk Taking

> "I take chances all the time. It's one of my worst qualities."
> —House, "Role Model"

A second striking aspect of House is that he seems to have a strong preference for taking risks. Normally, people are risk averse. For example, most people prefer a guaranteed 50 dollars over a 50 percent chance to receive 100 dollars and a 50 percent chance to receive nothing. Doctors should also be risk averse. After all, their work involves other people's health, and if their gambles do not work out, people may lose their lives. Yet people who feel powerful are much less sensitive to losses. Again, we see that House's behavior is an accurate description of the powerful. He also likes to take risks, even when a patient's life is at stake.

> Cameron: You can't diagnose that without a biopsy.
> House: Yes, we can, we treat it. If she gets better, we know that we're right.
> Cameron: And if we're wrong?
> House: We learn something else.
>
> —"Pilot"

The fact that a procedure is risky is never a reason for House to decide against it. In "Autopsy," House decides to temporarily kill and revive a nine-year-old girl by removing all of her blood, in order to do an autopsy. The fact that Wilson calls this treatment a "lottery shot" only makes it more appealing to House because he thinks it is her *only* shot. Yet sensing that something is someone's best shot is not how doctors usually decide. They usually follow protocols in difficult cases. Of course, to be fair, if you are treating patients who have such mysterious symptoms as those encountered by House, you cannot always follow protocols, and for many cases that House encounters, there are no protocols. Doctors therefore need to trust their instincts, abandon protocols, and take informed risks sometimes. House always listens to his instincts, though, and never follows protocols. Why is that the case?

First of all, powerful people are much more certain about themselves. The risks they take therefore appear less risky to them than to others. Second, to use the analogy of tigers again, they are more focused on their goals and dwell less on the negative things that might happen.

> Cuddy: How is it that you always assume you're right?
> House: I don't, I just find it hard to operate on the opposite assumption. And why are you so afraid of making a mistake?
> Cuddy: Because I'm a doctor. Because when we make mistakes, people die.
>
> —"Pilot"

Third, think back to the example of the 50–50 chance in the gamble for $100. One could say that we are irrational not to want to take the risk in this gamble, but most people wouldn't. This probably has to do with the fact that, psychologically, an uncertain $100 is not quite twice as good as a certain $50. Still, $100 is $100, so in some sense it can be rational to take more risks, and that is probably exactly how House sees it: "I take risks! Sometimes patients die. But not taking risks causes more patients to die, so I guess my biggest problem is I've been cursed with the ability to do the math" ("Detox").

Powerful People Lack Empathy and the Ability to See Others' Perspectives

"Humanity is overrated."

—House, "Pilot"

A third striking aspect about House is that he seems to lack empathy. Of course, we must realize that some degree of professional distance toward patients most likely helps doctors function. After all, they are confronted with pain, suffering, and death on a daily basis, and if they let all of this affect them too much, their jobs would become impossible: "If we were to care about every person suffering on this planet, life would shut down" ("One Day, One Room").

Such professional distance can be found more frequently among people with power. In the best interests of the country, presidents have to make decisions that can lead to a lot of pain and suffering. They therefore find it useful to talk about people in terms of statistics. In battles, generals may need to sacrifice a battalion to save an army. Thus, they prefer to speak of military personnel killed or missing as KIAs and MIAs. Using such abstract terms helps them suppress feelings of empathy that they would normally feel and that would impede their ability to make cold, rational decisions. Note that House uses a similarly abstract way of rationalizing in "Maternity," in which he opts for giving two dying babies different treatments in order to find out what caused their sickness and to be able to cure other babies.

Foreman: What the hell are you doing?
House: Therapeutic trial to find the cause of the infection.

It almost seems that for House, interacting with patients is a necessary inconvenience when trying to diagnose and treat illnesses. This cynicism is a welcome change from the stereotype that doctors carry all of the suffering of the world on their shoulders, but it is also a nice illustration of how power decreases empathy.

Foreman: Isn't treating patients why we became doctors?
House: No, treating illnesses is why we became doctors.

—"Pilot"

Yet power not only decreases empathy, it also reduces one's ability to see other perspectives in a more general way. Many people—even those without power—have difficulty realizing that other people have different views on matters. For example, people who prefer 1980s music over 1960s music believe that most people share their preference for 1980s music, but people who prefer 1960s music believe that the majority shares their preference for the 1960s. This bias—when people underestimate that others can have different views on things—is much stronger among those who feel powerful. The powerful often do not bother with what others think of their actions. We see this, for example, in "House Divided," where House organizes Chase's bachelor party (complete with strippers) in Wilson's home, without asking his permission.

> Wilson: This is my apartment. You can't do this.
> House: Clearly, reality begs to differ.

This does not mean that the powerful cannot see other perspectives. They are simply unmotivated to do so. When the powerful do want to understand other people's perspectives, they can often do so quite well. House is a master at this. In many episodes, he spots small inconsistencies in the patients' stories and finds out that they are withholding embarrassing information from him. He is also an expert at guessing other people's thoughts.

> Cuddy: How do you know? You don't have access to the hospital's mainframe.
> House: No, but "partypants" does.
> Cuddy: You stole my password?
> House: Hardly counts as stealing; it's a pretty obvious choice.
> —"Acceptance"

Powerful People Exercise Freedom of Expression

A fourth and final effect of power is that it makes people freer in their expression. Powerful people do not have to fear condemnation as much as other people do. A positive consequence of this is that the experience of power is psychologically liberating. Powerful people can generate more creative ideas and express opinions that conform less to those of others.

A negative effect of the intellectual freedom that the powerful enjoy is that they are more likely to use stereotypes, because they spend less effort trying to control or moderate their initial impressions. Most, if not all, people use stereotypes on a daily basis. This is because in many social situations, stereotypes offer an easy explanation. Given that our social environment is so complex, people often simply cannot resist the simplicity of a stereotype. If you see a hardworking colleague from Korea, you may unwittingly think of the stereotype that Asians are industrious. If you see a woman who can't make up her mind, you might flash on the stereotype about women being indecisive. Of course, you often quickly suppress these ideas because you know that you should not judge a book by its cover. Not all Asians or all women fit these generalizations. Yet the connection with the ethnicity or the gender of the person has already been made and can influence your thinking. Powerful people stereotype more often, because they are less likely to censor themselves in that way. House is a prime example of this. Hardly an episode goes by in which he does not offend some social group (although this is often accompanied by a comment that he is intentionally not discriminating).

> House: I can't ask the black guy or one of the chicks to do it; it'd be insensitive.
>
> —"Mirror, Mirror"

> Nun: Sister Augustine believes in things that aren't real.
> House: I thought that was a job requirement for you people.
> —"Damned If You Do"

Does Power Corrupt?

Having reviewed four common effects of power and illustrated how House's behavior is an example of them, here are three important questions to answer. First, does this mean that—as Lord Acton claimed—power corrupts? Many of the effects reviewed previously are quite negative: if people feel powerful, they take too many risks, they ignore other people's perspectives, and they voice stereotypes.

House: Can we forget my vices and get back to my virtues?
—"Merry Little Christmas"

This is certainly true, but, on the other hand, feelings of power also produce assertive people who can focus on the bigger picture, who are not too afraid to take risks, and who are more likely to generate creative, novel ideas. The better description is that power does not corrupt but that it changes the person. The effects of feelings of power are both positive and negative.

The best thing to do, therefore, would be to manage these effects. The negative effects need to be pruned so that the positive effects can blossom. One way that these negative effects can be pruned is by making people aware of them. If we explain to House that because of his power, he is apt to be influenced in a number of negative ways, he should be able to guard against these negative effects. You know, however, that House would not follow this advice. There are some episodes in which House seems to realize that his behavior makes him lonely, but he makes no real effort to change it. This is also the case for other people, including ourselves. A great deal of our behavior is difficult to control, especially when we have strong habits of behaving a certain way or when we gain a hidden advantage by acting in a certain manner. For these reasons, it seems very unlikely that House would change the negative aspects of his behavior.

A better way to curb people with power is to change their feelings of power. They should be made aware that their power is not God-given but is conferred on them by others. Research by Joris Lammers and colleagues has shown that the side effects of power can be effectively blocked by making powerful people aware that others might see their power as unfair and undeserved. This finding illustrates, from a psychological point of view, the importance of democracy and the separation of power. Power corrupts, but by ensuring that the powerful are controlled by others and cannot take their power for granted, the corrupting effect can at least be mitigated.

Limiting people with power is a very difficult thing, though—and limiting House is almost impossible. On the show, this Sisyphean task rests on Cuddy's shoulders. As dean of medicine, she is House's superior and the only one who can restrict and bridle him.

> I am the only one that can control him.
>
> —"Half-Wit"

Although she is not always successful, Cuddy is the only factor that puts a limit on House's bizarre behavior. This is good for the series. If House would—as Cuddy puts it—run around the hospital like a monkey in a banana factory, the series would lose its appeal. The struggle between Cuddy and House, even though her attempts rarely succeed, keeps the series fresh. Moreover, it is good for House and the hospital. If House were allowed to do whatever he wanted, at some point he would derail completely. Yet most important is the wider meaning: powerful people need to be controlled.

This important lesson extends beyond *House*. In this chapter, we have tried to explain House's behavior using what we know about the effects of power. As social psychologists, we believe that people's behavior can, at least to a great extent, be explained by looking at the social situation they find themselves in. This reductionism may seem somewhat simplistic, but we do not want to claim that these effects can explain all behavior. Not everyone who has power is necessarily like House. As psychologists, we discover order, patterns, and laws in human behavior. These patterns explain a good deal of the differences among people, but they do not explain everything. Success generally leads to happiness, but not all successful people are happy. Power leads to overassertiveness and risk taking, decreases empathy, and increases stereotyping, but not all powerful people are overassertive risk takers who frequently stereotype others and have little empathy. By seeing patterns in our experiments, we can predict that people are more likely to behave in this manner in certain situations. Even though House's behavior is clearly a caricature, it still can serve as an (exaggerated) illustration of how powerful people as a rule behave. As such, the series can help us understand the effect of power on the behavior of others and ourselves.

SUGGESTED READINGS

Galinsky, A. D., D. H. Gruenfeld, and J. C. Magee (2003). From power to action. *Journal of Personality and Social Psychology*, 85, 453–466.
Lammers, J., A. D. Galinsky, E. H. Gordijn, and S. Otten (2008). Illegitimacy moderates the effects of power on approach. *Psychological Science*, 19, 558–564.

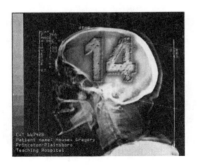

House on the Brain

ANTOINETTE MILLER

In "No More Mr. Nice Guy," a patient named Jeff is admitted to the intensive care unit (ICU) at Princeton-Plainsboro. What sets Jeff apart from every other patient there is that he seems almost too nice. He appears unnaturally trusting, optimistic, and patient, as we see in his initial meeting with House.

> House: Sir, why do you have two lunches in front of you?
> Jeff: Been here for two meals.
> House: You're happy with that?
> Jeff: No, I just don't see much use in complaining.
> House: Seriously? It's a very useful tool. You complain, make people miserable, and they do what you want and make the misery go away.

House becomes slightly intrigued at this point, and to test whether Jeff's case is really worthy of his attention, House slams Jeff's foot with his cane. Jeff's wife, Deborah, objects, but Jeff himself is pretty relaxed about it:

Jeff: Ow!
Deborah: What the hell?
Jeff: I'm sure it was an accident.
House: Is he Canadian?
Cameron: Uh, he's a low priority.
House: Is that a yes?
Cameron: He's just . . .
House: Happy. I've gotta stop this before it spreads.

This exchange prompts House to take on Jeff's case. The question that intrigues House is whether Jeff's niceness is a simply a part of Jeff's personality or a symptom of his medical condition. Maybe something is happening in Jeff's brain. In some general sense, of course, everything we do and feel is happening in our brains. House makes this point when he argues with Deb about the nature of Jeff's personality:

Deborah: He's not sick, he's nice.
House: Nice in the sense that your toaster is nice for making breakfast. It's the only thing his wiring will let him do. He has Williams syndrome. Your husband is missing the genes that make him suspicious.

In general, our brains determine our behavior—even without our conscious intervention. In fact, they even determine our conscious intervention. In this chapter, we review some cases from the Princeton-Plainsboro files to see what they can tell us about the relationship between our brains and our thoughts, feelings, and behavior. Why are we nice? Why are we mean? Why do we fall in love? How do we know who we are? Why might we see sounds or hear colors and feel limbs that are no longer there? How can we be blind, yet not know it? We take a case study approach—examining a wide range of symptoms and then exploring the brain functions that underlie those symptoms.

Do You See What I See? Sensation, Perception, and *House*

> House: You see grace because you want to see grace.
>
> Wilson: You don't see grace because you won't go anywhere near her.
>
> —"Autopsy"

Case Study 1: The Woman Who Heard with Her Eyes

"The Right Stuff" opens with a harrowing scene. As Greta (an aspiring air force pilot) flies her Stealth fighter jet over a desert landscape, she suddenly begins to see flashing, vibrant, unnatural colors on the landscape before her as an alarm beeps in the background. While she is lost in the waves of color, she loses control of the jet and crashes it.

To our relief, we (the intrepid audience) realize it's only a simulator, and although she manages to put up a brave front after the cockpit opens, the experience has shaken Greta considerably. She wants to be an astronaut, but NASA would never take her now! She comes to House begging for his help.

> Greta: Something is wrong. With my eyes, my ears.
>
> House: Well, if it's fixable, the air force will do it for free. If not, doesn't matter.
>
> Greta: There are a hundred applicants ready to take my place who don't need to be fixed. I need to do this off the books. I did the research, you're the best, you break rules, and you don't care about anyone except yourself.
>
> House: Well, let's say that's true. You get a new job, the hospital gets a nice wad of cash, what do I get?
>
> Greta: I crashed a flight simulator, because I started to hear, with my eyes.

House is understandably intrigued, and it's not by the wad of cash she dumps on his desk, although $50,000 is no small wad! In fact, he's intrigued enough to agree to see her "off the books" and send the thirty-plus doctors who are competing for the coveted positions on his diagnostic team to find the answer. As he says to the candidates: "Thirty-year-old female, with synesthesia. New rules. You generate a lab report—you shred it. X-ray—you melt it. No notes, no records, nothing. As far as you're concerned, the patient is Osama bin Laden, and everyone not in this room is Delta Force. Any questions?"

While the black ops of medicine disperse to root out the cause, Greta is thrown into a multicolored world again; during a procedure a monitor beeps, and (to Greta) strange colors fly about the room. This, in combination with her increasing fear that she'll be "outed" (she's terrified that NASA will hear of her condition and disqualify her from its program), inspires her to break away from the doctors and barricade herself in the hospital chapel.

> Candidate 10: She had another episode of synesthesia, it set off a psychotic attack, and now she ran in there and must've jammed something in the handles.
> House: So you called me, the guy with one good leg and zero leverage.

What is this "synesthesia" they keep talking about? Is Greta psychotic? Is she tripping? No, not at all. Synesthesia is a neurological condition—the word literally means "sensations together"—one sensory experience (like hearing a sound, such as a beep) may cause an involuntary second sensory experience (such as seeing a color or flashes of color). It comes in many different forms: for some people, it means that certain letters have their own inherent hues; for others, numbers or days of the week have their own special "personalities"; or some (as in Greta's case) see colors when they hear certain sounds. Here, beeps (first the alarm in the flight simulator, then the monitors in the hospital) are triggering the color waves that scare her so badly. The experience of synesthesia is automatic, it's involuntary, it's highly memorable, and it often has a strong emotional flavor. And speaking of flavor, there is even a kind of synesthesia where words have their own special flavors!

So, What's Going On?

What explains Greta's symptoms? Consider, first of all, that we are continually bombarded with information from the external world. Our senses were designed to bring that information into the parts of the brain where it can be processed and interpreted as needed. That's their function. Information about the things we see goes to the visual processing area of the brain (our *occipital lobes*) and is broken down according to its characteristics, such as color, movement, and location. Sounds we hear go to the auditory-processing areas of the brain (our *temporal lobes*), things we taste and touch are also processed in their own areas (the *parietal lobes*), and so on. The world we experience is cut up, analyzed, and eventually put back together again into something that makes sense.

What happens, though, if a short circuit occurs, and things overlap before their time? You may then begin tasting shapes and hearing colors—and you're a synesthete. Some doctors believe the condition reflects the way our brains put information back together again (it just happens a bit differently in people with synesthesia), and others think that certain brains don't separate out the sensory signals as they should. Or, because every sense has its own "map" of the world on the brain, these maps might overlap a little too much. It's still not entirely known how synesthesia happens; however, what was once thought to be either a hallucinatory or a drug-induced experience is now accepted as a real neurological condition, and usually it's something that we're born with. In Greta's case, though, this mixing of the senses can sometimes be an indication of an underlying medical problem, especially if it comes on suddenly. Greta is ultimately diagnosed with a condition that produces multiple cysts in her lungs. The oxygen deprivation caused by those cysts is driving the synesthesia, and once the cysts are removed, the mixing of sensation stops. Although House first lies, telling everyone (including Greta) that he's notified NASA of Greta's condition, we learn later on that he kept it to himself, and we are left wondering whether she goes on to realize her dream of becoming an astronaut.

Case Study 2: Failing to See What Is There (or, Hey, Where'd You Go?)

In the previous case study, the patient experienced what could be described as an *excess* of perception—seeing and hearing things that aren't there or experiencing an unusual mixture of senses. Sometimes, though, the opposite happens. People experience too little perception. Here we present a pair of cases, a man who can't see things when they're in motion, and a man who simply can't see.

"Son of a Coma Guy" brings us Kyle, whom House identifies as a case just by tossing a bag of chips. The episode opens as House sits, enjoying his lunch (using "Coma Guy" as a tabletop) and the television. Wilson finds him there, and as House waxes on about the irony of putting color TVs in the rooms of patients who never can use them, Coma Guy's son (Kyle) enters the room. As Wilson (understandably embarrassed) tries to cover for House's apparent callousness, we see House begin to show an interest in Kyle. He inexplicably gets up, begins flashing the room lights on and off, and he picks up his bag of chips. He offers the chips to Kyle and then tosses the bag at him gently. Kyle stands and allows the chips to hit him, apparently unaware of their flight path. Then things get even stranger. House asks, "Wanna see something really cool?" He stands up and starts to walk toward Kyle, and we (the audience) watch from Kyle's point of view as House suddenly disappears and then reappears right in front of Kyle's face. Kyle is clearly startled (as anybody would be after seeing someone suddenly teleport across the room).

> House: I saw you leaving last Tuesday; practically tripped over two guys on your way out. But you had no problem opening doors. It's called akinetopsia. You can't see things when they move. And since you haven't been hit by a bus, I assume it's intermittent.

As House has correctly determined, Kyle is now akinetopsic; he has become motion-blind.

So, What's Going On?

Our brains have specific centers that process the various aspects of what we see; one such area (called "V5," found in the occipital lobes near where they meet the temporal lobes) is tuned to how and where things move. Damage that area, and things become invisible to us when they're in motion. A person with this condition may be able to see things perfectly well while stationary (such as when House is sitting and talking to Kyle, or when he is holding the bag of chips), but once the object moves, it becomes essentially invisible (as when House tosses the chips—they disappear while in flight, as far as Kyle is concerned). It becomes impossible to pour tea, coffee, or any liquid without overflowing the cup (the liquid appears "frozen" midstream) or to cross the street safely (cars pop in and out of existence, seemingly at random). Conversation can be difficult because the lips of speakers look all herky-jerky, and any gestures made are lost entirely on the akinetopsic listener.

Motion blindness usually results from brain damage—stroke, head injury, or a tumor. The most famous case of akinetopsia was a woman in her midforties who suffered a blood clot that damaged the motion-sensitive areas in her brain in the 1970s. Although there was no treatment for her motion blindness, she has learned to cope somewhat and modify her life. As House notes, however, Kyle's motion blindness is intermittent, so something else must be going on. (Again, even though Kyle hasn't yet been hit by a bus, crossing the street can be very dangerous for the motion blind!) Based on Kyle's symptoms and family history, House diagnoses him with a rare condition called red ragged fiber disease, in which people suffer from a variety of problems that include seizures and intermittent motion blindness. While no cure exists for red ragged fiber disease, House and his team can at least treat Kyle's symptoms.

Whereas Kyle's akinetopsia keeps him from seeing objects once they are in motion, there is another brain disorder that leads us to miss what is right in front of us. We can be at least partially blind, yet not know it. This happens to Foreman in the two-part episode "Euphoria." A cop is brought to the hospital after having been shot and shrapnel lodges in his head, yet he is still laughing uncontrollably. Even while he is being treated in the ER, he remains giddy until he goes blind, begins experiencing horrible intractable pain, and eventually dies. This is bad enough, until Foreman himself begins to giggle.

After Foreman and Joe (the cop) are put into isolation at the end of part one, House insists on doing a brain biopsy (taking a small slice of tissue for testing) to try to nail down the source of infection. Because the chance of contagion is so high and the nature of the disease is unknown, it's left to Foreman to do it while in the isolation chamber. (Foreman is still experiencing the symptoms himself; though he is not yet in pain, he knows it is coming.) Foreman grabs the pick and the hammer (it's tricky to biopsy the brain), and all seems to be going well until House notices that Foreman has missed Joe's head entirely. Instead, he's biopsying the mattress beside Joe's head. Foreman seems completely unaware of his mistake, insisting that House take the sample to test. He's completely blind, yet he doesn't know it.

So, What's Going On?

First Joe and then Foreman have become blind, not because their eyes are affected but because their brains are being attacked by a parasite. They are victims of *blindsight*, a paradoxical condition in which a person can be apparently blind but still be able to detect movement and, in some cases, locate objects in space. We have more than one visual system in our brains: one is our primary, conscious pathway and the second is a less conscious backup pathway. When the occipital lobe is damaged (which is where the conscious processing of visual information truly begins), this second pathway can still be spared. As Chase notes here, "Physically, his [Foreman's] eyes are fine. Problem is isolated to his brain. Damage to the occipital lobe extends from the visual primary cortex."

In some cases of occipital lobe damage, the patient may insist that he or she can see (Foreman continues to tell House to test the mattress sample he's biopsied), regardless of all evidence to the contrary. This is called *Anton's syndrome*, and as Foreman does here, the patient may *confabulate*, or fill in the missing pieces of his conscious experience without realizing it. While Foreman is successfully treated for the infection (with some initial side effects), blindsight is a real (and really debilitating) condition. Confabulation can be seen in many neurological conditions, including impairments of memory.

And Who Are You, Again? Memory and *House*

"Temporal lobe controls speech, hearing, memory. She loses those things, she's gonna be a terrific date, but beyond that . . ."

—House, "Not Cancer"

Case Study 3: Just Another Empty-Headed Model?

Imagine living always "in the moment," moving from event to event, experiencing each as if it were the very first time. This experience is associated with *amnesia*, the loss of memory. In "Skin Deep," a young model named Alex picks a fight and then falls to the ground during a fashion show. She is rushed to the hospital, and her tox screen is positive for both alcohol and heroin. Because House doesn't trust what either Alex or her father (also her manager) tells him, he orders a rapid detox. Her father claims that this was the "first time" and that Alex isn't an addict. As Chase says, "Heroin chic in a model? Shocking." During the procedure, Alex's heart stops, leaving her brain without blood flow or oxygen for several seconds. When she awakens from the procedure, the real strangeness begins.

> Alex: Are you mad at me, Daddy? I let you down.
> Dad: No, no, not at all, sweetie.
> Alex: I should have been more mature. I should have handled the pressure.
> Dad: Stop, stop. We're going to get you better, all right. Nothing else matters.
> Chase: Excuse me. We've got you on what we call a banana bag: vitamins, nutrients.
> Alex: I got the cute doctor. [*Then repeating herself*] Are you mad at me, Daddy? I let you down.
> Dad: What's going on?
> Alex: I should have been more mature. I should have handled the pressure.

So, What's Going on?

There are several different types of memory that can be teased apart by the *length of time* they last and the *type of information* that is stored. One type, called *short-term memory*, if left on its own, will decay rapidly, deteriorating within twenty to thirty seconds. Another kind of memory, *long-term memory*, is the "Twinkie" of memory, having the longest shelf life of all. Theoretically, once a long-term memory trace is successfully created (and not all information makes it successfully, by any means), it can presumably last as long as the brain in which it is stored does. The trick may be in reaccessing the memory once it's been squirreled away. We also can experience memory *losses*, and in Alex's case she has become an amnesiac, unable to remember anything for more than that critical twenty to thirty seconds that it's held in her short-term memory. Once Chase leaves her bedside, it's as if he has been erased from her memory, and she starts fresh.

But why? How does a temporary loss of oxygen wipe away memory? As it turns out, a variety of brain areas are involved in the creation, maintenance, and retrieval of memories. One structure, called the *hippocampus* (due to its seahorselike shape), is crucial in moving things from the temporary storage of the short-term memory to the more permanent long-term memory. Yet although this fairly small structure (well, *structures*, because we have two of them) is so very essential to maintaining our memory, it is also very sensitive to oxygen loss. Alex is similar to one of the more famous cases of amnesia, a man known only as R. B., who also experienced a brief loss of blood flow to his brain during surgery. Once he awoke, he had a dense *anterograde amnesia*, a disorder in which people can't form permanent memories anymore (as in Alex's case). While R. B. never recovered from his condition, Alex at least seems to recoup some of her memory function by the end of the episode, but as we learn later on, she (or is it "he"?) has other problems to deal with.

Case Study 4: Filling in the Gaps

"Histories" finds House where he least wants to be: the clinic. Yet one patient (named Jodi) catches his eye. She is completely confounding two medical students by repeatedly changing her story about how she injured her wrist (first it was that she fell off her beach house steps, then it was that she fell off her horse, and so on). After sending them on various wild goose chases (including the hint "It starts with 'C'") House finally confronts Jodi in a strange and interesting exchange.

> House: Hi, Jodi, I'm Dr. House. What brings you to the hospital?
> Jodi: My wrist.
> House: How did that happen?
> Jodi: I was riding the Ferris wheel and this huge seagull flew right at me. [*We can see that there is a picture of a Ferris wheel on the back of House's clipboard and a bird pin on his jacket.*]
> House: How horrifying.
> Jodi: I swung my arm at the bird, but I hit the Ferris wheel. [*House turns to the medical students.*]
> Student 2: She's making it all up?
> House: No, her wrist really does hurt.
> Jodi: I'm not lying.
> House: Of course, you are. You have no idea what happened. You have no memory.

No memory? After they leave the examination room, House further explains, "Korsakoff's syndrome. Her brain is damaged by excessive drinking or insufficient diet; pretty obviously the latter. She has no new memories, no new ideas, can't even process that idea. So her brain fills the gaps as best it can using visual clues."

House then returns to the patient's room, to prove a point.

> House: Hi! Jodi, I'm Dr. House. What happened to your wrist?
> Jodi: There was this weird old guy, he had a cane.
> House: See? It's like it never happened. Perfect forgiveness.

So, What's Going On?

While Alex the model may not have been able to form *new* memories, *retrograde amnesia* is a disorder in which people are unable to recover the memories that have already been put into the long-term store—this can result from stroke, it is seen in the more advanced stages of Alzheimer's disease, and it also occurs in a condition called Korsakoff's syndrome. Korsakoff's can result from prolonged malnutrition (most often seen in excessive drinkers), which then causes a loss of thiamine (an important B vitamin). Because of the Korsakoff's, Jodi is having major memory issues (presumably, both anterograde and retrograde amnesia), but her mind is struggling to fill in the blanks with things that make sense. She's confabulating, and in this case Jodi is filling in the blanks with things she sees around her: one medical student is wearing a shirt with a horse on it, so Jodi fills in those gaps with a horseback-riding accident. Another has a surf scene on his clipboard, so Jodi imagines that she must have been at a beach house when she fell. And finally, the "weird old guy" is our own House, and obviously his cane was the cause of her injury. The most interesting thing about Jodi is that she has no real awareness that her manufactured memories aren't real, and until she is treated for her nutritional issues, she won't be aware. Yet at least House implies that she *can* recover her memories. Other such cases (particularly those that result from the alcoholic version of Korsakoff's) may not be so lucky.

What's That You Say? Language and *House*

"Left brain has language, arithmetic, rationality. Right brain is a mute loser."

—House, "Both Sides Now"

Case Study 5: Gobbledygook

"Failure to Communicate" involves a patient named Fletcher, a reporter preparing for a speech. After striking his head, his words become jumbled beyond understanding. While Chase and Foreman attempt to take a history, it becomes very clear that Fletcher is impaired.

Chase: Have you been taking any drugs?
Fletcher: I displaced my function . . . back late.

Elizabeth [*Fletcher's wife*]: He used to drink regularly, but he's been clean and sober for nearly a year.

Foreman: Mr. Stone, you think you're speaking normally, but your speech is impaired. [*Turning to Elizabeth*] He knows what he wants to say, but when he reaches for a word, he finds something else.

Fletcher: I grapple average. Cancer glisten.

Elizabeth: He doesn't know that he's saying it wrong?

Foreman: It all sounds right to him.

So, What's Going On?

There are highly specialized areas in the left hemisphere of the brain that have developed to produce and process language. This is the case in better than 90 percent of the population; the remaining population may share the work across the hemispheres or, in the rarest cases, language is processed on the right side instead. For spoken communication, the major players include Wernicke's area (which aids in the comprehension of language), Broca's area (which is intimately involved in the production of language), and the arcuate fasciculus, which connects the Wernicke's and Broca's areas. Other brain areas are involved as well, but these are the primary ones, and damage or disruption to any of them can cause language disorders called *aphasias.*

Here, Fletcher is talking in a *word salad*, tossing words together in a nonsensical way. This is symptomatic of more than one aphasia. When Wernicke's area is damaged, the patient may toss words and phrases out with great fluency, but his speech is completely nonsensical, and he is unable to understand what is said to him. Yet Fletcher seems to understand everybody else just fine, so what else could it be?

While conducting the usual tests (including a brain scan), Foreman is confused by the results; although there are indications of brain damage (which is ultimately attributed to a malarial infection contracted during off-the-books brain surgery—only on television!), he notes, "The scarring is not in the area of the brain normally associated with conduction aphasia." *Conduction aphasia* occurs when Wernicke's area and Broca's area are disconnected.

Even though the patient may understand what is being said to him, he is unable to repeat things that are said or to respond in a coherent manner, and although he is aware of the errors, he has difficulty in correcting them. This can happen through brain injury, but in the case of Fletcher it seems his aphasia is merely symptomatic of the cerebral malaria. That infection is ultimately treated, but Fletcher is left with a host of other problems that go beyond his language issues.

Come to the Dark Side: Executive Functioning and *House*

"I have no reason to feel guilty. It doesn't make sense, unless there's something wrong in the limbic area of my brain."

—House, "Under My Skin"

Case Study 6: One Scary B . . .

In "Remorse," House is intrigued by Valerie, a patient who is initially brought in because of a series of symptoms, including ear pain and heart arrhythmia. As she is evaluated by the team, however, it becomes patently clear that Valerie is one scary chick; she has apparently been sleeping with a coworker and stealing his work, as well as drugging him to get him fired. When Thirteen finds out about her shenanigans, Valerie files false sexual harassment charges against her. As we said, she's one scary chick. While Valerie is undergoing a brain scan, Thirteen engages her in a conversation that should have evoked some emotional responses, with some surprising results.

Thirteen: Look what's lighting up.
Foreman: Lateral frontal cortex, Broca's area—so what?
Thirteen: I told her it was customary to talk during MRIs, to relax. I spent the last thirty minutes asking her about everything in life that she loves, then hates, then feels any emotion about at all.
Foreman: There's nothing in the paralimbic system, amygdala.

> Thirteen: Because she's using the language part of her brain and bypassing the emotional. She can understand love and pain and empathy, but she can't feel them at all. She's a psychopath.

So, What's Going On?

The prefrontal cortex (PFC), found at the very front of the brain, is responsible for a number of the more "human" characteristics that are at play in Valerie's case: impulse control, planning, classifying things as "good" and "bad," and various aspects of the personality. Many of these are called executive functions; one portion of the PFC (ventromedial) is interconnected with the limbic system that is involved in many emotional responses. Another section (orbitofrontal, so named because it is located just behind the orbits of the eyes) is important in regulating behavior and inhibiting inappropriate impulses and may help us learn the consequences of our behavior.

As House notes, the limbic system is involved in guilt (as well as in other emotions), and although Valerie should have been feeling very emotional about what she and Thirteen were discussing, those areas were quiet on the brain scan. Her Broca's area was working just fine (remember that this is involved in speaking), but that seems to be it as far as the frontal lobes are concerned. They call Valerie a psychopath, and though it's later revealed that she truly isn't, it has been found that psychopaths do seem to have less activity in their limbic systems than nonpsychopaths do in certain situations. They process emotionally laden things differently, and this may be in part to blame for their behavior. There's also some evidence that prefrontal areas may be malfunctioning in psychopaths, who show a diminished capacity for remorse and poor behavioral controls.

Back to Valerie, though. After further investigation, we learn that Valerie wasn't always this way and that she in fact suffers from Wilson's disease, where the body builds up excess copper in a variety of organs (including the brain). Presumably, the condition has affected her limbic and prefrontal areas, essentially disconnecting her from emotion. After Thirteen begins the treatment to remove the excess copper, Valerie begins to feel emotions again, much to the dismay of those around her.

So, What *Does* All This Brain Stuff Have to Do with Psychology, Anyway??

This small sample from the case files of the Princeton-Plainsboro Teaching Hospital illustrates quite vividly how our brains are intimately involved in our perceptions, our memories, our communications, and our feelings. As House once describes it in "Big Baby," "The brain's like the Internet; packets of information constantly flowing from one area to another." Fortunately for us, the information usually gets to where it is supposed to go, but, as so many of the patients in each season of *House* find out, even the smallest disruption in that network can have dramatic consequences.

SUGGESTED READINGS

General Resources

Banich, Marie T. (2004). *Cognitive Neuroscience and Neuropsychology.* New York: Houghton Mifflin.

Gazzaniga, M. (2000). *Cognitive Neuroscience: A Reader.* New York: Wiley-Blackwell.

Perception

Carey, B. (2008). Blind, yet Seeing: The Brain's Subconscious Visual Sense. *New York Times*, pp. D5, D7.

Cytowic, R., and D. Eagleman (2009). *Wednesday Is Indigo Blue: Discovering the Brain of Synesthesia.* Cambridge, MA: MIT Press.

Grossenbacher, P., and C. Lovelace (2001). Mechanisms of synesthesia: Cognitive and physiological constraints. *Trends in Cognitive Sciences*, 5(1), 36–41.

Heywood, C., and J. Zihl (1999). Motion Blindness. In *Case Studies in the Neuropsychology of Vision* (pp. 1–16). Hove, England: Psychology Press/Taylor & Francis.

Hirstein, W. (2004). *Brain Fiction: Self-Deception and the Riddle of Confabulation.* Cambridge, MA: MIT Press.

Ramachandran, V., and E. Hubbard (2001). Synaesthesia—a window into perception, thought and language. *Journal of Consciousness Studies*, 8(12), 3–34.

Shipp, S., B. de Jong, J. Zihl, and R. Frackowiak (1994). The brain activity related to residual motion vision in a patient with bilateral lesions of V5. *Brain: A Journal of Neurology*, 117(5), 1023–1038.

Weiskrantz, L. (1992). Unconscious vision: The strange phenomenon of blind-sight. *Sciences*, 22–28, 32.

Memory

NINDS Wernicke-Korsakoff Syndrome Information Page, accessed May 1, 2010, www.ninds.nih.gov/disorders/wernicke_korsakoff/wernicke-korsakoff.htm.

Shimamura, A. P. (1992). Organic Amnesia. In L. R. Squire (ed.), *Encyclopedia of Learning and Memory* (pp. 30–35). New York: Macmillan.

Language

NIDCD Aphasia Information Page, accessed March 22, 2011, www.nidcd.nih.gov/staticresources/health/voice/FactSheetAphasia.pdf.

Executive Functioning

Blair, R. (2008). The amygdala and ventromedial prefrontal cortex: Functional contributions and dysfunction in psychopathy. *Philosophical Transactions: Biological Sciences*, 363(1503), 2557–2565.

Kiehl, K. A., et al. (2001). Limbic abnormalities in affective processing by criminal psychopaths as revealed by functional magnetic resonance imaging. *Biological Psychiatry*, 50(9), 677–684.

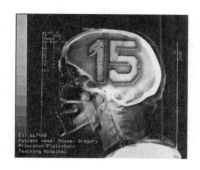

A Hospital Full of People but Only Five Personality Dimensions

The Big Five Personality Factors

PETER J. RENTFROW AND JENNIFER A. MCDONALD

"Is this isn't just about the sex. You like her personality. You like that she's conniving. You like that she has no regard for consequences. You like that she can humiliate someone if it serves. Oh, my God. You're sleeping with me?"

—House, "Don't Ever Change"

House has this rather disturbing epiphany when he finds out that his best friend, Wilson, is dating Amber (aka "Cutthroat Bitch"), who behaved ruthlessly when she fought to secure a spot on House's diagnostic team. House realizes that Wilson is attracted to the same combination of characteristics, or traits, that he possesses—his own personality. Simply put, personality is something that psychologists infer from behavior in order to explain differences between individuals and to help predict how people might act in a given context. It is a distinguishing pattern of thinking, feeling, and behaving that differentiates us from others and leads us to act consistently across situations. Because personalities can provide important clues, House often pays close attention to those of his patients, and because they are interesting, we are captivated by the personalities of House and his colleagues.

"The Down Low": What Is Personality?

The Distrustful Man. The Offensive Man. The Arrogant Man. The Surly Man. The Reckless Man. The Unpleasant Man. The Mean Man.

These labels might seem like synonyms for House, but they are actually the titles of some character sketches created by Aristotle's pupil Theophrastus more than two thousand years ago. In *The Characters*, the Greek philosopher provided definitions of a certain type of person and then described the sorts of behavior that could be expected from such a person. For instance, the Unseasonable Man is someone who does things at the worst possible time, the Flatterer says anything to win the favor of others, and the Surly Man lacks courtesy in his words. It can be said that Theophrastus's *The Characters* was the first attempt at studying personality.

It is impressive that Theophrastus's characters still live among us today. We see them in our own daily interactions, as well as in watching the doctors and the patients of Princeton-Plainsboro Hospital—such as every time Chase sucks up to an authority figure or House calls someone an idiot. What is most noteworthy, however, is that the archaic character sketches reflect a current and widespread view of personality. When people describe themselves or others, they do so in terms of personality traits. Traits are consistent and stable patterns in the ways people think, feel, and behave. So when we say that someone is awkward, charming, secretive, or cutthroat, we are using a trait descriptor and implying that the person tends to behave in a particular manner over time and across situations. In "Honeymoon," when Wilson tells House, "Be yourself: cold, uncaring, distant" (to which he sarcastically replies, "Please, don't put me on a pedestal," in typical House fashion), Wilson is describing some of House's enduring traits. The fact that we use words to describe personality has formed the very basis of trait theory.

You could probably come up with a massive list of adjectives that can describe people. In fact, psychologists in the 1930s scanned the dictionaries and identified more than seventeen thousand words that could be used to depict someone's personality. Yet having too many adjectives could create chaos in what should be a scientific discipline, so personality psychologists have taken advantage of a statistical procedure called factor analysis to organize the multitude of trait descriptors in a meaningful way. Factor analysis reduces a large number of variables down to a smaller set of factors, and, when applied to personality traits, this technique reveals a small number of distinct personality factors that consist of traits with similar meanings. Just as House whittled down a room full of forty qualified applicants to three new fellows, each offering something different, we can reduce thousands of personality descriptors to a few broad dimensions (well, in a *much* more systematic way). These personality dimensions are commonly referred to as the Big Five.

Because the Big Five represent the basic dimensions that people use to describe themselves, and they are the most widely studied personality factors, this chapter will now explain each of the Big Five using examples from Princeton-Plainsboro. We will then address issues surrounding trait psychology, such as whether our personalities and behaviors are actually as consistent as trait psychologists and House, who apparently has "been alienating people since [he] was three" ("Detox"), seem to suggest. Finally, we will discuss how personality manifests in everyday life and can predict important life outcomes.

"Simple Explanation": The Big Five

So, what are these Big Five personality dimensions? The most popular labels spell the acronym OCEAN: openness (intellect), conscientiousness, extraversion, agreeableness, and neuroticism (emotional instability). Before describing these factors, it is essential to note that they are indeed *dimensions* and not personality *types*. Although you might say that someone is an "extravert," you are really saying that the person is high in extraversion. The terminology represents the high end of a pole, with introversion at the low end; likewise, this label does not necessarily define the individual. A person might indeed be extraverted but could also be quite agreeable, unconscientious, emotionally stable, and intellectual. The Big Five factors provide a very broad overview of what someone is like. Each dimension comprises more specific traits, which provide a more precise depiction of someone's personality. For instance, although House appears to be unsociable and thus not extraverted at all, he often acts in ways that are indicative of some of the smaller facets of that personality factor, such as assertiveness and excitement seeking. When we consider all aspects of the Big Five and their unique combinations, we get a better understanding of the person. As you will see, the meanings of the Big Five labels are generally consistent with how nonpsychologists use them in their daily lives.

Extraversion

> House: What, you're saying I've only got one friend?
> Wilson: Uh, and who . . . ?
> House: Kevin, in Bookkeeping.
> Wilson: Okay, well, first of all, his name's Carl.
> House: I call him Kevin. It's his secret "friendship club" name.
> —"Detox"

Truth be told, both Wilson and House don't have many friends. They do have each other, but nobody would say that they are especially gregarious or talkative or love being part of a group, which are common features of extraverts. They are comfortable spending time by themselves, and they avoid large crowds, which suggests that they are much closer to the introversion end of this personality dimension. Extraversion is essentially the tendency to direct one's energy externally, toward others and the environment. Conversely, House and Wilson tend to direct their attention inward and focus on their own thoughts. Other than when House is considering differential diagnoses with his fellows, interrupting or teasing Cuddy, or being forced to see a clinic patient, he is typically bantering with Wilson or sitting alone, twirling his cane and reflecting on his latest medical mystery.

Besides enjoying time alone, introverts tend to be quiet and low-key; while extraverts are typically energetic, assertive, confident, and active. The episode "5 to 9," which unexpectedly centers on a day in the life of chief hospital administrator Cuddy, presents some examples of Cuddy's extraverted behavior. In particular, we can see how incredibly active and fast-paced her lifestyle is, which includes several meetings with a variety of different people. Although she secretly feels overwhelmed at times, Cuddy confidently and assertively holds her ground and is successful in her dealings of the day.

In general, Cuddy's leadership is evident, but at times there is a power struggle with House, who similarly wants to be in control and often gets his way. As far back as the pilot episode, House tries to push Cuddy's limits and challenge her authority, even though he is her subordinate. With the exception of perhaps Foreman, the various team members do not show House's or Cuddy's level of assertiveness—in "Deception," House once described Cameron's leadership skills as "Nonexistent. Otherwise excellent." House himself demonstrates another aspect of extraversion, which is seeking excitement (e.g., taking dangerous risks, such as electrocuting himself to have a near-death experience in "97 Seconds"). Yet although it is not evident in the definition, extraversion is also synonymous with enthusiasm, because extraverted people often experience positive emotions and demonstrate a love for life. It is probably safe to say that House is not one of those people.

Agreeableness

"House doesn't have Asperger's. The diagnosis is much simpler, he's a jerk."

—Cuddy, "Lines in the Sand"

Along with extraversion, the other interpersonal factor of the Big Five is called agreeableness. This reflects the tendency to be warm, helpful, friendly, and trusting. Agreeable individuals get along easily with others and maintain social relationships over long periods of time. They are altruistic and caring, such as Cameron, Wilson, Foreman, Thirteen, and the like, putting others' interests above their own and showing much concern for humanity.

The opposite end of the dimension, disagreeableness, is exemplified by showing little concern for others and being uncooperative, antagonistic, and suspicious. Sound familiar? Just watching and listening to House effectively defines disagreeableness. People who are disagreeable might appear "abrasive and annoying and come on way too strong, like . . . vindaloo curry," as House's ex-partner Stacy Warner tells him in "Failure to Communicate." Their distrust might also lead these individuals to say things like "Everybody lies," and they might frequently insult others. When they actually do something nice, it might be so rare that it prompts people to ask, "So does this guy have pictures of you being nice to him?" as Wilson inquires of House in "Who's Your Daddy?" In addition, they might talk back to people, even to those who are close to them, and ask their doctor whether he or she is "a moron," as does Nate, the unforgettable chess-playing patient in "The Jerk." House has finally met his match in this teenager with the personality that is so aggressive and bratty, the diagnostics team mistakes it for a symptom.

What else makes House the poster boy for disagreeableness? How about his lack of modesty? Even House's name exemplifies this aspect of the dimension: "First, 'Hector does go rug' is a lame anagram. Want a better one for Gregory House? 'Huge ego, sorry.'"

In "House Training," House suggests a more appropriate anagram for his name than the one Wilson came up with. The new one illustrates the tendency for individuals who are low in agreeableness to have high opinions of themselves. Well, at least House is willing to admit it.

Conscientiousness

"You're not happy unless things are just right. Which means two things: you're a good boss, and you'll never be happy."
—House to Cuddy, "Humpty Dumpty"

Cuddy is a conscientious person. She is likely one of the most efficient, well-organized, and responsible people at Princeton-Plainsboro. As the leader of the hospital, she follows all of the rules and the norms, thinks before she acts, and demonstrates the ability to control her impulses. She is very self-disciplined and takes pride in maintaining order; House is correct in saying that she is not happy if things are not perfect. When Cuddy first becomes a foster mother to Rachel, she is overwhelmed by this unfamiliar new chaos in her life as a stay-at-home mom to an infant. Consider this conversation between Cuddy and Wilson in "Painless":

> Cuddy: I let House supervise himself. That's like handing a twelve-year-old the keys to the liquor cabinet and the car.
> Wilson: You passed the inspection. The patient lived. The car is still in the driveway. . . . Did I mention you passed the inspection?
> Cuddy: I passed by their meager standard. I failed by mine.

Although Cuddy does meet the home inspector's expectations, she expresses disappointment that the place was a "disaster" (in her high-achieving mind) and is upset that her time off work leaves House unsupervised. Actually, she is probably justified in worrying about House, because he isn't exactly the most responsible person in the medical profession. In fact, you could say he is the opposite of Cuddy on the dimension of conscientiousness.

Unconscientious people tend to be impulsive and unreliable. They are also disorganized, inefficient, and perhaps even lazy. Like House, they might watch soap operas and play handheld video games when they should be working or may eat lunch in odd locations, such as the morgue, to avoid getting assigned a new task. Unsupervised or not, they have the potential to be quite irresponsible and break the rules, as when House, being the reckless and immature jerk that he is, leaves a rectal thermometer in a disgruntled clinic patient and takes off from work early in "Fools for Love." Unfortunately for him, the wronged "clinic guy" turns out to be Tritter, who spends much of the third season trying to get House in trouble for possessing Vicodin without a prescription. This brings us back to rule-following Cuddy, who displays some uncharacteristic behavior when she commits perjury to protect House from Tritter's wrath in "Words and Deeds." Yet maybe she does that to put things "just right" again?

Neuroticism

> House: You don't feel angry?
> Wilson: Ah. I'm a little disappointed.
> House: Disappointment is anger for wimps. You don't have to be so gentle about everything. It's okay to get angry once in a while.
>
> —"Wilson"

As House implies, most people show anger sometimes, as Wilson eventually does in the episode about him, aptly called "Wilson." After being told he is a wimp for feeling disappointed, rather than angry, about his friend Tucker's misguided actions, he places an offer on the same condo that Cuddy has her eye on, as a way to punish her for hurting House. This angry act is a onetime thing for Wilson, but repeatedly experiencing anger and other negative emotions such as sadness might indicate a high degree of the fourth personality factor: neuroticism, or emotional instability. Like House, whom Cameron alludes to as being "insanely insecure" and an "angry, misanthropic son of a bitch" in "Heavy," individuals who score high on this dimension often experience insecurity, angry hostility, and irritability. Emotionally unstable individuals also tend to feel vulnerable and anxious and be quite emotional and moody. Conversely, emotionally stable people experience few mood swings, handle pressure well, and are quite calm.

Foreman is a good example of emotional stability because nothing really seems to faze him. Considering his stressful job, he rarely gets upset or emotional, prompting his colleagues to call him boring or even imply that he is a robot. In "The Softer Side," Taub refers to Foreman as "T-1000, built by Cyberdyne Systems," just before doing a rather humorous impression of Foreman's mechanical expression of emotion or lack thereof. The funny thing is, if Foreman had witnessed Taub's impression, he likely would have kept his cool. What's great about personality traits is that they can help us to predict or expect certain behaviors and reactions from others. Take this exchange between Foreman and Chase in "Lucky Thirteen" as an illustration:

> Foreman: Do you think I'm boring?
>
> Chase: Yes.
>
> Foreman: You're saying that just to screw with me.
>
> Chase: Yeah! Why would you expect anything else?
>
> Foreman: I expect House to pull my strings, I expect Cameron to make me feel better, I expect the new team to kiss my ass, and I expect you to be honest, 'cause you don't give a crap.
>
> Chase: Yes. You're boring. That speech was boring.
>
> Foreman: Thanks so much.
>
> Chase: You don't let other people's problems affect you. You don't let your own problems affect you, and it's the screw-ups that make us interesting.

It is important to note that the meaning that personality psychologists give to the Big Five personality dimensions is not exactly the same that given by nonpsychologists. For instance, when personality psychologists talk about neuroticism, they are referring to a normal degree of emotionality, insecurity, and anxiety that healthy people experience. This usage is quite different from how some nonpsychologists think about neuroticism, which is typically considered some sort of mental illness. Although the words that compose the Big Five framework are based on common English terms, in some cases, such as neuroticism, the meanings of those words are not always the same for psychologists and nonpsychologists.

Openness

> "You know how some doctors have the Messiah complex—they need to save the world? You've got the Rubik's complex—you need to solve the puzzle."
>
> —Wilson to House, "DNR"

House repeatedly demonstrates his curious desire to solve the challenging medical puzzles that his patients are facing. Not only does he seek out the most ambiguous and mentally stimulating cases possible, he typically goes about unraveling them in a creative and unconventional way. For instance, in "Half-Wit," when a traditional test does not show anything in the fMRI, House comes up with an interesting new plan: to ask the patient, a musical savant, to pretend to play the piano on his leg. Once the patient does this, the brain function is clearly visible, thus prompting a "Cool, huh?" response from mastermind House.

House often uses unorthodox means to determine whether patients are lying. In "Known Unknowns," he walks into a hospital room playing Metallica music, hands the patient some makeshift drumsticks, and tells her, "I want you to rock out to the music the way you did last night," when she apparently played a video game called Drummer God and then jumped a fence. When the patient looks confused, House says, "Go on, this is a classic medical test. Hippocrates used it. Let's go." Then, once she attempts to "rock out," her arms stop moving, and this leads House to deduce that "there's no way she could have climbed the stairs and then a fence to the pool," meaning that their initial diagnosis was incorrect. "Be careful. Our patient's a big fat liar," House warns. The Drummer God experiment was probably the farthest thing from a "classic medical test," but it takes an open person such as House to think out of the box like this.

Curiosity, imagination, and unconventionality are all traits associated with the openness dimension. House's diagnostic team members are similarly open-minded and original, which they demonstrate with each differential diagnosis (and they have to be open-minded to put up with their boss). Of all of the fellows, Kutner displays the most creativity in solving cases, a characteristic that makes him stand out to his mentor. Open individuals are also intellectual, appreciate the arts, and like trying new things. In the words of the late Kutner, "I just like experience. If it's new, it's interesting" ("Mirror, Mirror").

Personality Stability: "Don't Ever Change"

"People don't change. For example, I'm gonna keep on repeating 'people don't change.'"

—House, "Don't Ever Change"

An important question surrounding the study of personality is whether traits are truly stable over time. House is a strong believer that personality is stable. In fact, in "Don't Ever Change," House is so adamant that the patient's unexpected behavioral transformation is a symptom of her illness, rather than a real personality change, that he almost does not solve the case in time. The patient, Roz, had gone from living in the "fast lane" as a record producer to slowing down completely when she suddenly embraced a strict branch of Judaism. Contrary to the views of his team, House will not accept that this radical change was something Roz made intentionally.

> House: Wegener's wouldn't explain the changed mental status.
> Thirteen: Actually, we've been trying to ignore that part of the whiteboard.
> House: Well, I wrote it in black. I'm always serious when I use black. Lupus would explain . . .

Like most people, House attributes the patient's behavior to her personality and struggles to accept that her personality really changed. In the same episode, however, after House's attempt to bribe Amber to break up with Wilson fails, House realizes that she has changed—that she is not the same "Cutthroat Bitch" who would do whatever it takes to obtain success.

Although people behave slightly differently from one situation to another, there is a growing amount of evidence suggesting that people behave in a remarkably similar way across situations and over time. This makes sense because if people behaved drastically differently all of the time, it would make the world a very unpredictable and chaotic place. Even if we believe that we behave inconsistently at times, as Wilson does in the following dialogue, we might simply be responding to our environment, as House persuasively argues in "The Social Contract."

> Wilson: I'm not always nice. I'm not nice to you.
> House: Because you know nice bores me. Hence, still nice.

When we do perceive a change in someone we know well, this can seem quite alarming because it conflicts with our expectations about that person. For example, in "The Softer Side" when House starts acting polite and actually appears to be happy, this causes Kutner, Cuddy, and Wilson to suspect that something is wrong with him. It turns out that House's new traits are only a temporary result of being on a methadone treatment to reduce his leg pain. Unfortunately, House decides that having no pain is compromising his ability as a doctor, and he goes back to being a miserable jerk. Yet the sixth season gives us some indication that the then-newly Vicodin-free House is becoming nicer, even if he has regressed a bit of late. For example, in the episode "Remorse," House slips a check for $5,000 in his former medical school classmate's mail slot to help keep him from losing his home, even after he finds out he was not the cause of the man's misfortune. We don't know for sure whether House's generosity is motivated by guilt and remorse for having mistreated many people in his life (including Cuddy, whom he upsets, yet refuses to apologize to, in the same episode), or if he commits a truly unselfish act. On the surface, however, it appears that we may have caught a glimpse of a different side of House.

There is growing evidence that personality changes slightly throughout life. As people develop and take on new roles—from being a student and an employee and later a spouse and a parent—they take on new responsibilities and relationships, which elicit behaviors, thoughts, and feelings that are not as common at earlier stages in life. As a result, personality tends to change slightly during the life span—people become more agreeable, conscientious, and emotionally stable as they age. Maybe there's still hope for those who are like House.

"Meaning": Manifestations of Personality

We now know what the Big Five dimensions are, but why are they relevant? As you may have gathered, the traits that people possess can be linked to particular patterns of behavior. In the past, some psychologists believed that the specific *situation* that one finds oneself in is the best predictor of how one will behave in that context. Yet there is now consensus that personality plays a large role, too; that there are individual differences in behavior. It makes sense that people will differ in how they react to situations because of their consistent personality traits—can we really expect two diverse people such as House and Wilson to respond to a situation in the same way? Recently, the person-situation debate has subsided, and now "interactionist" theories, emphasizing connections between the person and the environment, are the norm. Research in this area is currently concerned with establishing connections between personality and common everyday behaviors, as well as important life outcomes. We will now consider some of these findings.

"Mirror, Mirror": Everyday Reflections of the Big Five

"You are what you sit in . . . your friends, your job, your furnishings. It all defines you."

—House, "Black Hole"

In "Black Hole," House isn't satisfied when Wilson refuses to pick out his own condo furniture, informing him that our daily activities, surroundings, and preferences define us. According to interactionist theories, House's statement is quite accurate. These theories propose that individuals choose and create (sometimes unintentionally) social and physical environments that reinforce and reflect elements of their personalities, self-views, and values. Research has indeed found connections between the Big Five and our daily surroundings—our social interactions, living spaces, Web pages, belongings, music collections, jobs, and so on.

To illustrate, consider that House listens to and plays everything from blues to classical to classic rock music, which fits right in with what the research suggests regarding the music preferences of open individuals. Openness is related to liking a variety of music genres, especially those that can be considered reflective and complex, such as classical and jazz. Similarly, Foreman is revealed as a jazz fan in a few different episodes, including "Fools in Love" when he invites the nurse he is dating to a jazz festival. The connection between personality and living spaces is nicely portrayed by Wilson in "Black Hole." He has a hard time following House's advice in picking out a sofa that "defines" him, opting to hire a decorator to furnish the condo instead, but he does select one piece of furniture on his own—Wilson surprises his roommate with a vintage electric organ. This item defines him more than a sofa ever could; the fact that he chooses the organ because he knows House will appreciate it is a perfect reflection of Wilson's kind and thoughtful personality.

We do spend a lot of time listening to music and hanging out at home, but we also spend much of our lives at work. So, does our personality also influence our career choices? The following exchange between House and Kutner in "The Greater Good" suggests that it does:

> House: People act in their own self-interests. You're all here because you're happy to be here. Or at least because it's your best option.
> Kutner: I'm here because I want to help people.

In fact, a growing amount of research suggests that personality is related to occupational preferences. For example, openness is positively related to having artistic or investigative occupational interests. The research suggests that open people seek out jobs and activities that are outlets for their creativity. We can speculate that had House not pursued a career as a diagnostician (which is pretty much a medical detective), he would have been either a criminal detective or a professional musician. Interestingly, Kutner's desire to help people is a common tendency among those working in health care. Although House argues in "Pilot" that "treating illnesses is why we become doctors; treating patients is what makes most doctors miserable," this is likely inaccurate. There is evidence that people working in the helping professions, such as medicine, are high in the trait of agreeableness. House is, therefore, more the exception than the rule.

Prognosis: Personality Matters

Wilson: Why did you make me the head of oncology?
Cuddy: Not because you have the most organs. You're thoughtful, caring.

— "Wilson"

The personality traits of individuals are clearly reflected in their typical surroundings or mundane daily activities, but evidence also suggests that the Big Five dimensions are linked to important life outcomes, from occupational and relationship success to physical health. For example, not only can we assume that organ-donor Wilson went into practicing medicine to help others because he is high in agreeableness, but we can suppose that he may also *excel* in his position because he possesses this very trait. In addition to occupational preferences, a lot of evidence suggests that personality is related to occupational achievement. Among the Big Five, conscientiousness is most strongly related to performance and success at a variety of jobs. Essentially, people who are high in conscientiousness, such as Cuddy, are dependable, organized, and efficient—the characteristics that all employers look for.

Another life outcome that is related to personality traits is relationship satisfaction. The Big Five factors that are major predictors of unsuccessful romantic relationships are neuroticism and low agreeableness. Based on interactionist theories, it is possible that emotionally unstable people experience dissatisfying relationships because their irritability upsets their partners, which in turn creates a tense environment. Or, people who are generally very uncooperative and untrusting might evoke similar tension or conflict. Unsurprisingly, House has not been able to sustain a romantic relationship since breaking up with Stacy.

A final, rather important, consequence of personality is our health and mortality. In terms of mental health, psychological disorders such as anxiety and depression appear to be strongly associated with high neuroticism and low extraversion, the traits most closely connected with negative emotions. Also, disorders related to substance abuse are associated with high openness and low conscientiousness, traits we revealed in House—the man who, in "Both Sides Now," lands himself in a psychiatric hospital and almost loses his medical license because of his dependence on Vicodin. In regard to physical health, research has shown that personality traits such as low agreeableness are related to factors that might cause disease. Also, conscientiousness and extraversion are connected to fighting the risk of disease, particularly because conscientious individuals engage in health-promoting behaviors (such as exercise and a healthy diet) and can control potentially dangerous impulses, and extraverts have helpful social support networks. The Big Five, especially extraversion and conscientiousness but also agreeableness and low neuroticism, are also related to living a long life.

We can see House (disagreeable), Foreman (emotionally stable), Cuddy (conscientious), and the entire staff of Princeton-Plainsboro in other people and in ourselves. All that we have to do is look around and within. These personality dimensions operate in our daily lives, and they are relatively stable during the course of our lifetimes. Moreover, our relative standing on these dimensions influences everything we do—from the type of music we listen to and how we decorate our living spaces to which jobs we pursue, our lifestyles, our success, and our health. We can't really be certain about what will happen to us—whether the prognosis is good or bad—but there seem to be some clues in our personality traits. Overall, it is clear that personality matters.

SUGGESTED READINGS

Gosling, S. D. (2008). *Snoop: What Your Stuff Says about You.* New York: Basic Books.

Ozer, D. J., and V. Benet-Martínez (2006). Personality and the prediction of consequential outcomes. *Annual Review of Psychology*, 57, 401–421.

Roberts, B. W., N. Kuncel, R. N. Shiner, A. Caspi, and L. R. Goldberg (2007). The power of personality: The comparative validity of personality traits, socio-economic status, and cognitive ability for predicting important life outcomes. *Perspectives in Psychological Science*, 2, 313–345.

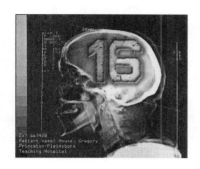

"You Are Not as Special as You Think"

The Political Psychology of *House, M.D.*

JESSE WYNHAUSEN, JOHN T. JOST,
AND GREGORY L. MURPHY

If House assumes that "everybody lies," what must he make of politicians? In the episode "Role Model," the following exchange occurs after House sarcastically dismisses the saccharine, overcoming-all-odds spin of a black Democratic senator and presidential hopeful:

> Senator: You a Republican, or you just hate all politicians?
> House: I just find being forced to sit through drivel annoying.

Like much of the U.S. population, House has little time, energy, or respect for the formal political process. After the same senator expresses a particularly inspiring (and apparently heartfelt) sentiment, House declares, "Well, that's very moving. It's a shame I don't vote."

Yet someone who seems to be rejecting politics is often doing politics, nonetheless. In this chapter, we suggest that House's attitudes toward institutions, religion, social issues, human nature, authority figures, and individual autonomy reflect implicit ideological stances, even as he professes to be above politics of any kind. We will diagnose House's political inclinations and use his (and others') behavior to highlight some of the defining characteristics of major political philosophies or orientations, such as liberalism and conservatism. In this way, we hope to provide you with a better understanding of the psychological basis of House's—as well as your own and others'—political mind-sets.

What's Politics Got to Do with Psychology?

Political psychology explores the interface between political science and psychology—how people's behavior affects and is affected by political institutions. The roots of modern political psychology can be traced back to Ancient Greek philosophers and the first recorded debates about how society should be governed in light of human nature. These themes were revisited centuries later in the writings of Hobbes, Locke, Rousseau, and many other European philosophers. Contemporary political psychology uses the tools of psychological science to shed new light on these classic issues.

Modern political psychology began around the turn of the twentieth century and came to flourish in the last quarter of the century. Graham Wallas was among the first to explicitly synthesize insights from psychology and political science. He argued that people ought to be made aware of the psychological processes that allow them to be manipulated by political elites, and he questioned the pervasive assumption that "every human action is the result of an intellectual process." Undoubtedly, House would share his skepticism.

It was the terror brought on by fascism and the effective use of propaganda by fascist leaders that provided the practical impetus for the scientific emergence of social and political psychology. As we shall see in this chapter, the one philosophy that House consistently espouses is the importance of acting according to one's own moral compass and not allowing oneself to be influenced by peer pressure or social conformity. It was the failure of so many in Europe and elsewhere to do this—and to allow themselves to be manipulated into committing unthinkable atrocities—that made the study of human nature and its relationship to political institutions an urgent matter for social scientists in the latter half of the twentieth century.

A Quick Look at the Left-Right Dimension in Political Life

Cuddy [*Surprised by House's sudden appearance*]: Where did you come from?
House: Apes, if you believe the Democrats.

—"Alone"

The left-right distinction in political philosophy originates with seating arrangements during the French Revolution of 1789. Those who supported *l'ancien regime* (the monarchy, the church, and the aristocracy) sat on the right side of the assembly hall, while those who opposed the regime and sympathized with the revolutionaries sat on the left. From then on, the "right-wing" label came to represent political views that are inherently conservative, supportive of existing authorities, and status quo oriented. "Left-wing" views, by contrast, came to be associated with social change and egalitarian ideals, as in liberal, progressive, and socialist traditions.

Two core aspects of the left-right distinction have persisted for the last two hundred years or more: (1) defending tradition versus advocating social change, and (2) accepting versus rejecting inequality. Thus, rightists (now typically called "conservatives") tend to be more accepting of inequality and resistant to social change (thereby preserving hierarchical traditions). Leftists (often called "liberals") tend to reject social and economic forms of inequality and advocate qualitative social change. To this day, conservatives are more likely to profess traditional cultural and "family values," including religious forms of morality, and to support conventional authority figures, whereas liberals are more likely to advocate policies and reforms aimed at bringing about more social and economic equality, such as welfare, social security, income redistribution, and affirmative action.

Why are some people drawn to conservative ideals such as hierarchy, stability, tradition, and preservation of the status quo, whereas others are drawn to liberal ideals such as equality, social change, progress, and diversity? An accumulating body of evidence indicates that left-right (or liberal-conservative) ideological stances reflect the influences of genetic endowment, parental socialization, and childhood temperament, among other factors. In other words, political psychology reveals that there are connections between an individual's personality and his or her political orientation.

Where Your Politics Meets Your Personality (and vice versa)

Most of us have intuitive theories about how personality types are associated with different political viewpoints, and it turns out that some of these possess a grain or more of truth. A straw poll of our friends and colleagues in which we asked them to guess House's political leanings drew more than a few responses that he must be a conservative. Why? "Well, because he's so . . . grumpy!" Certainly, there are many stereotypes associated with the adherents of various political ideologies, and research has produced empirical evidence that supports at least some of these. For instance, conservatives are (on average) more rigid and dogmatic than liberals. Liberals, by contrast, are more flexible but also more disorganized and messy. These differences (and others) can be understood in terms of the so-called Big Five dimensions of personality and in terms of basic orientations toward uncertainty and threat.

The Big Five Dimensions of Personality

During the last several decades, personality psychologists have determined that there are five major personality dimensions on which individuals differ. The first letters of these dimensions spell out the acronym "OCEAN": openness (to new experiences), conscientiousness, extraversion, agreeableness, and neuroticism. Research reveals that liberals and conservatives generally differ on the first two dimensions but not on the other three. More specifically, liberals tend to score higher on measures of openness to new experiences, whereas conservatives score higher on conscientiousness. Openness is characterized by traits such as curiosity, creativity, sensation seeking, and rebelliousness. Conscientiousness is characterized by traits such as conformity, rule following, orderliness, and deference to conventional authorities and traditions. By these criteria, House exhibits a fairly liberal temperament: He is curious, creative, and rebellious, and he is downright contemptuous of social order, conformity, rule following, and religious tradition. Indeed, these are perhaps his defining personality characteristics, which we will explore at some length.

The show includes other characters who provide a strong contrast with House when it comes to openness and conscientiousness. For example, Cuddy values social order and rule following much more than House does, although she is in fact more flexible and reasonable than many administrators in her situation might be. Vogler, the sinister board chairman, represents one extreme, demanding abject obedience from those who are subordinate to him in the hierarchy. His relationship with House is a match made in hell, and in "Babies and Bathwater," House's rebelliousness instigates Vogler's departure from the hospital.

Orientations toward Uncertainty and Threat

Left-right ideological differences have also been linked to more fundamental differences in orientations concerning the management of uncertainty and threat. Consistent with their greater openness, liberals are less likely to experience uncertainty, ambiguity, and unfamiliarity as psychologically aversive, and consistent with their greater conscientiousness, conservatives are more attuned to potential threats, especially threats to the existing social order. Here again, House's ideological posture resembles the liberal profile: he relishes the challenges posed by medical uncertainties, even as he seeks, playfully and irreverently, to determine the correct diagnosis. He asks, in "Resignation," "What's the point in living without curiosity?" House is acutely aware of biological and other threats, but he seems not to share his patients' anxiety about mortality or understand their attempts to cope with that anxiety.

> Wilson: You can't let a dying man take solace in his beliefs?
> House: His beliefs are stupid.
> Wilson: Why can't you just let him have his fairy tale if it gives him comfort to imagine beaches and loved ones and life outside a wheelchair?
> House: Are there seventy-two virgins, too?
> Wilson: It's over. He's got days, maybe hours left. What pain does it cause you if he spends that time with a peaceful smile? What sick pleasure do you get in making damn sure he's filled with fear and dread?
> House: He shouldn't be making a decision based on a lie. Misery is better than nothing.
> Wilson: You don't *know* there's nothing. You haven't been there.
> House: Oh, God, I am *tired* of that argument! I don't have to go to Detroit to know that it smells.
>
> —"97 Seconds"

In summary, House appears to have many of the characteristics typically associated with liberals; however, these personality traits are merely indirect clues toward understanding a given individual's political orientation. Clearly, more information is needed. Let us return to the two core philosophical dimensions that separate left from right: attitudes concerning tradition (vs. change) and attitudes concerning equality (vs. inequality).

Tradition and Authority: Rules Meant to Be Broken?

If one thing is clear, it is that House has nothing but contempt for tradition, conformity, and conventional forms of authority, including religious authority. He is not only an atheist himself but frequently ridicules the religious beliefs of others. He mocks nuns in "Damned If You Do," refers to a Mormon medical resident as "Big Love" (e.g., "97 Seconds"), and in "Don't Ever Change," he derides deities as "imaginary friends." He concludes in that same episode that "Religion is a symptom of irrational belief and groundless hope."

House's confrontational atheism is also consistent with his attitudes on two major social issues, namely, abortion and euthanasia. When a woman's life is threatened by her pregnancy in "Fetal Position," House has no qualms about terminating the pregnancy and insists on using the label "fetus" as opposed to, for example, "unborn baby." In "Informed Consent," House resists the euthanasia option only when he believes that the patient has been misled about his prognosis. He has no moral objection to euthanasia in itself, and Wilson alludes to the fact that House has helped people end their lives in the past. So, when it comes to religion and two important social issues that are associated with it, House's ideological alliances are clearly with the liberals.

Authority and Rebellion

House's attitudes concerning conformity to authority and respect for rules, conventions, and the status quo in general are similarly impudent: "We can all applaud the doctor who's willing to break all the rules. But the real hero is the unsung doctor, toiling in anonymity, because he broke the rules without getting caught" ("You Don't Want to Know").

To repeat the obvious, conforming is simply not part of House's behavioral repertoire; he despises conventionalism. He is relentlessly independent and unwilling to bend his will for the sake of adhering to social norms, professional ethics, hospital rules, or even the needs and desires of his friends and colleagues. He frequently attempts to subvert or simply ignore Cuddy's official decisions as dean of medicine, lies to a transplant committee in "Control," and even condones the cover-up of Chase's murder of one of his patients ("The Tyrant"). Although he frequently exploits the rules (whether the rules of bureaucracy or of friendship) to get what he wants, this is only a means to an end. It does not reflect a belief in the validity of the rules or the system that gave rise to them. House is impertinent and rebellious in ways that are minor (e.g., refusing to wear his lab coat or do required paperwork) and major (flagrantly violating medical ethics and the law).

House disdains authority, but he has a special contempt for those who defer to it, probably because he sees their behavior as either mindless or disingenuous. The essence of House's position is captured in the tale of the Buraku, a telling chapter in House's "creation mythology." While visiting a Japanese hospital, an adolescent Gregory passes a janitor in a hallway. This janitor turns out to be a doctor and also a member of Japan's "untouchable" caste.

> House: He wasn't accepted by the staff. He didn't even try. He didn't dress well. He didn't pretend to be one of them. The people that ran that place, they didn't think that he had anything they wanted. Except when they needed him. Because he was right. Which meant that nothing else mattered. And they had to listen to him.
>
> —"Son of a Coma Guy"

Clearly, the notion that this man could earn respect while remaining outside the system appealed to young House—indeed, he seems to have modeled his life and career on it. Although the Buraku has no choice, nonconformity is a path that House has deliberately chosen. Perhaps it was in reaction to his father's cold, authoritarian parenting style; in "One Day, One Room," we learn that his father was a cruel disciplinarian. Whatever the cause, contempt for the usual ways of doing things (and especially for the slightest degree of haughtiness) has been part of House's personality since well before he graced the halls of Princeton-Plainsboro Hospital.

Ethical Dilemmas

In "Informed Consent," Dr. Ezra Powell, an aging medical researcher who believes he is terminally ill, asks the team to help him die. A heated debate ensues about legal rules, medical ethics, the role of the physician, and the rights of patients to control their own bodies. This debate echoes many that take place in our society (e.g., the Terri Schiavo case), in which various interest groups—patients, lawyers, physicians, and family members—try, often in vain, to negotiate a mutually acceptable solution.

> Chase: It's his call.
> Foreman: So what do we do? We put a plastic bag over his head and get it over with?
> Chase: No. We give him a syringe full of morphine. Every doctor I've ever practiced with has done it. They don't want to, they don't like to, but that's the way it is.
> Foreman: I haven't, I won't.
> Cameron: I couldn't do it, either.
> Chase: You just said we should respect his decision!
> Cameron: Respect it doesn't necessarily mean we honor it.

House simply does not engage in this debate. He even seems to mock his residents' sincerity, commenting dryly, "Certainly a lot of interesting things to consider." Instead, House just acts. He fools the patient into thinking that they are helping him to die, when in fact they induce a coma that will allow treatment to continue. House does not bother to defend this brazenly unethical step with a long monologue—his implied defense is, as always, that he is almost always right. After giving careful thought to the moral intricacies of the arguments presented to him, he sums up his position as follows: "Oh, come on. He's old and sick and tiny. We can do whatever we want to him."

House's nonconformity is not merely a personality trait; it is a crucial element of his ideology, which he feels driven to impose on others. He insists not only that *he* be allowed to do what he wants to do but also that the *other doctors* do what *they* want to do—even when they are not so sure they want to do it. If he suspects that someone is acting purely to comply with his anticipated wishes, he will quickly turn against that person. If he believes that someone is making a decision because of social convention or religious belief, rather than personal conviction, he will argue against the decision and even attempt to circumvent it.

Ultimately, the staff cannot help Dr. Powell, and he is condemned to a painful death. The issue again arises as to whether they will help him die, now that everyone agrees that his condition is terminal.

Cameron finally makes the decision to aid the dying man, despite her personal animosity toward him. Afterward, House says, "Good for you. You did what you thought was right." The fact that Cameron violated the law and (perhaps) medical ethics gives House confidence that she was true to herself.

House demands moral courage (or perhaps simply nonconformity) from everyone, not only from the other doctors. As we have seen, he often insists on trying to get the patients to renounce their belief in God, their subjugation to their parents, their faith in true love, and so on. To House, all of these things are masks behind which people hide to avoid taking responsibility for doing what they truly believe is right—or what House believes they believe is right. One of the original creators of *House*, executive producer David Shore, has said of the character:

> [House] enjoys pursuing the truth, and he knows we all see the world through our own lenses. He's constantly trying to strip himself of those biases, to get a clean, objective view of things.*

House is not satisfied to strive for objectivity on his own; he is driven to compel others to do the same. House as moral instructor has one main lesson: "To thine own self be true."

No Bleeding Heart

From a political psychology perspective, House's rebelliousness, disrespect for authority, and refusal to abide by rules and regulations might indicate a left-leaning orientation. Yet he hardly exhibits the compassionate, "bleeding heart" mentality that is frequently associated with liberals. Rather, he is tough-minded and unromantic, and he despises knee-jerk liberals just as much as he dislikes unthinking

---

*Diane Werts, "Fox's Medical Marvel Stays on Top: 'House' Reaches Its 100th Episode," *Variety*, January 29, 2009, www.variety.com/article/VR1117999278 .html?categoryid=3530&cs=1.

adherents to religion or convention. Above all, he refuses to countenance ignorance on the left or the right.

Consider the young mother in "Paternity" who refuses to vaccinate her child because "I think some multinational pharmaceutical company wants me to think they work. Pad their bottom line." One might expect House to approve of her skepticism concerning powerful institutions that try to tell her what to do. Instead, he takes the child's toy frog and says,

> All natural, no dyes. That's a good business: all-natural children's toys. Those toy companies, they don't arbitrarily mark up their frogs. They don't lie about how much they spend in research and development. The worst a toy company can be accused of is making a really boring frog. . . . You know another really good business? Teeny, tiny baby coffins. You can get them in frog green or fire engine red. Really. The antibodies in yummy mummy only protect the kid for six months, which is why these companies think they can gouge you. They think that you'll spend whatever they ask to keep your kid alive. Want to change things? Prove them wrong. A few hundred parents like you decide they'd rather let their kid die than cough up forty bucks for a vaccination, believe me, prices will drop *really* fast.

Thus, House values nonconformity only when he believes that it is intelligent and well-informed. He mocks attempts at nonconformity that strike him as mindless, as in "Kids," when House rejects a young musician for a position in part because he has a kanji symbol tattooed on his forearm.

> Dr. Spain: Wow. I thought you'd be the last person to have a problem with nonconformity.
> House: Nonconformity, right. I can't remember the last time I saw a twenty-something kid with a tattoo of an Asian letter on his wrist. You are one wicked free thinker. You want to be a rebel? Stop being cool. Wear a pocket protector like

he does [*gestures toward Wilson*] and get a haircut. Like the Asian kids who don't leave the library for twenty-hours stretches, they're the ones who don't care what you think. Sayonara. [*Dr. Spain leaves.*]

Wilson: So should I go through all the résumés looking for Asian names?

House: Actually, the Asian kids are probably just responding to parental pressure, but my point is still valid.

Clearly, when it comes to tradition and the status quo, House's sensibilities are generally liberal. At the same time, he is openly contemptuous of jejune, knee-jerk propensities to rebel against authority merely for its own sake.

"Everyone's Different, Everyone Gets Treated Different"

We noted earlier that liberals are consistently more in favor of policies designed to effect greater social and economic equality, such as progressive taxation and affirmative action, in comparison with conservatives. Several clues pertaining to House's attitudes about equality and inequality can be found in "TB or Not TB." In this episode, the team treats Dr. Sebastian Charles, a well-known humanitarian who divides his time between treating tuberculosis in Africa and campaigning to make TB medication more available to the world's poor. House finds all of this intensely irritating but not because he doubts that there is a genuine problem—it's more that he disagrees with Charles's methods and is suspicious of his motives. House is intensely skeptical of any efforts to try to make the world a better or more just place: "Welcome to the world. Everyone's different, everyone gets treated different. You try fighting that, you end up dying of TB." This does not mean that House finds unequal access to medical treatment to be acceptable. In a rare moment of emotional honesty, he expresses sympathy for the tuberculosis victims, accusing Charles of "cheapening everything they're going through" by engaging in a publicity stunt, namely, refusing treatment for his own TB.

So, how do we reconcile House's indifference to those who challenge inequality with his evident sympathy for its victims? He offers a valuable clue when he tells us (in multiple episodes) that *life isn't fair*. In "Spin," Cameron suggests that a patient's illness may be karmic retribution for having used steroids. House replies, "The only problem with that theory is it's based on the assumption that the universe is a just place." So, there is no paradox in House's philosophy. He perceives the universe as unjust—he simply doesn't think that there is anything to be done about it. There is a subtle but important ideological difference between believing that inequality is a pervasive reality and believing that it is morally justifiable. He displays a sardonic, jaded, even fatalistic acquiescence to the lamentable realities of inequality and injustice, but he does not go so far as to believe that they are legitimate or deserved. Thus, he cannot be described as a "system-justifier," that is, someone who is motivated to rationalize the status quo as fair and just.

This again places him left of center, politically. That is, liberals are less likely than conservatives to endorse belief systems such as the Protestant work ethic or belief in a just world, which assumes that "hard work breeds success" and that people generally "get what they deserve and deserve what they get," respectively. Liberals are less likely to stereotype poor people and members of disadvantaged groups as lazy, stupid, or otherwise responsible for their plight. Interestingly, research suggests that this is one reason why liberals are not as *happy* as conservatives: when conservatives are exposed to inequality, they find ways of seeing it as legitimate and just; liberals, by contrast, are more bothered by inequality. It is probably impossible to know how much, if any, of House's persistent malaise is due to his assumptions that the world is unfair and that unjustified inequality is unavoidable, but his general outlook more closely resembles that of a gloomy liberal than a complacent conservative.

Yet if House is so concerned about inequality, how do we explain the outrageously politically incorrect language that he uses to harangue, well, *everyone*?

House on women: I know it sounds sexist, but science says you're weak and soft; what can I do? ("Airborne")

House on Jews: "They killed our Lord. Are you going to trust
   them?" (the aptly titled "Insensitive")
House on racial equality: "You know, I have found a difference. Admittedly, it's a limited sample, but it's my experience in the last ninety seconds that all black people are
   morons. Sorry, 'African Americans.'" ("Humpty Dumpty")

These group-based insults are heavily laced with sarcasm, and
House seems concerned with egalitarianism only to the extent that
everyone is equally deserving of his derision. Therein lies the key to
understanding the obnoxious slurs and taunts that make him seem, on
the surface at least, to be a bigot in the tradition of Archie Bunker. For
House, not only does political correctness reek of insincerity, it does
a disservice to people by assuming they will be unable to cope with
and respond to what is essentially a form of teasing that lampoons
the stereotype more than the target of the stereotype. His barbs
are designed to keep people on their toes; it's how he flirts, how he
keeps people distant and then brings them closer, and how he raises
the tension level to avoid boredom. Thus, his comments about other
groups may sound like those of a right-wing extremist, but they are
delivered with a self-conscious, ironic tone that communicates a leftist sensibility.

Consider his attitudes toward women (or his statements about
them, which may not be the same thing):

Cuddy: Your attitude toward supervisory personnel is disrespectful, and a disturbingly large proportion of your comments are racist or sexist.
House: That top makes you look like an Afghani prostitute . . .
   would be an example of that.
   —"No More Mr. Nice Guy"

References to Cuddy's body and attire are woven through every
encounter, but it is also obvious that she elicits considerable respect
from House in general. Despite the tumultuousness of their relationship and his relentless jibes, his apparent "sexism" is a comic ruse—a

devious tactic, perhaps—but probably not an indicator of genuine prejudice. Thus, his attitude is much closer to that of Stephen Colbert or Bill Maher than Archie Bunker.* A similar dynamic can be seen in his treatment of African Americans, Jews, people with disabilities, religious people, and so on. He gets a kick out of offending people, taking a shot at political correctness, *and* mocking bigotry, all at the same time. Certainly for House, others are inferior to him, but this is not because of their skin color, religion, or gender; it is simply because they are not . . . him. The correct diagnosis, it seems, is narcissism. Thus, what looks like conservative ethnocentrism probably is not. He feigns social intolerance, but only because it suits his crabby, self-centered persona.

Is House a Libertarian?

It is not difficult to imagine that House is a libertarian, defined as the privileging of individual freedoms over all forms of social control, including governmental control. Libertarians generally believe that people should be left to pursue their goals unfettered, at least as long as these do not impinge on the freedoms of others (and sometimes even if they do). This sounds quite a bit like House. In "Deception," Foreman says, "House is not a hero. A person who has the guts to break a bad rule, they're a hero. House doesn't break rules, he ignores them. He's not Rosa Parks, he's an anarchist."

The problem is that House is too selective, purely self-serving, and controlling of others to be considered a true libertarian. He pursues his own freedom, to be sure, but he hardly respects the freedoms of others—most notably, the patients whose choices about their own lives and bodies he frequently overrides. His medical demeanor is best described as *paternalistic.* To the extent that libertarianism can

---

*Perhaps this is why House once displayed a picture of Stephen Colbert—a leftist who masquerades as a rightist for comedic effect—in his office. See "Stephen Colbert Makes a Cameo on 'House,'" No Fact Zone, February 17, 2009, www.nofactzone.net/2009/02/17/stephen-colbert-makes-a-cameo-on-house.

be summed up by the old saw "live and let live," House is much less interested in the second part.

Foreman is right: House often engages in unprincipled actions and rarely takes principled stands. When it comes to House's views on freedom, we might be better off borrowing a term from international relations and conclude that House subscribes to the doctrine of *exceptionalism*—in this case, the belief that *he* is exempt from the rules that govern others. This is why the judge needs to admonish him in "Words and Deeds": "Rules and laws apply to everyone. You are not as special as you think."

So, if House is a libertarian, he is a selfish, ungrateful one, and he probably wouldn't be the first (or the last) to earn such a description. He flagrantly neglects and undermines the system around him, exhibiting nothing but disdain for the institutional structures that make his brilliant career possible. Where would he be without the hospital, its administration, medical schools, internships, insurance companies, governmental support, emergency responders, police officers, the legal system, and so on? At no point does House even acknowledge that the system he flouts so enthusiastically is also what makes his life livable and his work workable.

Final Diagnosis

Although the show is primarily a medical drama, political questions are often central to the characters' motivations. Indeed, House's team members frequently serve as political foils, with Cameron taking the role of the traditional liberal, Foreman that of a neoconservative, and Chase espousing the views of an apolitical pragmatist. House's political genius is that he can clash with all of them simultaneously. Much of the dramatic tension arises from debates over hot-button political issues, such as individual rights, abortion, euthanasia, social class, racial differences, the role of religion, and so on. It is not surprising that one of the show's writers and producers possesses a strong political background, having worked as chief speechwriter for Vice President Al Gore.

So, what *is* House's political ideology? Is he a disaffected liberal with attitude? A closet conservative whose true colors come through in his treatment of others? Or perhaps he is a go-it-alone libertarian, for whom independence and personal freedom trump all other considerations? We have discussed some of the ways in which one might go about trying to answer these questions. With respect to the core dimensions of traditionalism and hierarchy, House comes out decidedly left of center. Like liberals, who tend to be relatively high on openness and low on conscientiousness, House is curious and creative but irreverent and rebellious and has no problems slaying the "sacred cows" of others. Like a typical leftist, he is not particularly fearful of uncertainty, ambiguity, or change; he likes a little bit of chaos.

Yet we have also seen some of the ways in which his mind-set is more typical of a conservative. He is tough-minded, dogmatic, and suspicious of any attempts to make the world better or more just. House may flirt with libertarian themes, such as prioritizing individual freedom over social control, but his defense of freedom is selective and self-serving. He also feigns bigotry, largely for comedic effect, but he is capable of controlling and berating others in the manner of a genuine authoritarian. All in all, House is a complex, self-contradictory mix of competing ideological proclivities, and in that respect, he may not be so special after all. To paraphrase Walt Whitman, "we are large, we contain multitudes."

Part of the show's brilliance emanates from the fact that the writers cultivate enough ambiguity for viewers to interpret House's attitudes and behaviors as consistent with their own ideological worldviews, whatever those happen to be. In a 2007 Norman Lear Center/Zogby poll report on culture and media, *House* was singled out for appealing to nearly equal proportions of liberals and conservatives.[*] This was a rare distinction, insofar as the same poll revealed that the consumption of popular culture reflects ideological polarization more than ever. Given these results, it may well be an exercise in futility to try to diagnose House's ideology with any degree of precision. One thing is for sure, though: when it comes to predictions and diagnoses,

---

[*]See "The Zogby/Lear Center Surveys on Politics and Entertainment: 2007," Norman Lear Center, www.learcenter.org/html/projects/?&cm=zogby/07.

the good doctor should stay away from politics and stick to what he knows.

> House [*To black senator*]: Trust me—you're not going to become president either way. They don't call it the White House because of the paint job.
> —"Role Model," first aired April 12, 2005

It would seem that House is *almost* never wrong.

SUGGESTED READINGS

Jost, John T., and Orsolya Hunyady (2005). Antecedents and consequences of system-justifying ideologies. *Current Directions in Psychological Science*, *14*, 260–265.

Jost, John T., and Jim Sidanius (2004). *Political Psychology: Key Readings*. New York: Psychology Press/Taylor & Francis.

Napier, Jaime L., and John T. Jost (2008). Why are conservatives happier than liberals? *Psychological Science*, *19*, 565–572.

PART FOUR

The Awe-Inspiring: House Rocks!

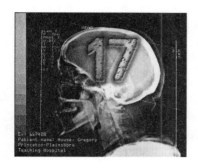

House and the Hero's Journey

LEONARD L. MARTIN AND MATTHEW SANDERS

What are we to make of House? Sure, he's a brilliant diagnostician, but his positive features pretty much end there. He breaks into people's homes, he embarrasses patients by revealing truths they had hoped to keep secret, he hides in the hospital chapel to watch television and to avoid clinic duty, he puts his name on all of the Secret Santa gift cards, and he intentionally leaves a thermometer up one patient's butt. Even the people closest to House don't use positive terms to describe him. They call him a misanthrope, an obsessive son of a bitch, a real jerk, and a drug addict who flaunts his addiction and refuses to get treatment. They accuse him of talking only to people he has to, then insulting them while showing off how insightful he is. Last, but not least, House has been described as a limping twerp. House's assessment of himself? "I'm pathetic" ("Ignorance Is Bliss").

This is not the stuff of heroes. House is no Superman, Indiana Jones, or Luke Skywalker. These characters are heroes in the classic sense. They are pure, selfless, and noble. They ride in on a white horse (or a red cape or a land speeder), save the day, get the girl, and ride off into the sunset to live happily ever after. Although House may save the day, he never gets the girl; he is not pure, selfless, and noble; and he is rarely happy.

This has led some to conclude that House is not a hero but an antihero. He is more like Batman than Superman. More like Dirty Harry than Indiana Jones. He saves the day, but he breaks a lot of rules along the way, and he has a dark, even antisocial, side to him.

It is difficult to disagree with this conclusion—but we are going to. House is not an antihero. He is a hero. In fact, he may be the best representation of a hero of any of those we just mentioned. How can we say this? Our claim makes sense if we think of House as the kind of hero described by Joseph Campbell—a mythic hero.

In this chapter, we define what it means to be a mythic hero. Then we outline the typical hero's journey, and we show how House's life maps onto that journey. By the time we arrive at the end of the journey, we will have learned a lot about House. We'll also have learned something about Wilson, Cuddy, and the others at Princeton-Plainsboro Teaching Hospital. And because House is a mythic hero, we may even have learned something about ourselves.

Myth and the Hero's Journey

Before we can say what a mythic hero is, we have to say what a myth is. Think of a myth as a story that conveys a truth but that in itself is not meant to be taken as true. For example, was there really a Prince Charming who slew a dragon and woke a Sleeping Beauty to find true love? That seems unlikely. On the other hand, have you ever had to overcome a personal challenge to accomplish your goals? That seems more likely. So, in that sense, there was a Prince Charming. He was you. You slew your own dragon and woke your own sleeping love. Although myths may be false at the descriptive level, they are true on a psychological level. According to Joseph Campbell, myths show us how to face the struggles all humans in all times in all cultures have had to face.

So it is with House. Whereas he struggles with his addiction to Vicodin, we may struggle with eating too much junk food or watching too much television. Whereas House has a physical limp, we may be hampered by our shyness or our less-than-perfect looks. Whereas House desperately needs to develop social skills, we may need to be a little bit kinder or a little more patient. We are not House, but we may be able to gain some insight into our life struggles by watching House deal with his. As Joseph Campbell put it in *The Celebration of Life*, "Myths provide inspiration for aspiration." They inspire us to overcome our weaknesses and live life to the fullest.

How do heroes provide this inspiration? By going on a hero's journey. Exactly what does that mean? If you've seen almost any popular movie or read a few best-selling novels, you already know. Many of our favorite stories take the form of a hero's journey. Consider *The Wizard of Oz*.

The story begins on an ordinary farm with Dorothy feeling that something is not exactly right. She longs to fly over the rainbow. To make matters worse, Miss Gulch is trying to take Toto away. So, Dorothy gathers Toto up and runs away from home, but she does not get far. A traveling magician convinces Dorothy to go back home. Before she can make it home, though, a twister carries Dorothy away and deposits her in Oz. Here, she has to navigate a road of trials to see the Wizard and make her way back home. Dorothy survives with the help of the Scarecrow, the Tin Man, and the Cowardly Lion. Ultimately, though, it is through her own power, a power she had with her all along, that Dorothy is able to return to Kansas. Back home, she is happier and wiser and able to live in harmony with her loving family.

This is a classic hero's journey. The elements are the same whether the journey is that of Dorothy, Superman, Luke Skywalker, House, or you.

1. *Ordinary world* (Dorothy on the farm)
2. *Initial call to adventure* (wanting to be over the rainbow, Miss Gulch threatening to take Toto)
3. *Refusal of the initial call* (Dorothy starts to go back home after meeting the magician)

4. *Undeniable call to adventure* (the twister)
5. *Road of trials* (the yellow brick road, flying monkeys)
6. *Guides* (Scarecrow, Lion, Tin Man)
7. *The abyss* (Dorothy is captured by the Wicked Witch; the adventure seems doomed to failure)
8. *Slaying the dragon* (killing the Wicked Witch)
9. *Refusal of the return* (the Wizard takes off in the balloon without Dorothy)
10. *Reconciliation* (there's no place like home)
11. *The return* (back on the farm, happier with the family).

We can see many of these elements in House if we consider the series as a whole. In short, we see House embark on a classic hero's journey, and in seeing this, we may come across some truths—truths that, according to Joseph Campbell, apply to all of us in all times in all cultures. Exactly what are these truths? We can find out by walking side by side with House as he makes his way through his hero's journey.

House and the Hero's Journey

1. The Ordinary World—Except in House's Case, It's Not That Ordinary

A hero's journey always begins in the ordinary world with things going generally well for the hero. Even so, the hero may have some sense that things are not quite right. Is this true of House?

We know he used to be physically active. He used to skateboard and play baseball. He was also on the varsity lacrosse team, and he became a cheerleader. He met Stacy while playing paintball, and he had his infarction while playing golf. In short, he was not always the limping twerp we now see. He did well in school, learned multiple languages, and learned to play the piano and the guitar. He had at least two romantic relationships (Stacy and Cuddy), and his friendship with Wilson began before he came to Princeton-Plainsboro.

So far, nothing totally out of the ordinary. Yet early in every hero's life, there comes a sense of unease. For House, this comes in large part from his father—who House correctly suspects was not his biological father, in "One Day, One Room": "He liked things the way he liked them. And he believed in discipline. He was right, I suppose, because I hardly ever screwed up when he was around. Too scared of being forced to sleep in the yard or take a bath in ice."

House's father was a Marine Corps pilot. He was stationed in a variety of places around the world, so House moved a lot as a child. It is unclear how this frequent movement might have influenced House's ability to form close relationships, but we know one important influence it had. It exposed House to the Buraku. The Buraku was a skilled physician who was also a descendant of Japan's untouchable community ("Son of Coma Guy").

> House: He wasn't accepted by the staff. He didn't even try. He didn't dress well. He didn't pretend to be one of them. The people that ran that place, they didn't think that he had anything they wanted. Except when they needed him. Because he was right. Which meant that nothing else mattered. And they had to listen to him.

Sound familiar? House is essentially the Buraku of Princeton-Plainsboro. If he is right in his medical diagnosis, then nothing else matters.

What else do we know about House's life before his hero's journey? House was kicked out of Johns Hopkins Medical School based on allegations of cheating, and he was fired from five positions in ten years before Cuddy hired him at Princeton-Plainsboro.

In short, House had a typical hero's start. He had some good times and some bad times, and he seems to have had a sense that things were not exactly right. He was not sufficiently moved at this point, though, to make a dramatic change. That came with . . .

2. The Undeniable Call to Adventure: Starting off on the Infarcted Leg

For Dorothy, it was the twister. For Superman, it was the destruction of Krypton. Luke Skywalker did not start his journey until he found his aunt and uncle killed and the farm burned. In most cases, the hero is thrust unwillingly into the adventure when his or her old life is irretrievably lost. There is no going back. What forces House out of his ordinary life? I think we all know the answer to that: his infarction.

> House: It's what happens when the blood flow is obstructed. If it's in the heart, it's a heart attack. If it's in the lungs, it's a pulmonary embolism. If it's in the brain, it's a stroke. I had it in my thigh muscles.
>
> —"Pilot"

Because of the infarction, House cannot go back to the life he had before, even if he wants to. As Stacy and Cuddy note, however, House is not much different after the infarction compared to before it. So, what did the infarction actually do?

Certainly, it started the pain and the addiction, but perhaps more important, it leads House to rearrange his priorities—a common after-effect of traumatic experiences. When people have part of their lives taken from them, they often open up to other parts of their lives. What is of value now? What can I hold on to? What do I need to let go of?

House answers these questions in this way: "The only thing I can do is think. I can pretty much do that anywhere. As long as no one's bugging me" ("Euphoria, Part 2"). In short, the infarction leads House to prioritize logic, problem solving, and intellect over emotions and social niceties. He may have always had these leanings, but the infarction exaggerates them. In fact, this is exactly the conclusion Wilson suggests to House in "No Reason":

> House: I don't define myself by my leg.
> Wilson: No, you have taken it one step further. The only way you could come to terms with your disability was to some way make it mean nothing. So you had to redefine every-thing. You have dismissed anything physical, anything not coldly, calculatingly intellectual.

House's fixation on rational problem solving not only creates interpersonal problems for House, it also makes him susceptible to

hurting himself. His search for answers leads him to take nitroglyc-
erin, LSD, and antidepressants—in quick succession. He subjects
himself to deep cranial stimulation, which brings on seizures and
a coma, and he injects himself with the blood of a patient to see
whether the patient's symptoms could have been brought on by a
transfusion. He even sticks a knife into an electric socket to see what
he can find out about life after death.

Part of the hero's job is to get in touch with his or her authentic
skills and values, but that is not enough. The hero ultimately has to
live in the real world and has to reconcile his or her personal goals
and values with those of society. Although House identifies his unique
skills, he fails miserably with regard to reconciliation.

So, that, in essence, is House's journey. He has to reconcile his
cold, rational, intellectual, problem-solving self with the part of himself that needs other people and wants a close relationship. He has to
learn to live in harmony with others. At the descriptive level, this may
take the form of dealing with pain, addiction, hospital rules, or boring
clinic duty, but these are just the trappings of the mythic journey. The
real journey is one of reconciliation. Fortunately, House does not have
to make that journey alone—none of us do.

3. Mythic Helpers: I Get By with a Little Help from My Friends

Dorothy had the Scarecrow, the Tin Man, and the Cowardly Lion.
Luke Skywalker had Yoda and Obi-Wan Kenobi. Who does House
have? He has the staff and the patients of Princeton-Plainsboro.
In ways big and small, intentional and unintentional, these people
have acted as sounding boards to help keep House on the road to
reconciliation.

Perhaps the main mythic helper for House is Wilson. Wilson's
chief trick is keeping House from taking himself too seriously.

> Wilson: That smugness of yours really is an attractive quality.
> House: Thank you. It was either that or get my hair high-
> lighted. Smugness is easier to maintain.
>
> —"Occam's Razor"

On another occasion, Wilson learns that House has been look-ing through his personal file without his permission, in "Histories." Wilson finds out because House makes fun of Wilson based on what he read in the file:

> House: Wilson, James. Boy wonder oncologist. You know him?
> Wilson: You know, in some cultures it's considered almost rude for one friend to spy on another. Of course, in Swedish, the word *friend* can also be translated as "limping twerp."

Notice that Wilson does not respond with anger, nor does he simply ignore the incident. He good-naturedly points House back to himself—to his lack of social skills. In this way, Wilson turns House's social faux pas into a teachable moment.

Whereas Wilson helps House at a personal level, Foreman is in many ways House's mythic guide on a professional level. This is true not only because of Foreman's high degree of competence (Foreman runs the lab when House goes to rehab) but also because Foreman differs from House in terms of his professional ethics (then again, who doesn't?). Foreman will take some chances and even lie but only within the parameters of the profession. As he explains to a patient in "Need to Know," "Confidentiality rules stop me from telling your husband the truth. But my obligation to lie ends there." From Foreman, House can learn how to play within the rules without being a complete conformist.

Cameron, of course, is the empathic, emotional member of the Princeton-Plainsboro staff. Although House sees this as a weakness in Cameron, it is precisely this feature that makes her a good mythic guide for House. As we all know, House treats diseases, not patients. Cameron's focus is just the opposite. For her, caring takes precedence over curing. She even marries a man she knows has a fatal disease. Why? Because "when a good person dies, there should be an impact on the world" ("Acceptance"). In Cameron, House gets to see a mir-ror image of himself.

Although Chase is generally considered to be the yes man of the staff, there are times when he stands up to House—and these times are very telling. For example, in "Ignorance Is Bliss," when things are not going well in a diagnostic meeting, House belittles Chase by saying, "Give me something, or I'll get your ex-smarter half on the phone and ask her." Because Chase and Cameron are having relationship problems at the time, this is an especially cruel remark from House. Chase's reaction? He walks out of the meeting—but on the way out, he sucker-punches House, knocking him to the floor. Some interpersonal feelings are worth standing up for. Maybe House will think of that before his next snide remark about someone's relationship.

Cuddy's role as a mythic guide is more complex. She represents what Joseph Campbell referred to as the temptress. The temptress is a figure (male or female, depending on the story) who is extremely alluring to the hero, but who, precisely because of this allurement, can turn the hero from his or her path. Think of Odysseus and the Sirens or Frodo and his "Precious." Give in to the temptation, and your quest is over.

House is romantically interested in Cuddy, but Cuddy is also head of the department. As such, she is the rule giver, the enforcer of conformity. This presents House with a dilemma. Does he conform to the rules to win Cuddy's affections, or does he stay true to his nonconformist personality and risk losing a passionate relationship? Thus, in one person, House can see both sides of his dilemma. What do you have to sacrifice in order to get what you want?

House has also been helped on his journey by numerous patients. Dr. Charles in "TB or Not TB," for example, reminds House that doctors deal with real people, not only diseases. "When you have millions of people dying, the correct perspective is to be yelling at the top of your lungs."

Sidas is an extremely bright person who is taken to Princeton-Plainsboro when he loses the ability to move his hand, in "Ignorance Is Bliss." He is also married to a woman who is clearly his inferior with regard to intelligence. Yet Sidas loves her and is not bored with her inane conversations. To House, this reaction is a clue about the patient's condition. Sidas is intentionally taking cough medicine to lower his intelligence. It is the only way he can stay in the relationship. When faced with a choice between a loving social relationship and intellectual accomplishment, Sidas chooses the relationship. The exact opposite of House.

In "Autopsy," House faces a mythic triple team. A nine-year-old girl knows she is dying and she wants to be kissed before she dies. She chooses Chase, the cute one, not House. After observing the kiss, Wilson turns to House and notes, "She enjoys life more than you do."

In sum, the staff members and the patients provide House with frequent lessons about life on the other side of the street, the side where emotions and relationships matter. They show House how to open himself to the pain, vulnerability, and messiness that can come with close relationships. For the most part, though, House seems to learn little from these lessons. The problem, ironically, is his diagnostic genius. It continues to work for him. Of course, House is not in a stable relationship, he has lost his staff, he is shot by a former patient, he is almost fired by a rich hospital patron, and he is arrested by Officer Tritter. Even so, he is doing fine, isn't he? I mean, in general, more or less.

Then, Kutner commits suicide.

4. The Abyss: "I'm Melting . . ."

Although Kutner's suicide catches everyone by surprise, it has the most profound effect on House. After all, House is the guy who diagnosed an entire waiting room of patients after seeing them for only five minutes. How can he not see Kutner's suicide coming? Why does Kutner do it? Why does House miss it?

Then, there is the bachelor party for Chase. House invites a stripper he knows, and he encourages Chase to drink a shot from her body. The problem, though, is the stripper is wearing strawberry body butter, and Chase is allergic to strawberries. Shortly after Chase drinks the shot, he becomes unconscious and has to be taken to the hospital. House knows of the body butter and of Chase's allergy. Why does he fail to put the two together?

There is also the diagnostic meeting in which Taub bests House. House recommends giving a patient total body radiation. Taub suggests prescribing the patient a drug that will make the cancer stronger. Then they can find exactly where the cancer is and treat it directly.

Taub's recommendation is better. How can that happen? Is House losing his ability? If he loses that, then what else does he have?

From a mythic standpoint, House is in the abyss. He is at the lowest point in the hero's journey. This is the point where the hero either succeeds or fails—and right at this moment, failure seems to be the most likely outcome. House's first reaction is everyone's first reaction. Retreat to the familiar. In House's case, that means Vicodin.

The retreat only makes things worse. House overdoses and begins hallucinating. Then, his unconscious takes over in the form of Amber, Wilson's old girlfriend. Eventually, House finds himself groveling shamelessly on the floor near his toilet, trying desperately to recover his last Vicodin. Then, miraculously, Cuddy appears. She helps House detox, and she shares an intense, passionate night with him. Except there is no Cuddy, no detox, and no passionate night. Just the drugs, the hallucinations, and the degradation.

When House realizes what is happening to him, he plays his trump card. He tries to diagnose and treat his problems, but he fails. He fails for a good reason. He is in the abyss. Old solutions don't work in the abyss. At this point in the journey, the hero is utterly alone. There are no helpers and no set ways to solve the problem. The hero must turn inward to find the one answer that is right for him or her, right then and there. House has only one strategy left. He reaches out for help.

5. Slaying the Dragon: We Have Met the Enemy and He Is Us

There is only one way out of the abyss. The hero must die to his or her old self and live out of a newfound wisdom. In psychological terms, the hero must slay his or her ego. This can be scary. It is not surprising, therefore, that people avoid this, if possible.

When House first arrives at Mayfield Psychiatric Hospital, he acts as though his problem is a simple drug overdose. He does his detox and is ready to return home. His therapist, though, Dr. Nolan, says he will not recommend House for a return to medical practice unless he undergoes additional therapy. So, House is compelled to stay. He is not compelled to cooperate, so he does not. The old self dies hard.

House refuses to take his medication, he lies repeatedly, and he leads a patient uprising. His meddling even causes one patient to injure himself by leaping from a parking deck. That's when it happens. House finally realizes he cannot continue with his old ways. He opens himself to therapy, and he starts to die to his old self.

House 2.0 is first revealed when House begins to fall romantically for Lydia, the sister of a patient at Mayfield. Although House has very strong feelings for Lydia, he is unable to maintain a relationship with her. She has to move away—and House is sad. Yet this is good. It is a sign of progress. It is why Dr. Nolan agrees to write House the letter that will allow him to resume practicing medicine.

> Nolan: Well, two things just happened: You got hurt, which means you connected to someone else strongly enough to miss them. And more important, you recognized the pain and came to talk to me, instead of hiding from it in the Vicodin bottle. The fact that you're hurting and you came here, the fact that you're taking your meds, and the fact that we're talking right now.
>
> —"Broken"

In short, during his time at Mayfield Psychiatric Hospital, House dies to his old self and opens up emotionally to other people. He has slain his dragon. He reached the turning point in his hero's journey. He has not reached the endpoint, however.

6. Refusal of the Return: The Joys of Cooking

In mythic terms, after the hero has slain the dragon, he or she gets the prize. This could be a princess, a treasure, or perhaps an elixir of immortality. The real prize, of course, is psychological. For House, it is a newfound vulnerability and openness.

Unfortunately, after obtaining the prize, the hero may find it difficult to return to his or her old life. What if the hero loses the prize? What if other people do not accept the new person the hero has become? How can the hero live in the ordinary, mundane world, while still holding onto the insights he or she has gained? Because this can be difficult to do, heroes are often tempted to refuse the call to return. House is no exception.

When he returns to Princeton-Plainsboro, he offers this simple greeting to Cuddy: "I quit." He moves in with Wilson and starts cooking all day. He spends his nights watching *The Biggest Loser* and eating ice cream.

Of course, if this is all House does, he will not be a hero. The hero must take the insights he or she has gained and return back home.

> House: I was about to take the pills. I went online, I found people posting medical problems. And my leg stopped hurting.
> Nolan: Oh.
> House: Oh?! I'm supposed to be changing my life. This is not a change.
> Nolan: Well, maybe I was wrong.
> House: Says the guy making sand castles in my brain.
> Nolan: We need to keep you from using. Taking your job away—the medical puzzles—nearly drove you back to it. Maybe diagnostic medicine is the key to keeping you clean.
>
> —"Epic Fail"

So, House returns to his old job but not back to his old life. This is a new and improved House. He has survived the abyss, he has slain his dragon, and he is learning to live in harmony with real people in the real world. House is now ready for the last stage of his journey.

7. Reconciliation: There's No Place Like Home

Recall that the hero's journey is ultimately one of reconciliation. House has to reconcile his past with his present, his intellect with his emotions, and his conscious with his unconscious. Now that he is back in the ordinary world, he must use the insights he gained for the betterment of those around him.

In season 6, we can see House begin to do this. He keeps Wilson from giving a speech that can hurt his career (albeit by drugging

Wilson—but at least this time, House's inappropriate behavior is for an interpersonal good, not merely a medical one). He also lies in court about Alvie's DNA test. He counsels Cuddy on how to deal with her responsibility to the hospital board while juggling insurance contracts, and he helps Nolan deal with his terminally ill father.

Perhaps the most dramatic sign that House has changed comes when he tends to Hannah, a woman who got pinned under a fallen building. Cuddy and the emergency medical technicians want to amputate Hannah's leg to free her. Hannah says no—as does House. "Am I the only one who knows the value of a leg?" ("Help Me").

Eventually, though, House realizes amputation is the best course of action, and he makes a confession to Hannah:

> House: I did this very risky operation, and I almost died.
> Hannah: But you saved your leg.
> House: I wish I hadn't. . . . I'm in pain every day. And it changed me. It made me a harder person, a worse person, and now . . . now I'm alone. You don't want to be like me.

House also holds Hannah's hand to comfort her while she is trapped. This from the person who once asked famously, "What would you want? A doctor who holds your hand while you die or a doctor who ignores you while you get better?" ("Occam's Razor")

Sadly, Hannah dies. Her death hits House very hard. He returns to his bathroom, crashes his mirror, and retrieves a hidden stash of Vicodin. No more pain. . . . At that moment, though, Cuddy shows up. This time for real. She tells House it is his choice if he wants to go back on drugs. Then, she makes a confession.

> Cuddy: I'm stuck, House. I keep wanting to move forward. I keep wanting to move on, and I can't. I'm in my new house with my new fiancé, and all I can think about is you. I just need to know if you and I can work.
> House: You think I can fix myself?
> Cuddy: I don't know.

House: 'Cause I'm the most screwed-up person in the world.
Cuddy: I know. I love you. I wish I didn't, but I can't help it.
—"Help Me"

House and Cuddy kiss, and this time it is not a hallucination. House is no longer running from his pain, and he is opening himself up to meaningful relationships.

And They All Lived Happily Ever After

The truth of the matter is, we don't know how things are going to turn out for House. In the real world (and in television dramas), people have to deal with the problems that life continues to present to them. The hero is the one who can cope with these problems in ways that are consistent with his or her authentic skills and values and who can live in harmony with others while doing this. This is what House is learning to do. By watching him, we can be inspired to make our own journeys and slay our own dragons. That is why House is a hero.

SUGGESTED READINGS

Campbell, J. (2008). *The Hero with a Thousand Faces*, 3rd ed. Novato, CA: New World Library.

——— (2002). *The Celebration of Life* (audio CD). San Anselmo, CA: Joseph Campbell Foundation.

Martin, L. L., W. K. Campbell, and C. D. Henry (2004). The roar of awakening: Mortality acknowledgement as a call to authentic living. In J. Greenberg, S. Koole, and T. Pyszczynski (eds.), *Handbook of Experimental Existential Psychology* (pp. 431–448). New York: Guilford Press.

Tedeschi, R. C., and L. G. Calhoun (2004). Posttraumatic growth: Conceptual foundations and empirical evidence. *Psychological Inquiry, 15,* 1–18.

Contributors

The PhDs of Princeton-Plainsboro

Miranda L. Abild is a graduate student at the University of Lethbridge. Her research interests include evolutionary theory, sexuality, and gender psychology. She continues to lose sleep wondering whether House would have sounded even more snarky with Hugh Laurie's original English accent. She thanks the creators of *House* for the delightful respite their show has provided to offset her workaholic lifestyle.

Dr. Mark Alicke is a professor of social psychology at Ohio University. His major lines of research are on the psychology of the self and blame and moral judgment. Prior to writing his chapter, he had never seen *House*. Now he has seen almost every episode and is grateful for the opportunity to conduct research by watching TV.

Dr. Fiona Kate Barlow is a postdoctoral fellow and lecturer at the University of Queensland, Australia. She has published work on race relations in Australia, the cross-group contact hypothesis, and the impact of perceived rejection on prejudice. She currently has two primary lines of research: the first on meta-emotions, meta-cognitions, and intergroup relations, and the second on the relationship between social identities, norms, and sex. She originally thought that she and Dr. House might be romantically suited. After seeing Dr. Cameron and Dr. Cuddy fail in their attempts to change the irascible Dr. House, however, she has reevaluated.

Adam T. Cann is on the path to becoming a psychologist. He has done research on the role of the media in our lives and is preparing to build a career by joining the social psychology program at Texas Tech University. He aspires to the wit of Dr. House and the tolerance of Dr. Wilson.

Dr. Arnie Cann is a professor of psychology at the University of North Carolina, Charlotte. His lifelong fascination with humor eventually led to his developing workshops for workers in high-stress careers to help them learn to use humor effectively. During the last twenty years, he also has published multiple articles on humor and health and humor in relationships. Although he enjoys the humor on *House*, he truly believes that Greg House needs a humor coach to help him balance his humor styles.

Dr. Ted Cascio recently obtained his PhD from the University of Georgia, where he conducted research on individual differences in self-esteem and authenticity and, later, moral reasoning and judgment. Now, he's teaching psychology at University of Deusto in the Basque region of northern Spain, a place where people really appreciate their *cerveza, jamón, fútbol*, and *dios mio*(!), even their *Casa, M.D.*!

Dr. Bella DePaulo is a visiting professor of psychology at the University of California, Santa Barbara. She is the author of *Behind the Door of Deceit: Understanding the Biggest Liars in Our Lives* and more than a hundred scholarly publications. After spending decades studying lying, she decided to do something different and became a scholar of single life (instead of just a practitioner). *Singled Out: How Singles Are Stereotyped, Stigmatized, and Ignored, and Still Live Happily Ever After* was her first book on that topic. The new term that she coined—singlism—is as unevenly appreciated as her fondness for quoting House in polite company.

Dr. Anne Gast is working as a postdoctoral fellow at the University of Ghent. Being a learning psychologist, she wonders why a brilliant observer like House never seems to learn that any diagnosis that he makes before the thirty-sixth minute is necessarily wrong.

Dr. Brian Goldman is an associate professor of psychology at Clayton State University. He is a social psychologist who studies the role of authenticity and self-esteem in psychological well-being. He finds Dr. House's more recent transformations from a reformed drug addict and maladjusted elitist into a more authentic, well-rounded character worthy of a sequel to this book (but in the meantime, he hopes they don't yuck up House's "evolution" too much).

Dr. Edward R. Hirt is a professor of social psychology at Indiana University. His research interests are quite broad, including such topics as creativity, allegiance and sports fanship, mental depletion, and self-protective behaviors such as self-handicapping. Married to a physician, Hirt has a genuine appreciation for the thrills and frustrations of medical diagnosis and practice. A notoriously nice person, Hirt delights in vicariously simulating House's acerbic wit and sour disposition while watching the show.

Katherine Jacobs (BA, University of Virginia) is a graduate student at the University of California, Riverside. She studies the course of well-being in romantic relationships and the mechanisms of increasing happiness. She's considerably happier than House, so she thinks she's on the right track.

Dr. Jolanda Jetten is a professor of social psychology at the University of Queensland, Australia. Her published work is concerned with intergroup processes relating to discrimination and prejudice, and she explores the way stigmatized groups respond to their disadvantage. She also examines group processes relating to leadership, conformity, normative behavior, deviance, and the relationship between social identity and mental and physical health. Professor Jetten's husband bears a striking resemblance to Hugh Laurie, to the degree that he has been asked to have his photo taken by *House* fans. Luckily, her husband is marginally less cantankerous than House.

Lile Jia is a doctoral candidate in social psychology at Indiana University. His research interests lie in various unconscious processes of goal pursuit, self-regulation, and creativity. He is notoriously cunning and manipulative in various board and card games. As such, Lile wishes he could have a friend like House, so that he could play Wilson.

Dr. John T. Jost started as a pre-med major at Duke University, where he roomed with Dr. Ken Jeong, now a big-shot Hollywood actor who barely even has time for his old friends on Facebook. Jost hated organic chemistry, so he majored instead in psychology. He is now a professor of social psychology at New York University. Jost has been watching (too much) television for years, but his colleague, Gregory Murphy, and his wife, Orsi Hunyady, are responsible for his interest in the misanthropic Dr. House.

Dr. C. Raymond Knee is an associate professor in the Department of Psychology at the University of Houston and the director of the Interpersonal Relations and Motivation Research Group. As on *House*, his research team is a small army of curious and highly motivated graduate students and research assistants who actually do all of the important work while he does his best to take credit for it when they are right and blame them when he is wrong.

Dr. Megan Knowles is an assistant professor of psychology at Franklin & Marshall College in Lancaster, Pennsylvania. She is a social psychologist studying social rejection and belonging needs, self-regulation, and parasocial attachments to favorite television characters. She notes that in a way, Dr. House embodies her research interests, in that he frequently berates, insults, and rejects others while struggling to rein in his impulses—whether to down Vicodin or to torture Cuddy. Dr. House is also a television character whom many people report as being their favorite, but they don't necessarily become attached to Dr. House or see him as a friend, as they do other TV characters. Why? Well, see the previous sentence.

Dr. Joris Lammers is an assistant professor in social psychology at Tilburg University, the Netherlands. Because he is primarily interested in power plays and struggles but cannot stand the sight of blood, he had a mixed experience watching the *House* series as a preparation for this chapter.

Dr. Sonja Lyubomirsky is a professor of psychology at the University of California, Riverside. Her honors include a Templeton Prize and an NIMH grant to conduct research on increasing happiness. Her book *The How of Happiness: A New Approach to Getting the Life You Want* (New York: Penguin Press, 2008) was translated into seventeen languages. She would be a competitive match for Wilson on the tennis court.

Dr. Samuel J. Maddox is an assistant professor of psychology at Clayton State University in Morrow, Georgia. His areas of interest include clinical, child, and community psychology. He became an avid *House* fan because of the similarities between House and a supervisor he had in graduate school. He likens himself to the character of Foreman because they both seem to always struggle with the same question regarding their mentors: "Is this guy brilliant or insane?"

Dr. Leonard L. Martin is a professor of social psychology at the University of Georgia. His initial difficulties in writing the chapter were overcome when it was pointed out to him that he had been reviewing episodes of PBS's *This Old House*, rather than *House, M.D.* After he switched shows, everything fell into place.

Jennifer A. McDonald, M.Phil, is a doctoral candidate in the Department of Social and Developmental Psychology at the University of Cambridge. She studies real-life music listening behavior from both personality and social psychological perspectives. She is a huge *House* fan, but she swears that she didn't go to Cambridge just because it is Hugh Laurie's old stomping ground. She does, however, wish that she shared the actor's talent for faking accents.

Dr. Antoinette Miller is an associate professor of psychology at Clayton State University in Morrow, Georgia. She has published several research articles in psychophysiology and a variety of case-based instructional materials. At one time, a sprained ankle required her to use a cane and did nothing to improve her disposition. Apparently the resemblance was striking enough that her students called her "House." She took this as a compliment of the highest order.

Dr. Gregory L. Murphy has watched television since about 1960. In between shows, he studies cognitive psychology at New York University, where he is a professor. In addition to Dr. House, his role models include Perry Mason and David Letterman.

Dr. Delroy L. Paulhus is a professor of psychology at the University of British Columbia. His research on the Dark Triad (Machiavellianism, narcissism, and psychopathy) naturally led him to ponder the character of Gregory House. Inevitably, Del began to model himself after the brilliant but grouchy House. Del's students agree that except for the brilliant part, he has succeeded in that aspiration.

Dr. Peter J. Rentfrow is a university lecturer (assistant professor) in the Department of Social and Developmental Psychology at the University of Cambridge and a fellow of Fitzwilliam College. His research concerns person-environment interactions and focuses on personality expression through preferences for music and film. His research is also concerned with geographical variations in personality. He would enjoy rocking out on his drums alongside House on the electric guitar.

Lindsey M. Rodriguez is currently at the University of Houston obtaining her doctorate in social psychology and health. Her research focuses on interpersonal relationships from a motivational perspective.

This includes social network interactions; relationship initiation, maintenance, and dissolution; and examining conditions that reduce conflict and defensiveness within close relationships. Like House, Lindsey is often able to solve life's mysteries while doing things such as throwing a tennis ball against the wall and talking about fishing.

Matthew Sanders is a doctoral candidate in social psychology at the University of Georgia. He is currently working on theories of self-regulation and control. Matt often finds himself wondering whether graduate school is more or less the same as House's process of eliminating candidates for his team.

Nancy L. Sin, MA, is a social/personality psychology doctoral student at the University of California, Riverside. She has research interests in positive psychology interventions, physician-patient interactions, and patient adherence to depression treatment. A romantic, she suffered a vicarious heartbreak when Chase and Cameron separated.

Haran Sivapalan, MA (Cantab), is a researcher at King's College London with interests in the neurobiology of mental illness, addictions, and psychiatry in film. Having studied experimental psychology at the University of Cambridge, he is the author of the paper "Khantzian's Self Medication Hypothesis and Films by Martin Scorsese," published in the *International Review of Psychiatry* (2009). While writing this chapter on campus, his house was broken into, his fridge raided, and swabs of his crockery taken.

Jesse Wynhausen is a practicing psychologist (in his home country of Australia) and is currently a graduate student in social psychology at New York University. While he could never aspire to House's genius, he strives daily to emulate the bitter sarcasm and cutting insults. His wife would prefer he simply concentrate on the genius part.

Index